K2

SAVAGE MOUNTAIN · SAVAGE SUMMER

BY JOHN BARRY

The Oxford Illustrated Press

Dedication

For Coco, who has climbed a K2 of her own.

© John Barry, 1987

Reprinted 1987

Printed in England by J.H. Haynes and Co. Limited,
Sparkford, Nr. Yeovil, Somerset.

ISBN 0–946609–42–X

Published by:
The Oxford Illustrated Press Limited, Sparkford,
Nr. Yeovil, Somerset.

Published in North America by:
Haynes Publications Inc, 861 Lawrence Drive,
Newbury Park, California 91320, USA

British Library Cataloguing in Publication Data:
Barry, John, 1944
   K2 : Savage mountain, savage summer.
   1.   Mountaineering – Pakistan – K2 (Mountain)
   2.   K2 (Pakistan : Mountain)
   I. Title
   915.4'6   DS485.K193
   ISBN 0-946609-42-X

Library of Congress Catalog Card Number
87-80506

Contents

Acknowledgements

My thanks to those who supported the British 1986 K2 Expedition with cash or kind or kit and especially our principal sponsor, Fullers Brewery.

Kath for typing through all those dark days.

My father for assiduous checking and some wisdom.

John Porter for graciously stepping aside and for his contribution.

David Wilkinson for his contribution.

Jane Marshall for encouraging and bullying as appropriate.

Brian Hall and Jim Curran for appendices.

Mountain magazine for permission to lift extensive pieces.

Anthony Smee for skilfully making fine mountains out of inelegant molehills.

The British Embassy and their Club who made our stay in Islamabad more comfortable.

The British Mountaineering Council and Nazir Sabir of Mountain World for their time and advice.

For a full list of sponsors please turn to the appendices.

'. . . what does the mountain care?'

'All men dream: but not equally. Those who dream by night in the dusty recesses of their minds wake in the day to find that it was vanity: but the dreamers of the day are dangerous men, for they may act out their dream with open eyes, to make it possible.'

(Seven Pillars of Wisdom T.E. Lawrence.)

I had plenty of advice and almost everyone said the same: 'Don't write just another expedition book'. I agreed. There were far too many of them already. But that was as far as the advice went. Never a word on how this might be achieved, and I bet that the authors of expedition books have been scribbling hard to evade that 'just another' taint ever since expeditions ceased to be events of remark. That would have been long ago.

The very first scribblers had an easy run of it, but now, hundreds of expeditions later, there's little that is novel left to essay: easy pickings are long gone. The question is how hard to consciously strike for novelty. A wilfully obscure, chronologically askew, vainly veiled yarn might be a greater offence. The trouble with expeditions is that they are but stories, and like stories comprise beginnings, middles and endings—and not much more. Expedition books too. Nor is the traditional plot something to inspire wild flights of unfolding fancy: a mountain is a mountain, give or take a face, a ridge or a buttress. Endings sometimes vary though—but only between getting up and down and not getting up and down, and there's not much of a denouement to be wrung from those ingredients.

That was one problem. Another was objectivity. I can write for only one soul—and anyway, as Orwell noted, everyone writes as a partisan. So I have sneaked out the easy way: there has been no attempt at objectivity. My facts will be in dispute. It is my own tale and I must be my own judge of what I say. Some of the others have told their bits and have told them fairly. I wish they had been more—everyone had the opportunity to tell as often and as freely as they wanted. I hope these bits give my story some balance—though it may not be considered balance enough. Justice to K2 1986 will not be done by this book alone.

A much bigger problem was the mountain. In a way you could blame Reinhold Messner and Peter Habeler. In 1978 they climbed Everest without bottled oxygen—and in doing so moved the goal posts. No longer could it be entirely satisfactory—at least not in the minds that mattered, mountaineers' minds—to get to the top of big mountains by any means; no longer would a summit successful justify any means. For though mountaineering is a game without regulations (or rules or referee), it has regulation, which we call, a touch grandly, ethics.

Some of these ethics are that the mountain must be given a chance, the best chance; that the outcome must be in doubt to the end; that when someone does a bolder thing and moves the goalposts that there's no bringing them in again, though they may be moved beyond. And they are—always.

So bottled oxygen on the world's highest mountain is now something akin to a foul, the professional foul of soccer perhaps. You *can* do it but you feel . . . there is a feeling . . . most of the players feel . . . that the game would be a better one if you didn't. The greater god of mountaineering frowns on it, but it's a yellow card at most; no sending off.

But it's not all Messner's fault. There is another very good reason, some might say a better reason, not to take oxygen to K2. Cash. It's expensive to bottle oxygen, and very expensive to have it carried the 12 days to Base Camp. Even then you have to get it up the hill to a point where it makes sense, if not ethics, to use it. That costs effort, lots of it.

Incidentally, physiologists say that it is a happy coincidence that the highest summit on earth is 8,848 metres, because that is as high as a man is able to climb on thin air. They used to say that our ceiling was lower than that when, after nearly half a century of trying, no-one seemed to be able to improve on the 7,535 metres that Mallory and Irvine attained on Everest in 1924. You could forgive them their error when all the best evidence, empirical evidence at that, strongly suggested a ceiling around 8,500 metres.

Then Messner and Habeler proved them wrong, and soon after others proved them wronger. But it isn't so simple, or so easy. People still die at altitude of altitude. Messner called the space between 8,000 metres and the top, the Death Zone. The phrase was a bit too melodramatic for the average Anglo Saxon ear and a deadly serious matter was treated lightly. Then Whillans made the phrase respectable, at least to all Britons, when he said (at Plas y Brenin in 1984) that he thought the death zone was just that. A nation was converted in an instant; there were no doubters now.

That's not the end of it. In 1986, an American scientific team measured the mountain by some new method. They made it 9,022 metres high—over 150 metres higher than Everest's accepted height. So is K2 now the highest mountain in the world? Even at a comparatively lowly 8,610 metres it has long been regarded as the hardest. Everest is a big lump and by the South Col, its easiest route, of no great technical difficulty, though not yet the Yak Trak it has been nick-named. Over 100 people have stood on top, but only a handful of those got there on thin air.

K2 is steeper, rises more sheer into an only slightly lesser sky. There are no easy routes. It is all ways steep, all ways hard. Children draw their mountains not as Everests but as K2s; symmetrical, steep at the sides, pointed at the top: hard, and harder still if it is now higher than Everest. Whether it is indeed higher is hard to say—though everyone seems to have an opinion. The same method of measurement needs to be applied to Everest. Then what? The possibilities are endless and fun to conject. K2 *is* higher than Everest: the peak fee will go up—and out of all proportion to the increase in altitude. Pakistan will be delighted with its new stature—so will all those who have climbed K2 but not Everest. They can die (or may have died) happier and higher mountaineers. Those who have climbed Everest but not K2, and very few have done both, will be disappointed and will either have to settle for second best or gird themselves for a bigger battle. It is, of course, possible that K2 is indeed 9,022 metres and that Everest is actually 9,100 and something metres, in which case, according to our physiologists, it is impossible. This time the evidence seems to be against them. And if both K2 and Everest are higher than was thought, then why not all the other mountains of the Himalayas? Which may mean that there are many more than 14 peaks above the magic (and deadly?) 8,000-metre mark, which in turn, means that those engaged in the 8,000-metre pursuit should stay on their bikes a while longer, and that Messner, who'd thought he'd won, should get back on his—if he still cares. Another possibility is that no-one will think it matters very much. Somehow I think they will.

Anyway, up until 1986 K2 had been climbed by 39 people at the cost of 12 lives. This year, the summer of 1986, another 16 climbers reached the top and thirteen more died. That is the gruesome arithmetic, figures to give the scale.

Traditionally only one or two expeditions a year have been granted permission to tackle K2. In 1986 the Pakistan authorities allowed an unprecedented ten expeditions onto their sides of the mountain: up to ten times the usual K2 population. I'm not a statistician and I'm not sure whether more potentially unlucky climbs result in more unlucky climbers—but it's hard to avoid the conclusion that it is unlikely that the toll would not have been proportionally less given fewer expeditions. Pakistan has since announced that in future they will be restricting the number of expeditions to one a summer and that may slow down the rate of attrition—not that I think Pakistan is in any way culpable. Mountaineers live and die and make their own contracts with time and place and chance.

But there was a bigger problem. Ours was an unhappy trip; and not just because it was unsuccessful, nor only because of the death of Alan Rouse, the leader, though that was certainly our greatest unhappiness. (Al had been to K2 twice before. This would be his last go, he had said—damn the prescience—he didn't want to have to go again. And for all his faults he was one of Lawrence's 'dreamers of the day', and would have been one of his 'dangerous men'.) For us the end of this story will never quite lie down. On death; it is much easier to tell the truth about the living. Death bestows favours, enhances, promotes; it forgives as mourning bleaches out the stains. To deal in death takes courage and I have not the guts for it, and a soft heart is wrought all up in a tangle of loyalty and friendship. None of which is to titillate, only to think aloud and late.

Here are no great secrets, no revelations; nor lessons. It is an ordinary tale of ordinary lives, small happenings, little people. It is filled with little things: it is a little thing. And if it belongs anywhere in literature at all then it is on the shelf marked 'defeats'.

A Beginning?

'My dear Ram', interrupted the giant, 'I have not the least notion what you are talking about. If you would have the kindness to begin at the beginning, I should be vastly obliged; all these stories that begin in the middle simply jog my wits.'
(Translated from *Le Bélier* [*The Ram*], by Count Anthony Hamilton, soldier and author.)

The beginning, start at the beginning, someone advised. But they didn't tell me where it was and look as I might I can't find it. So by way of a beginning, a beginning as far back as I can associate anything with K2, I might (and might not) be forgiven an autobiographical indulgence, or two. Now there's subjectivity for you.

After a seven-year stint (and some good years they were) at Plas y Brenin, the National Centre for Mountain Activities, I left to work for a company that likes to describe itself as 'experts in extreme locations'.

The company had married engineering to mountaineering, and a happy marriage it made. They specialise in working in places few can get to or at—the undersides of bridges or the uppermost tops of bridges, the tallest skyscrapers in the highest skies, the biggest holes in the deepest ground; inaccessible structures and damn near anything that no-one else can reach. When I joined they were small, but getting big fast. Now they're big and getting bigger faster. Unfortunately, my dreams of getting rich along with them foundered on the rock of what the laws of libel insist I call misunderstanding.

But perhaps I wasn't so much misunderstood as inept. See here. We got a contract to examine the skin of two 26-storey buildings in the centre of Birmingham. The plan was for our climbers to abseil down the outside, inspecting for cracks and other superficial damage as they went. The flats were newsworthy and so were we, so the aim was to make good news together. The MD decided to hold his first ever press conference, and what's more, hold it on site. He, besuited in a voluminous double-breasted number that was much more than two breasts too large, I, in jacket, tie and nearly clean shirt, drove down from Manchester. The conference was to be at ten. I was to be 'Safety Officer' for the day—though just what that entailed was never explained. But that oversight does not excuse, or even explain, the comic catastrophe that befell me that day.

While the MD addressed the journalists I was dispatched in the lift to the top of the building to see what the lads were up to. The lads, as talented a bunch of climbers, grafters and mickey-takers as you'll ever be cajoled by, were readying for the demonstration that was to follow the MD's opening spiel. I hung about while they rigged their tackle and dropped ropes some 300 feet down the building. When we at the top were all set, I switched on a hand radio and reported that we were ready when he was. There was no reply. I tried again but still there was no acknowledgement.

It seemed important that the MD knew that the lads were ready to go so I decided to carry the message myself. The lift doors were closing on the 26th storey as I arrived. Hoping to save the several minutes it would have taken to summon a departed lift back to floor 26, the Safety Officer thrust his fingers into the closing gap. The lads did this all the time. Why my fingers should have been regarded by that particular lift on this particular day at this particular time as any different from any of theirs I do not know. What I do know is that the lift doors continued to close inexorably on my fingers, taking a remorseless hold of all eight, leaving me two thumbs to drum with and two legs to dance. I bewailed my fate to some good tune but to no good effect. The lads were outside in a 26-storey wind and the MD far below. I shouted louder—as manful a 'help' as a fingerless man can be expected to muster. No one came. This is mugging territory and the 'help' ploy old hat. No one ever comes. I thought to shout 'I've got my fingers stuck in the lift' but even *in extremis,* as I surely was, the ridiculousness, the sheer improbability of such a cry got the better of my panic and I burst into laughter. And then into tears as I realised I might actually lose my fingers for good, that is to say, permanently.

There's nowhere as lonely as a home for several hundred people; one of the social ironies of the day. I had to get those doors open. I tried my nose. Have you ever tried opening a lift door with your nose? Don't bother. Unless you have a probiscus like a pruning fork, it doesn't work. My own was particularly unsuited for such an operation for, having been radically redesigned twice (talking when I should have been listening), it sports a broader than average front elevation, a flatter than average profile.

By now, my fingers had lost all feeling and I only knew that they were still mine because I was still attached to that damn door though by a now rather less than finger-width gap. I kicked; a kick that would have not been out of place on any football terrace in the land. But the doors were used to that. I withdrew to arm's length and ran their full length (all of 30 inches) full-tilt at the door. This shaved my fingers a little leaner and allowed the doors to close another inexorable micro-millimetre.

The button. The button! By now I must have been wild eyed with genuine, very unstiff-upper-lip-panic. I was certainly in pain. Perhaps I could get a foot to the lift's call button. Now, on a hot day, carefully warmed and with at least two nubile assistants, I can normally get my foot about as high as my waist—but who knows what might be done in an emergency? Panic and the probable loss of fingers consequent upon failure notwithstanding, I didn't get my foot within a yard of that taunting button. It was too near and too high.

Just when all seemed lost, voice hoarse with shouting, manful 'helps' mocking to the echo, all my gods deafened by prayers and my fingers offered up in bloody sacrifice—just then, the doors opened. I fell back in a corner and sank to the floor, writhing, sobbing and clutching shattered hands between quivering thighs, doubled up and frightened to look lest there was nothing to see. But who or what had opened the doors? Not prayer, not effort of mine, not electronic fluke, not even magic. No, there in the lift entrance stood the MD, a contingent of press pressed about him. I saw them all dimly through the pain and struggled to reduce my great shaking sobs to an inaudible whimpering.

'Ah, gentlemen, John Barry, our Safety Officer,' intoned the MD. 'He's leading an expedition to K2 next year. Our safety record is impeccable.'

From where I lay I could see that few believed any of these claims.

'Here we have a roof situation', he continued in transatlantic idiom as he led his entourage to the roof.

'All our operatives are experts' (though not all of his experts currently operative) 'and our access methods subject to vigorous testing. Anything or anyone who fails to measure up goes down the road.'

The press looked blank.

'Is fired.' They understood, some weak smiles said so. I looked bleak, bleak as my future. The MD was cast in the MacGregor, hire 'em an' fire 'em North American School of Management.

As I surveyed the bloody wreckage of what had once been two fine fists I wondered if I was of the right stuff for the white heat of the commercial world. I suspect the MD had his own thoughts on the subject.

But he hadn't entirely given up hope for me. Not long after I was told that I was to accompany him to Glasgow, this time in the guise of Marketing Manager. Because I had no idea what a Marketing Manager did for a living he was to show me how it was done. I was anxious to learn from the expert, and equally anxious to perform rather better in this new camouflage than I had as Safety Officer. Besides, 'Manager' sounded like promotion—if only for the day.

Our appointment was with the City Architect's Department. We were there to persuade them that their city's several hundred tower blocks were falling apart and that our company should inspect them by abseil.

'How much per tower block?' they wanted to know.

'Between two and three thousand pounds,' the MD replied.

That was more than twice the price Birmingham had been charged. Then I cottoned on. In one of his lectures on the principles of marketing, the MD had told me that it was bad practice to turn down a job when the same result could be achieved by deliberately pricing yourself out. 'Clever bugger,' I thought, 'he's clearly seen some reason why we shouldn't do it and he's making sure we don't get the job.' I was learning fast.

Out on the street again, I turned to the MD, and said:

'That was clever.'

'Why thank you JB. What was clever?'

'Overpricing by about times two. You didn't want the job, right?'

'Sure did. We'll get it too.'

And he did. A contract for half a million. Clearly, I was no Marketing Manager either—and the white heat of commercialism was badly scorching my flimsy capitalist armour.

I was demoted to Salesman (though again only for a day) and sent packing to one of the London Boroughs there to persuade the Borough Architects that all their tower blocks were falling down (which they were) and that we should inspect them. By now I had affected the MD image and had arranged to borrow his leather-bound, combination-lockable briefcase which did rather more for appearances that my floppy canvas mountaineer's job.

I sped down the M6/M1 with a few thousand other salesmen, marketing managers, safety officers and executives, feeling every inch Betjeman's

I am a young executive. No cuffs than mine are cleaner;
I have a Slimline brief-case and I use the firm's Cortina.
In every roadside hostelry from here to Burgess Hill
The *maîtres d'hôtel* all know me well and let me sign the bill.

You ask me what it is I do. Well actually, you know,
I'm partly a liaison man and partly P.R.O.
Essentially I integrate the current export drive
And basically I'm viable from ten o'clock till five.

The architects' office was enormous which was as well for there seemed to be dozens of architects—though handfuls of them could have been borough engineers, borough housing officers, borough commissars—this was good old GLC, President Livingstone days. A copy of the *Guardian* crossword, two clues entered, lay across a desk. Coffee came in gallons, brown sandwiches came crustless; stress came not at all. Why ever we were here, it didn't seem to be for work. As a result a very agreeable atmosphere prevailed.

'Now then, what have you got for us?' asked the richly-tanned Chief Architect.

I'd got a big, fat, leather-bound briefcase full of glorious technicolour for them, that's what. With a flourish I brought the briefcase from floor to knee and with what I hoped passed for practised ease, cocked my thumbs over the fastenings. Without looking I pressed them simultaneously, smiling confidently at the Chief Architect as I did so, and then glanced down to fish out all that glorious technicolour. I saw only leather. The lid remained the lid. I tried again, with slightly less panache, again with no panache whatsoever, and once more in growing desperation. It was locked; combination locked and I didn't know the combination.

'Hummm—could I use your phone a minute?'

'Fine, fine.'

I rang the MD.

'Got the contract sewn up?' he asked.

'All but. What's the combination on your attaché case?'

'Come on John, a six year old could crack it.'

Which was true, indeed a six year old had cracked it the previous weekend. I smiled at the Chief Architect.

'Could you just tell me and stop pratting about?' I asked in a most reasonable voice.

I smiled again at the Chief Architect. He smiled back and gave me the distinct impression that things were progressing at a perfectly normal pace.

The MD gave in.

Armed with the combination I opened the case. It was upside down. The glorious technicolour spewed all over the floor.

We didn't get the contract.

The white heat of commercialism had burned me third degree. Industry and I did not get on. That was about the only thing the MD and I agreed on. I left the company shortly after on mutually agreed terms—at least that's what the MD calls them.

* * *

But now my memory, struggling to get a grip on something, is telling me that K2 began before any of that; a year before, when Al Rouse and I were in the Tyn-y-Coed, a hostelry where my often boorish behaviour was actually rewarded by the most elastic drinking hours imaginable. Hargreaves drank there too; he was to become our Base Camp Manager, but much more of him later. Al was effervescing. Conversation was one of his favourite competitive events but just now he offered a brief respite—though it could be a trick, a lure, you could never drop your guard against Al entirely, repartee had to be armour-plated as well as barbed and razor sharp.

'Wanna come to K2?' Al asked.

'Yeh.'

'Two more pints please.'

I think that's my earliest K2 memory. It's easy to get on these big trips when you know how.

* * *

Soon after, Al wrote:

23 Sept 84

Dear John,

Because of my personal circumstances I would like to hand over to you at this stage. It is highly likely that I will come to K2. Although I do not feel like it at the moment I am sure I will soon be back to normal and keen to go. The Royalty is obviously a problem. It is 30,000 Rps which must be sent in foreign currency, ie £s to the Pak Embassy in UK with the application. At my last enquiry about 4 weeks ago it was around 20 Rps to the pound. The Financial Times on Tuesday publishes a full currency exchange list. This makes it around £1,500, so I enclose a cheque for £300. I would suggest keeping the team as it is now. It can always be changed later if someone does not want to come or cannot come (obviously Andy may not be able to

12

come). Andy will certainly not have any money but if five of us pay £300 each that should do. I would tend not to invite anyone else at this stage—the trip is two years off and friends can be made and lost in that time. We could firm up the final team next autumn.

Applications need to be in by 30 October at the Pak embassy. That is for K2 in 1986. Other mountains you only need to apply one year in advance. I have told people 30 Sept as the date to give a margin, knowing how people tend to be last minute about things.

My scheme is to apply for another lower mountain for acclimatisation but that can be done anytime in the next thirteen months. It would be worth sending a note with the application to the effect that if we cannot get permission for 1986 we would like to roll over the application for 1987.

Embassy of Pakistan, Chancery Division, 35 Lowndes Square, London SW1 9JN (Tel 01-235 2044 Javed A Qureshi).

You will need to type out an application as per the enclosed form. All the words need to be typed out clearly. Any date of starting will do so long as it is not later than 15 June. (We can use another peak to climb before that period if they give us a June date). Basically we must have 15 June to end July for K2.

Scribbled at the bottom of the page was:

'Brian is doctor for purposes of this application,' and

'PS MAKE SURE YOU KEEP A COPY OF APPLICATION'.

The letter was typically Al: long on information, short on grammar, titbits packed in at every angle, second and third thoughts scribbled between the type, afterthoughts scribbled below. He would have hammered it out on his old typewriter in his bedroom office at Wayland Road, Sheffield 7, scribbled in all the ammendum and addendum and thrown it at an envelope, borrowed a stamp and chucked the whole at a letter box a minute or so later on his way to Burbage South, there to work out the moves on his latest problem—a climb which when solved he would have graded 6B—until it was repeated when it would be dismissed as a 5B scramble. Al's scrambles embraced climbs as hard as 5C, (London Wall at E4 for instance was for the most part '5C scrambling'). Then he might return to the office, hammer out his monthly bit for *High* magazine, grab a sandwich, go on down to the gym to train with the young rockstars, all of whom he could see off on finger-tip pull-ups—I know this to be true because he never stopped telling me—and thence to the pub for a few hours of his favourite competitive game, conversation.

The 'personal circumstances' he referred to in his letter were women problems of which Al had more than his share—though no more than his fair share (which applies to almost every mountaineer that I know). Andy is Andy Parkin who was one of Britain's best; a superb rock climber and a formidable mountaineer with routes such as a winter solo of the Walker Spur to his credit. Andy had been terribly injured in an accident when guiding on the Mitteleggi Ridge of the Eiger and it looked unlikely that he would be coming with us. Indeed it looked unlikely that he'd ever climb again. This was the first though that I knew of Andy's involvement in the K2 trip. Nor had I any idea who the rest of the team were. I didn't know Al well at this stage but I was beginning to see that his genius was frantic, frenetic and flawed—though genius of a sort he had indeed—and that his dealings wavered extreme to extreme, from rigorous to random, superficial to sedulous.

And that's how, entirely by default, and always with only temporary intent, I became the leader of the K2 expedition; never more than a purely administrative appointment.

Soon after I received his letter I rang Wayland Road intending to ask Al who exactly was in this team. I was told he was up at Jim's for counselling. Jim Curran was an expert on woman problems, which is to say that he was inexpert with women. Who isn't? But inexpert though his own traumatic record showed him to be, he was a veritable Solomon of the female mind compared with Al who had the romantic maturity of a fourteen year old and about as much understanding of the female mind as Rambo.

Al regarded Jim as a walking-talking agony uncle and to Jim's place he almost daily repaired for a dose of counselling. Not so much the blind leading the blind as the blind leading the purblind. I rang Counsellor Jim.

'Ask Al who's in the K2 team will you?'

Al came to the phone to tell me: 'Phil Burke, the twins, John Porter, Brian Hall, Andy, if he's fit, me if I'm sane, oh and you!'

I'd found the team.

We had still to get the mountain—this meant completing an application form. I hate forms of any sort. I'm allergic to them. Even the most straightforward, designed by some psychologist for simpletons to take in their stride, end scrunched up on the floor and reduce me to a steam of impotent, ridiculous rage as I fail to follow their progression. If there is a word for form-blindness then I'd like to plead it.

The K2 application forms were a classic of the post-colonial bureaucratic genre: 115 clauses, umpteen questions to be answered, preferences to be preferred, guarantees to be averred, explanatory notes—which for a man of my form-blindness needed their own explanatory notes—and annexes too many for one alphabet. The whole was crowned with a cryptic covering letter which began 'Kindly refer to our letter of even number dated 25th March 1982.' I had no idea what that jargon meant. I took a look, wrestled with it all for as long as I could bear, a period not much longer than 30 seconds, and handed it all over to Kath, my wife, who speedily completed the form, in septuplicate, as requested, rounded up shares of the deposit from the rest of the team and despatched the whole package to the Embassy of Pakistan.

The year was 1984.

Then no one did anything for a year.

That might have been the beginning.

But Jim Curran, poly lecturer, artist, film maker, wit, climber, postprandial prattler, repairer of shattered romances, and counsellor to those whose romances are shattered beyond repair: Counsellor Curran says there was another, an earlier beginning. Who can tell? That was the way of it. Al's way of it. Jim says this is how it began:

Al to Jim:

'Wanna make a film of K2?'

'Yeh.'

'Two more pints please.'

Which, being at least as good a start as any other, and the absence of a date notwithstanding, will do as the official beginning of the K2 trip, later to be known as the British K2 Expedition, still later to be known as 'The Fullers' Brewery K2 Expedition'. Doubtless there are as many beginnings, official or unofficial, as there were team members.

Later, Jim wrote, this would be early '85, to say, 'Before he went mad' (Counsellor Curran admitting failure!) 'Al said that if he went to K2 I could make a film of it. This is to say that I'm still on.' (Clearly he had forgotten his claim concerning the expedition's genesis.) I wrote back to say he 'was on'—though in truth there was nothing much to be on—but to be invited twice, in each case by a different leader, on a non-existent trip must be worthy of some remark. (Jim's 'what the hell's going on?' might be that remark).

In several respects already we were not just another expedition. We had two leaders, one retired as a semi-psychiatric case while the expedition was still at the 'two more pints' stage, the other reduced to apoplexy at the merest sighting of a form; a film maker with as yet no mountain to film, and a nebulous team that seemed to have been selected on the classic terrorist cell system whereby no single climber knew who were the other members—including, I suspect, Al, who'd engineered, if that is not too precise a word, the whole shooting match. Nor had we any mountain to climb, nor money to climb it with—though some of us (Curran, did you pay your £300?) were £300 pounds poorer and nothing to show for it. And there was K2—the second highest mountain in the world, one of the hardest; as yet no successful British ascent, plenty of British failures and only climbed six or seven times in all from any direction, by any nation.

1984 drifted into '85. We did nothing, heard nothing from Pakistan or their Embassy in London, wondered occasionally what had become of our £1,500 and still did nothing.

Still, it was fine to be able to reply nonchalantly to the over-the-pint 'got-any-trips-planned?' query, 'only K2'.

* * *

1985. I blundered into 'Experts in Extremes,' blundered out again and found myself jobless for the first time since leaving school, penniless for the umpteenth time. I sat for a few hours in my dingy flat in Manchester and surveyed what seemed to me to be the badly smouldering wreckage of a life—a dozen mid-life crises come all at once—which may read a touch melodramatic, but that's how it looked to me. It was certainly the lowest ebb of my life so far (I'm now sufficient of a realist to expect it to be surpassed sometime). Then I did what any other forty year old with no qualifications, or apparent prospects, would do on finding himself jobless for the first time in his life. I panicked; fled back to what had been intended as a temporary home in Wales and set about applying for every job under the sun. I threw together a C.V. (two jobs in twenty years takes very little throwing together) and stretched it to two sides of A4 by liberal interpretation of the 'never let your career shorten a good C.V.' theory, and sent it hither and thither in a random, nationwide, job search.

I didn't get the editorship of Paul Raymond's new men's magazine, and neither did I get the 'perfectionist with a breathtaking command of the English language' post advertised by a well-known women's magazine. Then I got an interview. The National Health Service were looking for general managers for their hospitals, and as such a job in Carlisle appealed. I applied. The C.V. fooled them and I was shortlisted. I hurtled northwards with some excitement. Carlisle was an extremely pleasant city and a salary in excess of £25,000 was worth telling a few white lies for. And such is the confidence of all Irishmen in their innate ability to bullshit that the facts that I'd seen the inside of a hospital only once in my life, that I knew nothing of hospitals or the NHS and possessed not the semblance of a qualification, deterred nor depressed me one whit.

Now my suit is of a light grey colour and that is important. I cut no sartorial corners, pressed suit, a newish tie, clean shirt, polished shoes, sober socks, clean finger nails, close shave, kempt hair, pencil and notepad—I couldn't see how I could fail. Surely I had young(ish), upwardly mobile, general manager written all over me. I sat in a corridor and waited my interview reading a sprinkling of NHS-orientated magazines and trying to commit certain key phrases to memory so that when the moment came I could stun the interview panel with lashings of NHS acronyms, jargon, argot, buzz-words—anything; the lot.

The door to the interview room opened and there emerged the preceding candidate. He looked a broken man. One out of the way I thought ruthlessly. A secretary warned me that I had about two minutes. I thanked her (in case she was asked for her impression) and strolled to the lavatory for a nervous pee, my head full of new-found information, my general demeanor that of the General Manager elect.

The hand basins boasted those taps that you push in to start and which then turn themselves off on some pre-ordained signal. I tried one. Not so much as a trickle. And another. And another. A great gout of water shot from the fourth tap with the force of a Niagara and, hitting the bottom of the curved bowl with awesome velocity, ricochetted at speed and in great volume, toward the handwashing interviewee—me. I was caught four-square by several gallons of very cold, NHS tap water. That it was undoubtedly sterile was scant consolation. The front of my trousers was soaked through, though my jacket had somehow largely escaped the torrent. I had about a minute and a half to go. On the wall at about shoulder height was a hot-air hand dryer but try what contortions I might, I couldn't get my trousers within feet of it—until it dawned. I took them off.

So there I stood, tie, shirt tails, socks and shoes and trouserless; trousers held to the hot air dryer which hummed happily away. Lacking any other diversion I whistled, no particular tune, just whistled. Just then the door swung open and a distinguished looking gent came in, eyed me with no little curiosity, went about his business and washed his hands. I whistled, no particular tune, just whistled, but a little more urgently.

Could he borrow the hand dryer, the distinguished gent wanted to know.

I replied that of course he could. It was as good as my hospital (though the confidence was under seige) and good managers treat their staff firm, fair and friendly, don't they?

As the distinguished gent submitted his hands to the jet of warm air, rubbing the while, as the instructions bade him, I stood to one side, trousers in hand, trying to look as if it was the most unremarkable thing in the world. But trying to look unremarkable with no trousers on is a lot harder than you'd think. I caught him regarding me out of the corner of one eye.

The dryer stopped. My discomfiture had ended. But no, the distinguished gent wasn't satisfied and fired the thing into action again. I went for a walk, not far, just up and down and around a bit, admired a non-existent view through a frosted window, tested a tap, tested all the taps, leaping back at the one I had forgotten as it tried to drown me a second time, at which the distinguished gent smiled a knowing and sympathetic smile and left.

When he'd finished I leapt to the machine, completed the trouser-drying operation, put them on, banged out the creases, straightened my tie, shrugged my shoulders a vigorous shrug or two, checked in the mirror that all was well, set the jaw to a managerial squareness and marched out.

'Ah Mr. Barry, they're ready for you now', the secretary said and gestured toward a closed door. I didn't thank her this time but I could make that up in the years to come. I opened the door and strode to a long table in a gait that I hope bore the mark of a NHS General Manager.

'Hullo Mr Barry. I'm the Chairman of this interview panel. Haven't we met somewhere before?' It was the distinguished gent speaking.

I didn't get the job; no reasons were given.

In Wales I had planned to live off my wits—as I always boasted I could—safe boast as long as I didn't have to. Trouble is those wits had long since atrophied, dulled by 20 years in subsidised employ—I was no match for the real world and took a severe beating round after round, and sulked between those rounds.

Sitting at home feeling sorry for myself, political views swinging violently to the left (refuge for the beaten I'd always said with disdain), I was approached by my eldest son Joseph.

'What's up Dad?' he asked.

I told him gently; told him as much as I thought a nine year old should know, and ended by saying that I was trying to work out ways of earning money.

Later I went into his bedroom. All his toys were in little piles around the floor. Each had a label, and every label a price.

'What you doing son?' I asked.

He replied that he was selling all his toys to raise some money since I didn't seem to be much of a hand at it. What was more, he was going to get a job in the local newsagent but was concerned that he might not be tall enough to see over the counter.

That did it. I surrendered a life insurance policy that I'd taken out a few years before in a rare responsible moment midst those halcyon days of fat, unconditional monthly salaries, and began to look for work, any work.

Jobs came in bits: writing articles and stories, guiding, a bit of advisory work, a video voice-over, ice-climbing for a TV film, felling trees, digging holes. I got on my bike, actually an airplane, but the promised ski-instructing job in the States foundered in a snowless winter. I returned an air fare poorer—slow learner.

Robbie Burns tried to console me:

> To catch Dame Fortune's golden smile,
> Assiduous wait upon her;
> And gather gear by every wile,
> That's justified by Honour:
> Not for to hide in it a hedge,
> Not for a train-attendant;
> But for the glorious priviledge
> Of being independent.

*   *   *

At last, in December 1985, permission for K2. Two years after applying, two years in which we'd invested £1,500, two years in which the price of K2 had risen by 15,000 rupees (£750), two years in which we heard not a whisper—suddenly here was permission to attempt the unclimbed NW ridge for 120 days from 1 May 1986.

Other than the occasional over-a-pint throw away 'only K2' I think most of us had given up hope. I'd almost got to the point of hoping that I didn't have to hope—you can't go sugaring off to K2 for months with no money, no job and two kids. Or can you? Inside I didn't see how I could go, outside I continued to act as if it was a certainty. So far we had not a cent in sponsorship, no kit and no plans though it was true that we'd had two planning meets. The first, held in a pub, went awry because two or three of the members turned up early and the rest of us never quite caught up. Still it was a grand night and if K2 could have been climbed on bullshit it was trampled all over that night.

On the way out Al tottered up to me and asked what I thought about the leadership. Since at that stage I was still the nominal leader I replied that I thought the leadership was absolutely splendid. No, that wasn't what he meant. Al sometimes had difficulty in saying what he meant, especially if what he meant was the least bit unpleasant. It was an endearing trait, one of his many endearing traits, though it could also be infuriating. He meant he wanted the leadership back. He felt he could cope now. It was a claim which, being of an equal condition I took with equanimity, but which would have astonished any sober witness to these proceedings.

'Fine', I said 'Have it. No sweat Al.'

But that was too easy for Al. 'We'll share it. Joint leaders', he said.

'OK,' I shrugged.

Joint leadership, I knew from experience, seldom works but there was little point in discussing it then. I hoped that Al would wake up leader the next day—it was a job that was rightfully his. He had initiated the whole thing, he knew ten times more about K2 than I. I had never assumed that I was doing more than holding the reins while Al sorted himself out. I should have pressed the point more firmly for Al persisted with joint leadership until it became an embarrassment. Had I still been at Plas y Brenin with all of that centre's resources at my disposal, it might have made sense. But that was no longer the case and joint leadership was our first mistake. I couldn't understand why Al didn't just take it back and re-assume his rightful role. It puzzled me then, was to puzzle me again, and still puzzles me even though I knew him much better at the end.

* * *

Then a terrible thing happened to a conscience already under seige. I was offered a job. The job was with the National Trust, managing one of their estates. At the interview they asked what I knew of the National Trust. I confessed that I knew little except that they had a rather dull image. When they asked me what I thought they should do about that I replied, casting caution to the winds, 'employ me'. They offered me the job. I broke K2 to them. They said they'd wait until July 15th—would I be back by then? I doubted it. Kath, then still my wife—just—was greatly relieved. She holds the National Trust in high regard and was appalled at the prospect of that august organisation employing a yob, and in a position of some prominence. She knew that I'd never be back in time. Nor was I.

But a lucrative two-week TV commentating job for an August programme was a target I could, and had to, hit—by then I would badly need the money.

* * *

March 1986: Al rang. No, no sponsor had been found but he was still hopeful. Failing a sponsor he reckoned we could do it on £2-3,000 each. Could I manage that? I said yes. I'm not sure if he believed me. I certainly didn't believe myself. Al asked if I could help with raising cash, did I have any ideas, would I get stuck in? I said sure.

The following, an article I wrote for *Sport and Leisure* tells the next bit of this beginning:

SPONSORSHIP FOR MOUNTAINEERING EXPEDITIONS
For we ordinary mortals, attracting sponsorship to underwrite our personal delusions of glory or grandeur is not easy. For super-stars it's as easy as falling off a log—though as Botham has discovered you'd better watch out when you're down, then everyone puts the boot in. The rule is don't fall too often or too far, and get up quick; or better, (paraphrasing Dylan), don't stumble if you've got no place to fall. But for super-stars, stumbling avoided, sponsorship is seldom a problem: break a world record and there will be an agent in hot pursuit, pencil at the ready, contract to hand, all the way round the lap of honour. From then on every step will make both rich, provided that the steps are quick enough—and, the rules of the jungle being

19

what they are, provided no-one runs quicker. Not so much a market-place; more an arena. Imagine, if imagination allows, a goal-scoring England striker. Now that would be a commodity so rare as to render sponsorship by the devil himself no more than a yellow card on the sprint to deification. Or then again take one of those extraordinarily unproductive individuals referred to, usually overgenerously, as 'personalities'. They may be realistic enough to thank their lucky stars that we all inhabit a world that prizes pap above most things. On the other hand they may believe that they are actually worth their asking price. In either case they need only know enough of the sponsorship jungle to know that they can afford to leave it all to their agent and accountant—and to hope that the Inland Revenue knows less.

But for us ordinary mortals, mortals whose solemn promise to the Acme Training Shoe Company never to be seen dead in any other product is something less than irresistible, whose similar offer to bedeck themselves, at any excuse, several feet thick, entirely and exclusively in the fine garments of the Go Faster Sportswear Company causes no ripple on that directors' board: mortals whose vow to immerse and gorge themselves solely on Speedo-Speedo Food and Drink products, and furthermore, to sing of the healthgiving, life enhancing, age-defying qualities of their elixirs to the earth's last horizon extracts not even so much as an acknowledgement from that ungrateful firm—far less an agreement to sponsor to the hilt the Inter Galactic Tiddlywinks Championship or the In Search of the Holy Grail Expedition (though that might be a starter); for all those mortals, which is most of us, there must be some other way, some other angle, some other avenue—or we remain armchair-bound and tele-glued for the rest of our days, watching a lucky, gifted and increasingly rich few. Fortunately it is in the order of things that there are billions of watchers, few gladiators; a sociology that brings continuing joy to manufacturers of armchairs, gloom to all those whose business is sport, and despair to the denizens of 16 Upper Woburn Place (The Sports Council) who would have it otherwise.

But what chance if mere mortal would-be sponsored of Milton Keynes indeed you be? Take some heart. The sponsorship business is still one where novelty stands a sporting chance—though an idea is unlikely to succeed on novelty alone, as the following cautionary tale illustrates. When I was asoldiering for Queen and Country in Borneo some years ago I had amongst my team a young and enterprising marine, a thug who I shall temporarily promote to the rank of 'lesser mortal', who complained bitterly that in the jungle fastness in which we had been incarcerated for 3 months (and were so to be for 3 more) shaving was a waste of time and money. There was, he argued, and not unreasonably, no-one to see us shaven or otherwise. I trotted out the usual litany about morale, self discipline, appearances, etc, ending my argument with an intellectually bankrupt 'and if you can't take a joke you shouldn't have joined'. He did rather better and wrote to Wilkinson, then engaged in internecine commercial warfare with Gillette saying that he thought that Wilkinson Sword Edge were the greatest and that here he was fighting off Indonesians with one hand whilst effecting the smoothest of shaves with the other; and that one single blade was so keen, why it had lasted a full 3 months of daily use; and that they could proclaim to the wide world that all this was true, and that he had said so. He enclosed a picture of himself in a rugged pose, all bandoliers and grenades, grinning through a soapy face, an ostensibly Wilkinson razor held triumphantly aloft. Some weeks later the reply fluttered from the skies by parachute—our existence was wholly dependent on air-supply. It thanked him for his testimonial and enclosed a further three months' supply, a solitary blade. At least they had a sense of humour.

My own bag is mountaineering, a game which for the two centuries that it has been played has defied satisfactory explanation of its rules, purpose or raison d'etre to an increasingly indifferent and incurious public. In addition to being inexplainable it is well nigh unwatchable—'aint box-office, aint prime-time.' Some years ago friends and I decided to have a shot at climbing K2, the second highest mountain in the world, generally regarded to be the hardest (it's much steeper than Everest and is only a few hundred feet lower) and unclimbed by any Britons. (See how easily the hype rolls off this new-practiced pen). The Himalayan countries—China, Pakistan, India and Nepal make the most of their gigantic geographical assets. The peak booking fee for K2 stood at £2,500—a nice little earner.

Eight of us coughed up £300 each, sent off our application to the Pakistan Ministry of Tourism (in septuplicate) and waited. Two years later (December 1985) we received a reply. The good news was that we were to be granted 120 days on the mountain beginning May 1st 1986, the bad, that the peak fee had gone up by £500. We covered the increase by recruiting two more team members at £250 each and set about some hasty but earnest planning.

Al Rouse and I, co-leaders, drew up an expedition budget which concluded with the depressing calculation that our non-box-office, non-prime-time, inexplainable and unwatchable venture was going to cost, at the very least, £25,000. The principal costs were something in the order of £5,000 for flights to Islamabad, a further £500 for freight, £7,300 for the hire of porters to get all our kit the 14 days' walk to a base camp at the foot of the mountain at 17,000', £2,000 on equipment and £2,500 on food. An inescapable remainder comprised insurance, medical, internal travel and the like. Faced with the prospect of finding somewhere between £2,500 and £3,000 from our own pockets we mounted an energetic but amateurish search for sponsorship.

I convinced myself that so fine an example of British endeavour, resourcefulness and enterprise as this expedition would appeal to the shortly to be 'privatised' British Airways and wrote straightway to Lord King along those lines, hoping that he might see his way to free flights and free freight—or, at very least, some lesser deal. I thought my letter—on specially printed K2 expedition notepaper—a masterpiece of the begging art and confidently awaited an award of free first-class air-tickets for the entire expedition, as many camp followers as we could muster, freight unlimited— cost no object.

The reply was prompt, polite, and devastatingly unhelpful:

'Our experience of the sponsorship of expeditions has tended to show that there are limited promotional returns to be gained from such involvements and consequently we have had to decline such offers of sponsorship.

However, although we are unable to offer free transportation, the Market Centre responsible would be prepared to consider offering an advantageous fare. If this is of value to you you should contact our General Sales Agent, Greaves Travel, on 01-487-5681.'

It was signed 'Wartnaby'.

I confess anger. In retrospect that was a silly reaction. My reasoning, perhaps at least as silly ran something like this: all sorts of celebrities and so called personalities are daily awarded freebies that neither their bank balance or their promotional return index justifies. Had I not, only recently, read that Joan Collins was in the habit of breezing into international airports and demanding and getting free flights to wherever her egotistical whim took fancy—first class, naturally; whereas here were we bent on the noblest deeds, deeds of the greatest national moment, utterly wholesome lads unable to scrounge even a bus ride to the airport. Now that the first flush of indignation has evaporated leaving a strain of commercial reality I have to agree that it is hardly fair to ask anyone other than a mountaineer to see K2 as anything other than an 8,500-metre pile of snow and rock or its ascent as other than a pretty daft way of spending £25,000 of the national exchequer and several zillion calories of personal effort in three unpaid months of unremitting slog; pretty daft. I further agree that given the choice of giving a lift to anyone of our team or to Joan Collins there is not the slightest doubt who'd be walking; K2 could wait.

Time was getting short, we desperate and prepared to try almost anything. Al recalled an enterprising ploy that he'd tried some years ago when attempting to raise cash to finance an expedition to Patagonia. Because no-one inhabits the mountains of this wild and relatively unexplored area of South America most of the unclimbed peaks are also un-named. A custom has grown whereby mountaineers give a name of their choosing to any un-named peak that they are first to climb. Al reasoned that a place in history, or at least in geography, must be worth a lot of cash and wrote directly to Idi Amin with the promise that the first virgin summit that fell to him would be known to posterity as Mount Idi Amin—for a price. He received no reply. Perhaps he wrote to the wrong address.

We drew up a list of the world's megalomaniacs: Bokasa had gone and Baby Doc too; and just as he rose to the top of our list Marcos got the boot. There simply wasn't a respectable megalo to be had—we both considered Gaddafi to be even beyond the pale of our indigence. Besides no-one can agree on how to spell his name: what hope was there of his receiving our letter?

I tried the long shots. Jeffrey Archer: gave him my best shot—ending in a mixture of hope and flippancy: 'It is just conceivable that you might know someone who has £30,000 and nothing better to do with it than sponsor an expedition. If it helps I have considered voting Tory, though I'm afraid that in our team I'm in a minority of one. However, you never know what a donation will do to a man's fickle political loyalties!'

The reply was undeservedly polite, wished us luck but brought no cash. Richard Branson the famous Virgin and Eddie Shah received similar letters. So far neither has replied. Perhaps none is deserved.

It seemed that we were stuck. Now for the seven years that I worked at Plas y Brenin, the National Centre for Mountain Activities, I had, when beaten turned to June Mack who worked for the Sports Council, at their Headquarters near Euston. One of her jobs was to advise and assist me in running the Centre. She never failed. (Another job was to keep me on the straight and narrow. Here her record is less than perfect, and none of the blame hers.) I wrote telling her the problem and the size of it. By return she sent a pamphlet, a computerised list of U.K. COMPANIES,

PRODUCTS AND THE SPORTS THEY SPONSOR— a Fort Knox-worth of sponsorship. Since none of them sponsored mountaineering—or owned that they did—I selected the first 100 (there were over 1,000 in the pamphlet) for a mail shot. Next I wrote a new spiel and casting modesty to the 9 good winds (not an especially difficult task) I made the most of all the positive aspects of the expedition, dwelling on anything I thought might be marketable or newsworthy. With the help of a word processor it was tailored to fit on one side of A4. I have no idea how much people need to read in order to part with £30,000 but I can't imagine that anyone could stomach more than a sheet of A4 of unashamedly self-promoting flannel. The finished product read thus:

'K2—Nearly Highest, Easily Hardest
The Mountain—K2, 'The Savage Mountain' is universally accepted as the hardest mountain in the world. It is also the second highest; at 8611 metres (28,250') only two hundred metres lower than Everest itself.

The 1986 British Attempt—A team of 8 top British climbers is to make the first British attempt of K2. They have elected to try by the N.W. Ridge which has so far repulsed two attempts, one by a Polish party, the other by an American. In all they will spend up to 3 months on this remote vastness high on the Pakistani-Chinese border.

The Team—Alan Rouse and John Barry are joint-leaders. Alan Rouse is one of our best Himalayan climbers. He has been on 15 expeditions, including the first ascent of Mount Kongur (25,200') with Chris Bonington.

John Barry, ex-Royal Marine Captain and ex-Director of Britain's National Centre for Mountain Activities is also an experienced Himalayan mountaineer and a leading alpinist.

All the other team members are similarly experienced. Alan and Adrian Burgess are identical twins, originally from Holmfirth but now resident in North America. Together they have climbed the likes of Dhaulagiri, 8172 metres (26,810'). John Porter, Brian Hall, Phil Burke and Mo Anthoine have been on over thirty expeditions between them.

The Film—A TV film will be made in co-operation with Trans World International, Inc., the world's leading sports film makers and distributors, who already report worldwide network interest in such a film. [That film later fell through but was rescued, generously, by Chameleon, a Leeds-based firm of filmmakers.] Sponsors will be rewarded with invaluable media exposure. The same climbing team has already made a film of 'Everest in Winter' which was networked at Christmas '85 on ITV, shown twice on PBS (U.S.A.) and has been sold to ten other nations.

Jim Curran, our film-maker and chief cameraman has made four films for television. His successes include a first prize at the Kendal International Film Festival and a second prize at the world's leading mountain film festival at Trento. This expedition offers a new filming challenge—for despite the fact that the Karakorum is spectacularly photogenic a good film has yet to be made of the range. And since no British team has yet climbed K2 by any route a good film will have little difficulty in attracting public interest.

23

The Book—A book, his third, will be written by John Barry. His most recent book, 'The Great Climbing Adventure', (Oxford Illustrated Press) enjoyed an enthusiastic reception (by all his immediate family—who freely share their copy).

The Media—Details of previous K2 expeditions have featured on News at Ten, BBC News and Newsnight as well as on Radio and in the national newspapers. Sponsors will get a good return.'

This wouldn't fit on the front of our expedition note-paper because that had been designed with the words K2 writ so large that they consumed about one sixth of the available area and try as I might, I couldn't précis the thing any tighter. I could shorten it by leaving out a paragraph, even two, but knowing nothing of the game I was attempting to play, I was concerned that the excised paragraph might have held the very lines that would have appealed to a prospective sponsor had it stood.

The solution was to print it on the reverse of the sheet with enough bait on the front to hook readers into turning over. It was while I was pondering the prose persuasive enough for this purpose, that I was struck with what I modestly consider to be a marketing ploy that will rank right alongside 'Go to work on an egg', 'Guinness pure genius', and whatever else has caught the public fancy these last few years.

And so a hundred letters hit the market headed, each with an identical text, but each with a unique, customised heading:

'The Acme K2 Expedition 1986?' or 'The Go Faster Sportswear K2 Expedition?'.

I went on to suggest that if they liked the title, they would surely like it better without the question-mark. And all that it would take to remove it was £30,000. I added what I hoped was a compulsive argument or two and concluded by saying:

'If you decide that the question mark should be erased please contact Alan Rouse or myself.'

Well that's the way it happens in the movies, isn't it? And in real life too. Two days later I received a phone call from Fullers Brewery. They were interested, could I come to London to talk? Not half. I was sure that it had been my great state-of-the-marketing-art headings that had done the trick. 'No' they said, 'it was your address—2, The Old Brewery.'

Well we talked and the talks bore fruit. An agreement was signed and an advertising agent hired—by our sponsors who were understandably keen that their investment should yield the highest possible return. And so a brewery, a team of climbers, and K2 are joined in what we will do our best to ensure is a mutually worthwhile venture. But it is not quite as simple as taking the money and climbing. There are debts of honour, promises easily made in London that will be harder to keep on K2, obligations readily undertaken in the heady atmosphere of a brewery boardroom that in the thin air above 6,000 metres will seem chores of Sisyphean oppression. For when you accept a sponsor, especially one as generous as Fullers, you sell your soul and much of what is in it. Another way is to pay from your own pocket.

Of the hundred companies approached in the first assault about half have so far answered—so far being, at the time of writing, 6 weeks later. They have all said no, usually very politely and often wishing us luck at the same time. It matters not now what they say but I wonder what if, in all that 1,000 that I had intended to approach, we had somehow missed Fullers Brewery, or not said something in that letter that struck a chord, or caught Fullers too late—after they had sponsored some other venture—what then? Hit and miss about fairly says it. (Especially since Fullers have never before sponsored anything beyond their local rowing club and may never wander off flat friendly water again.)

So mountaineers need not entirely despair at 'the limited promotional return' of their game (and there are plenty of satisfactions to be found in that limitation—privacy, secrecy, independence—you have to decide what price you put on those things). There is cash out there and it can be secured.

To date (April '86) in a short two months' campaign, the Fullers K2 Expedition 1986 has raised £30,000 from our main sponsor, £1,000 from Texaco (one of the team sells their petrol) and £2,000 from the BMC and Mount Everest Foundation. Newspaper and TV news rights will provide a little extra assuming that current negotiations bear fruit; a book will earn a contract and an advance in three carrot-shaped dollops, and the film, if it is half as good as we hope it will be, should realise a bob or two—albeit post expedition.

I have confined myself to the raising of finance but sponsorship may take the form of goods, food or equipment, all of which are actually easier to come by than hard cash. There are dozens of equipment manufacturers who regularly and generously support worthwhile expeditions with very good deals on tents, rucksacks, sleeping bags and clothing and other essentials. It would be difficult to be sure that I named them all but it is equally difficult not to name the most prominent. Karrimor, Berghaus, Mountain Equipment, Phoenix, Europa Sport, DMM, Wild Country, Troll, British Wool, Javlin. Nor would it be fair to conclude without mentioning those hundreds of food suppliers who have given freely of their time and products to countless expeditions—and usually for little more than a polite letter and a handful of slides showing their product to good advantage in some unlikely situation. Too often their reward is rather less even than that small price.

We leave in three weeks (May 1st) after which the onus will be on us to repay those who have so generously supported us with their money or equipment, or goods or victuals—partly to honour the debt and partly to make fund raising a bit easier next time—for us or for the next team.

A Whole New Order of Chaos

'Whatever you can do, or dream you can do, begin it. Boldness has genius, power and magic in it.'

(Goethe)

So in the two years, 1984 and '85 nothing, or next to nothing, had happened. Now it all happened in two months. Fullers had agreed to sponsor us by the end of March. We were planning to fly from Heathrow on the 29th April—about a month to finalise, as Al cheerfully described it, the details—or, as anyone with more than a toe-hold on reality would have said, to organise the entire trip from beginning to end.

The who's who of the team unfolded at last: Al, Brian Hall, John Porter, Aid and Al Burgess (the twins), Phil Burke, Dave Wilkinson and myself were the climbers. Andy Parkin was out, not yet sufficiently healed from injury—though healing better than most of us had dared to hope. Eight climbers were thought to be a handy number though Al had a theory that the more people that came along the cheaper the trip would be for all—for despite Fullers' generosity we still needed to make personal contributions of something like £1,000 in total. Like many of Al's theories, he alone was capable of its comprehension. This particular piece of mathematical wizardry he aired over a pint in the Byron, a pub in Sheffield. I can't recall exactly the audience but since the subject was sums, and Al was a Cambridge scientist, the theory went unchallenged for a few minutes until Jim Curran, who'd been staring into his half-full glass for minutes as if the meaning of life was to be discovered there, ventured:

'Does that mean that if sufficient people come the trip will be free and we'll break even? And if so why don't we take a couple of hundred and make a big profit?'

The logic of Jim's improvement seemed irrefutable to $2+2$ me but Al refuted it in seconds with a devastating counter-deduction and a grin and a chuckle. The grin and chuckle I understood, Al's logic, deductions and mathematics were a dozen moves beyond me. Sometimes I felt they were beyond Al too and it was all a game of bluff, and sometimes it was and sometimes it wasn't; all part of Al's mercurial make-up, most times endearing, odd times infuriating, other times infuriatingly endearing.

One of his infuriatingly endearing habits was to offer places on the K2 trip to anyone with whom he was drinking and to whom he took a shine—and since he tended to be in love with half the world by tennish most pub nights the team's number wobbled from eight to infinity. Whether Al's invitation stemmed from his innate generosity or from a belief in his own 'the more that come' theory was never clear but the result was always the same: by breakfast Al would be rueing his generosity or re-checking his maths and I, curiously regarded by Al to possess diplomatic and palliative powers, would be despatched to haul some new hopeful down to earth from the very summit slopes of K2 and his own private white windy presence of eternity.

'I wish you wouldn't do that Al', I'd say over a pint.

'Sorry mate, what ya having?'

You just couldn't be cross with him—well not for long anyway.

Now we held a meeting at Al's house to discuss the non-climbing expedition appointments.

Al was at his dancing, clowning, cajoling best; master of ceremonies, orchestrating; his shimmering wittiest best. There were new members to be found: a doctor and, because we were now financially secure, a Base Camp Manager.

'Anyone know anybody who'd want to be Base Camp Manager?' Al had asked a few days previously. I said that I did and that I'd sound him out. Jim Hargreaves was the man, long time friend, ex-school chum, ex-run-away-to-sea-merchant-seaman, ex-sergeant, ex-Plas-y-Brenin instructor, ex-canoeist (Colorado, Bio Bio, Cape Horn), business man, (no 'ex' expected or imminent), and street fighter. I called round at his home the very next Friday and while we (Jim, Bonnie his wife, and I) were chatting over a pre-Friday-night-in-the-boozer cuppa, I noticed a shotgun hooked to the wall. Such a thing may be unremarkable in many country households but I knew that Hargreaves had no interest in game, and doubted that he had ever fired a shot in his life—or ever wanted to. (In the army, he'd served in the PT Corps—officially a non-combatant unit—though to describe Hargreaves as a non-combatant is both to stretch the meaning of that term and to risk a punch on the nose.) Jim caught my eyes on the gun and shot me a 'don't mention the bloody shotgun' look.

So I asked him about the shotgun.

'Always fancied shootin' a bit of game, know what I mean.' I didn't, not exactly, but I knew precisely what he didn't mean which was that he'd always fancied shootin' a bit of game. Bonnie knew it too but, grinning hugely beneath a poker face said nothing; enjoyed Jim's discomfort.

'Bloody hell,' Jim said once we were outside. 'Bloody shotgun, bloody epic.'

The tale was told. Jim had run up a huge bill drinking on tick at our local. George, the landlord, surely the most tolerant in all the land, decided that three figures of tick needed a settlement and Jim, punctilious in these things (when reminded) signed a cheque in a trice, and, business man that he is, entered the amount on the stub. Some days later Bonnie asked how come he was paying the pub a three-figure sum and Hargreaves, sensing that the truth might finally exhaust twenty years of superhuman tolerance, announced that he'd bought from George a shotgun. Shotgun? I am at a loss to explain why the lie was a shotgun. Hargreaves too—and I have asked him the question a dozen times. But shotgun is what he said. Maybe that twenty years of crime, largely detected, often advertised, drives a man to wilder, more desperate deceits than the rest of us. Anyhow he said shotgun.

'Where is it then?' Bonnie wanted to know.

'Picking it up Friday.'

'It is Friday.'

'Er next Friday.'

And so, in order to give substance to the subterfuge he'd had to go out, the Friday next, and buy a second-hand shotgun for which he had not the slightest use. Which is why I'd got that look not to bring the subject up and why I'm so especially pleased now that I did.

I subjected Hargreaves to our rigorous selection procedure.

'Wanna come to K2?'

'Yeh.'

'Two more pints please.'

Much later he asked, 'What to do?'

'Base Camp Manager.'

'NFP' (no effing problem).

'And ride shotgun.'

It was an inspired selection. Hargreaves threw his awesome energy (and not much less awesome weight) into his new job and in no time the expedition rule was if you couldn't fix it or track it down, you passed the problem on to the BCM who would produce twice the requisite quantity at half the expected price. Take batteries. We calculated that we needed 200 for personal stereos and the like. Hargreaves volunteered to acquire them and at cost, if possible. When they arrived he thought the package looked a shade small but was loath to confess administrative error to the firm and so rang to tell them that they had inadvertently mislaid a nought on his requested sum. We could have illuminated half of Asia for a year.

The veterans of Filthistan, as Al managed to call it without attaching any great offence, all felt that a doctor in a place so remote and so high as K2 was a desirable thing. Bev Holt (MA, LRCP, FFA, RCS) Consultant Anaesthetist at Newcastle General Hospital, had enjoyed a varied career that included swapping hearts with Christian Barnard. Now he seemed suicidally eager to risk years of hard won reputation in this wild venture. Perhaps he sought psychiatric experience.

It may have been at this meeting, that Al produced a tape measure and called for a great collection of vital statistics that Javlin and Mountain Equipment needed for the clothing that they were tailoring for each of us. Hargreaves applied the tape to Curran, and as Al called for a measurement, Hargreaves produced a figure.

28

'Chest', calls Al. Curran puffs out to a mighty but momentary 42.

'42' replies Hargreaves as Curran collapses to a near normal 38.

'Waist', calls Al. At this Curran, of a sudden coy of his vital statistics, seizes the tape and retreats to another room whence, after a pause, we hear, 'Christ I don't believe it!' The distance (for distance it was) was communicated to Al in a whisper. Al noted the secret, added to it inches, gave it decibels and before long half of Sheffield knew. But the joke was later to be on us all. When Al took our measurements to Javlin the lady tailor surveyed them with a knowing glance, took out a pencil, and made to each of them an adjustment. When Al asked what she was doing she replied that with male statistics it was standard practice to deduct two inches from the chest and add them to the waist. One particular set of statistics she declared to be anatomically impossible, or did we have Mr Universe in our team? We did and he was called Phil—who to this day claims that his measurements were of unimpeachable accuracy and that as a result of falsification his clothes never fitted properly. The rest of us were adjusted to about the right degree.

*   *   *

Then Al bought a computer. What Al's formidable, if erratic, intellectual prowess could do once harnessed to a computer was too awful to contemplate. But contemplation we were spared. The result of this unholy alliance, man and machine, Amstrad and Al, was soon upon us: memos, lists, budgets, letters. Al now moved to a large house, Rupert House no less, of Rupert Road, and kept an office of impressive efficiency. 'I don't believe in capitalism but if I have to be a capitalist I'm going to be a bloody good'n.' He was as good as his word—though I always meant to ask him who it was said he had to be a capitalist. I have an inkling that, like most of us, he just wanted to be rich, and, to be sure, he was far better equipped than most of us to realise such a wish. The walls of his office, a large high ceilinged room in Rupert House, were hung with shelves and lined with tidily arranged files: Personal Finance, Income Tax (a smallish file) *High* Articles, Foreign Magazines, Guiding Commitments and many more. I was always impressed, I to whom more than three sheets of paper on any one subject represented a major organisational headache, an insuperable filing problem. The computer lived on Al's desk in a corner of the room, the focal point of this monument to self sufficiency, independence and initiative—the battle cries of the party that Al detested, yet whose values he so amply manifested. Al was nothing if not a tangle of contradictions—all part of his elusive charm. I never so much as dared touch the computer but I convinced myself that somewhere inside were all the Fullers' K2 Expedition 86 souls, and maybe, bursting to get out, K2 itself. Fanciful? Not when you saw the amount of information that Al force-fed into the thing and the reams, literal though not always literary reams, that it regurgitated on K2-related subjects alone—and I'm told that they can think of more than one thing at one time. Magic. That must be it.

*   *   *

Fullers called an Expedition Promotional Meeting for 1st April. The afternoon before, I travelled across to Sheffield for a 'pre-planning' meeting. This, it turned out, consisted of hauling me off to Burbage South to be emasculated on a succession of Al's 5C solo scrambles. My brief single triumph turned to utter dejection as Al recalled that probably it was only 5A after all. Afterwards to the pub for 15 pre-Queensberry rounds of ruthless repartee. About this last game: I have to say that, though by English standards Al was fairly adept, something of a local champion, in Ireland where the talking game was invented and where everyone plays everyone else and all at the same time, he wouldn't have got past the qualifying rounds. He didn't have the timing see, or the raw gut instinct for it. Cambridge smoothie, big words, fancy notions and all would only have kept an Irish kindergarten amused 'till the milk break. But by English standards he wasn't half-bad, not half-bad at all.

Next day we took the train to London, both squeezed into ill-fitting suits—Al's the iller I thought, rather smugly—but the both as ruddy a pair of rustics as W1 has ever disdained. Fullers were a customer of Smees Advertising Agency, and it was to that address that we reported. We were held at bay in the foyer by the not entirely welcoming gaze of a species of secretary bird whose job it seemed to be to imprison suspects in that gaze whilst at the same time smiling a welcoming 'go on up' to those of a more prepossessing appearance. That the two operations were simultaneously possible on the one face was a matter of some fascination to me. But for Al it was the fact that she could answer the telephone, make notes and coffee, sort the mail, do her hair, straighten her seams—yes for heaven sakes, seams—that got him all of a lather.

It had come as some surprise to me that there were things called Advertising Agencies that made a living from promoting and advertising other things. In this case we were the thing to be promoted—on Fullers' behalf.

I was to be further surprised, staggered I think this second time, to discover that Fullers were to spend more via Smees on our promotion than the sum by which they were sponsoring us. Al, the socialist, took it all in his stride. A particularly useless manifestation of capitalism he called it; advertising people don't actually produce anything, and create wealth only for themselves. I meant to ask him what part in the great Utopian scheme of things we mountaineers played who not only didn't create anything but spent other folk's wealth on thin air—literally—but I forgot to ask.

The secretary-cum-seam straightener had checked upstairs that we were indeed bona-fide visitors, and Anthony Smee, young executive to his Russell and Bromleys, appeared seconds later to whisk us in a substantial limmo to Fullers' headquarters at Chiswick. There followed a most cordial meeting between we three, plus Charles Williams (Managing Director) and Maureen McCleland (Press and Publicity Officer). I reflected that it really had been a massive piece of good fortune that had brought us to this right place at this right time. It was hard to imagine how we could have found friendlier, more helpful sponsors; sponsors moreover who made a product, albeit for a profit, that we could heartily and honestly endorse.

I said as much on the train back to Sheffield, but Al couldn't quite bring himself to shake off at least a professed suspicion of all things capitalist—I think for my sake as much as anything. In all, we attended three of these meetings in London with Fullers and Smees, and Al was distrusting to the end, never really relaxing until the money was banked in the Expedition account in Sheffield. I felt that Fullers were sincere from the beginning and I trusted them. Al said this was naive but if anything it was Al who was insincere, to begin with at least. He saw Fullers as a bunch of capitalists whose business it was to exploit, and who, therefore, were themselves a fair target for exploitation. Many of my left wing climbing friends take this view but for someone of Al's intelligence and abilities to hold, and not only to hold but to propound a view of such subconscious servility was something I could never understand—and I had cause not to understand a dozen times in the next four months. One result was that Al, distrustfully nervous at those Fullers meetings, would rush into promising them everything, anything, and would not be delayed by my attempts to slow him. At the first meeting we promised Fullers, who I think knew even less about mountaineering than we knew about commerce, the earth. What about the such and such deal I asked Al on the way back.

'Oh there's no way we can do that. Anyway they'll have forgotten about it by tomorrow. We've just got to get that cash in the bank.'

But they didn't forget. Anthony Smee followed up every meeting with a written record and details of our every agreement.

Al would ring: 'There's no way we could have agreed to that.'

'We did Al,' I'd reply.

But his boyish charm got him by these small, self-dug pitfalls. And in the end Fullers, brewers of beer, gave us the money and shored it up with honest goodwill and support beyond any commercial consideration to the bitter, the bitterest end.

*   *   *

Fullers asked for mug shots. We took them to London. On the train Al dug them out and I commented how odd it was that the twins could look so different. Aid and Al, Al and Aid were, in life, nearly identical, both cast of bronze by Michelangelo, rippling and angular of torso, and both what I think a woman's magazine might describe as ruggedly handsome of head; and both were more than pleased with all these things. Somehow the camera had lied in those mug shots. Aid's indeed looked fit to sit on David's shoulders but Al, by a contrivance of light and shade, looked as if he'd fallen off the back of a tractor and was unable to find his way, unassisted, to the next haystack. Al Rouse with that infectious chuckle of his, changed the names so that Aid the Adonis became Agricultural Al and Al of agriculture was promoted Adonis. The swop was a classic of Rouse's impish humour.

In the few weeks that followed, Al unleashed the joint product of his and his word processor's energies. One such was a *Memorandum*, no less. Knowing his audience and concerned that there might not be one, he had scrawled the entreaty, *'Please Read'* across the top in heavy inch-high felt-tip. A second and identical entreaty in the computer's own hand constituted the second line.

31

PLEASE READ

MONEY
The cheque for £30,000 from *FULLERS BREWERY* has now been banked. See attached sheet with a rough budget. The trip will not be entirely free for members and it is important that it is not seen as such, because of grants etc. If there is a surplus then the MEF grant will be repaid, etc. This seems most unlikely at present.

Each expedition member should bring a reserve of £400 in Travellers cheques. This gives an expedition reserve of £4,400 which can be used to cover the helicopter bond or for other purposes. In addition most expedition members have already contributed to the expedition as follows (check if this corresponds with your calculations and let me know of any mistakes): A.R. £700, J.B. £335, P.B. £335, J.P. £335, D.W. £500, J.C. £300, BR.H. £300, Al.B. £291 (329$ plus £65 from Everest Film), Aid.B. £339 (400$ plus £65).

Next weekend I will level out these contributions so that each person has put in exactly £300.

The financial conclusion is that the trip will cost each individual overall between £200 and £700. If you want to buy presents etc, then bring extra money above the individual £400 of TCs. Living costs, boozing etc, will come from expedition funds as long as we are out of the country.

TRAVEL
A.B., A.B., A.R., J.B., J.H., J.C. leave on PK 702, 29th April at 15.15 from Heathrow, arrive Islamabad 30th April 09.05.

P.B., D.W., BE.H., BR.H., J.P. leave on PK 786, 3 May at 13.15 from heathrow (sic) arrive Islamabad 4 May 0.500.
Tickets are open return.

BAGGAGE
Absolutely crucial that as much personal baggage as possible is sent out by freighting. This means bringing it on the weekend of the 20th. If in doubt bring all the things that you think you might possibly need and we can always reduce it. Personal baggage allowances are the standard 20kg and excess baggage is extremely expensive compared to freight so stuff must go early.

Most of the personal baggage allowance will be made up of film and camera gear, along with items not produced in time by manufacturers. Bring an exact list of everything that you are sending.

CONTACTS IN ISLAMABAD
We are hoping to stay with Embassy people but this is not yet finalised. A temporary contact address is as follows: British K2 Expedition, Nazir Sabir, Mountain World, PO BOX 1442, Islamabad. Telephone 822993.

Facing page: **Porters negotiate the bridge of two planks across the Braldu Gorge at the end of the first day's walk.**

MAIL
The above address can be used until we have fixed up arrangements out there. We will have a mail runner. Mail takes approximately 14 days from Base Camp using normal channels but this will be speeded up for ITN News and important messages can be sent this way.

SPONSORS
The terms of our sponsorship were negotiated by JB and AR on behalf of the expedition. We had to make on the spot decisions and apologise if we have made any mistakes. Although the terms look rather complicated the whole arrangement really boils down to us trying our best to give them publicity. They are very pleasant and reasonable people at Fullers Breweries. Several people we are dealing with are rather more moralistic than we are used to so be careful with obscenities. Fullers have employed Smees Advertising Agency to promote our expedition and we are therefore in a sense answerable to both parties. Anthony Smee is dealing with our trip and he is very cooperative.

A FEW IMPORTANT POINTS:
Our expedition is now called The Fullers' K2 Expedition and should be referred to as such at all times—particularly when dealing with the media. Try not to refer to any other sponsors as 'sponsors', call them equipment suppliers or any euphemism suitable. Fullers want to be known exclusively as our sponsors in NATIONAL MEDIA. Minor white lies may be needed on occasions here—a skill I am sure we all have developed to a more than sufficient level. I enclose a copy of the agreement which is more a letter of intent than a legal contract.

PRESS DAY—29th APRIL
At 11am there will be a press call at Fullers Breweries. After this we will go to Heathrow on the Fullers double decker bus. Those who are not flying should be able to get away by 1pm.

Please SEND BIODETAILS FOR FULLERS USE (ie age, background, general sort of bullshit) to me in Sheffield.

FILM
We were committed to make a film in order to satisfy our sponsors. We negotiated with several parties but in the end only Chameleon offered an appropriate deal, ie one which offered us the possibility to make a film without us having to pay for it. They provide us with the wherewithal to make a film and they do the so called post production. When the film is finished we get £6,000 some of which may be absorbed in expenses but basically most of it will come to the team members equally, thereby probably cancelling out any initial expenditure on individuals' behalf. Everyone's cooperation will be required to make a successful film but it will not in any way interfere with our climbing programme.

EQUIPMENT
What the expedition is providing for everyone;
Sun Hat, Sunglasses, Goggles, Face Mask, T-shirts misc, Umbrellas, Training shoes, Javlin Super S Salopettes and Jacket (stretch pile), One-piece Goretex suit of

2 layer rip stop, Base Camp tent (quality dome), Yeti gaiters, plastic boots, Karrimat (1 for base, 1 for bivis), harness, jumars, helmet, skis with touring bindings, skins, ski poles, socks, headtorch, foamie sleeping mat.

This list is not complete, a further list will follow.

STILL FILM

The expedition will be purchasing 250 roles of Fuji slide film. This will be available for team members to use as they wish. All photos taken will belong to team members who took them but other members can have any dupes they want. It is suggested that at the end of the trip everyone picks their best 20 slides and these are duped communally and a set given to each member; this would cost some money but from past experience is a highly practical solution to the problems of trying to get hold of each other's slides for years after. We could use any surplus money for this purpose if everyone is agreed.

BOOK

At a previous meeting we established a principle that a book advance would go to the expedition but that the author would take the royalties minus the advance. Both John Barry and John Porter have investigated book possibilities.

Can everyone bring about five books then there should be enough to read.

POST EXPEDITION WORK

Inevitably there will be a great deal of post expedition work to do relating to sponsors as well as producing reports etc. The costs involved should clearly be borne by the expedition so bear this in mind—if we spend all of our money we may need to ask everyone for a further contribution.

Please SUPPLY ADDRESS AND PHONE NUMBER OF ONE WIFE OR GIRLFRIEND TO WHOM YOU WANT THE NEWS PASSED ON FROM FULLERS (IF ANY)— to A.R.
Expedition postcards will be available.

Please bring a list of all sponsors and people who have helped in any way to the meeting on the weekend of the 20th April in Sheffield. Please categorise as follows: A—More than £1,000 or equivalent in goods; B—£50 – £1,000 or equivalent; C—Below £50 or other help. Please include address, phone number, way they helped, and any personal contact within firm or organisation.
RING IMMEDIATELY IF YOU HAVE ANY STUFF WEIGHING ANYTHING SUBSTANTIAL WHICH WILL NOT BE AVAILABLE FOR 20th APRIL.
Be prepared to have Fullers badges sewn on every thing that might move. IT COSTS £6 PER KILO TO MOVE STUFF FROM HERE TO BASE CAMP SO KEEP GEAR TO A MINIMUM. (Likewise reading matter, inflatable dolls and other aids).

EXTRA POINTS

Bring any rock and ice pitons/screws you have to meeting on 20th April. We can see then what we want. All contributions will be returned in kind.
Snargs wanted.

The Team

John Porter, climber

Alan Rouse, Expedition Leader, climber

Brian Hall, climber (photo: Jim Curran)

John Barry, climber (photo: Jim Curran)

Alan Burgess, climber (photo: Jim Curran)

Adrian Burgess, climber

Bev Holt, Expedition Doctor (photo: Jim Curran)

Phil Burke, climber

Jim Curran, film-maker

Dave Wilkinson, climber

Jim Hargreaves, Base Camp Manager

If anyone has a snow shovel please bring it.

INSURANCE

Expedition cover will be £4,000 rescue (which is all we need), £1,000 medical, £1,000 injury death per individual. More than this costs a lot and on previous trips we have acted as our own insurers. Think about this before meeting on 20th and we can finalise arrangements.

BUDGET
PLEASE TREAT AS CONFIDENTIAL

In Pakistan

Food Purchase (£1.25 per head per day—13 people for 70 days)	£	1,137
Cook gear	£	200
Fuel and stoves	£	100
Costs in Islamabad	£	1,000
Hire of vehicle to Skardu	£	400
Expenses in Skardu	£	400
Vehicles to road head	£	400
Wages of cook, LO, Mail runner, assistant cook	£	1,500
Travel back to Islamabad and expenses	£	1,000
Agents costs and customs etc	£	500
Total	£	7,640

Plus Porterage:
Assume 180 porters

1136rps wages plus 150rps overheads at 23rps to £1	£	10,000
Return journey assume 45 porters	£	2,500
Total Costs	£	20,140
Plus contingency 5 percent	£	1,000
Money to be taken to Pakistan = c £24,000 plus remainder of Peak fee	c£	1,100

= c £25,000

IN UK

Flights	£	5,500
Freight	£	2,000
Food	£	500
Equipment	£	4,500
Miscellaneous	£	1,500
Total	£	14,000

Overall total of money still needed (Peak fee is largely paid)	£	39,000

Money at present (approximately) assuming each person has contributed £300

Fullers	£ 30,000
BMC, MEF	£ 2,000
Texaco	£ 1,000
Personal after Peak fee	£ 1,500
Each person to bring £400	£ 4,400
Total	£ 38,900

Thus overall summary of costs is that each person will contribute about £300, the other £400 you are asked to bring will cover the helicopter bond and should be largely returnable as if the bond is used we are insured and the money will be returned.

The following week was a hectic one. Hargreaves became the scourge of British industry; he hounded, chased and bullied and never once failed to deliver. Brian Hall co-ordinated the assembly and collection of tents, clothing and footwear. John Porter rounded up grub, and the rest of us chased after the rest, Al and Amstrad conducting from a haphazard score with relish and fortissimo: tin foil from Rio Tinto, Angelsey; radio from Plessey; tents from the USA; beans and things from Liverpool; hardware from Bethesda; skis from Kendall; gas from Germany; stoves from France; something it seemed from almost everywhere. Rupert House grew daily more like a well-stocked climbing shop or supermarket. Boxes of goodies spilled into every ground floor room and Al, at the helm of this gathering mountain, rejoiced at it all.

Curran, in comparative isolation in Bristol, hard-bargained a film deal with Chameleon (to which Al has already referred) and then hit us all with a ream of his own. Since it is the only advice I have ever encountered on the subject I reproduce it in its entirety—it may serve aspiring Peckinpahs; it certainly served us well enough (see appendices).

* * *

Sometime during all the preparations, an ugly head, where there should have been no head at all, was raised again.

'What'll we do about this leadership problem, JB?' Al asked.

'Have it Al, take it. It's your show. There's no problem.'

'It's really important to me professionally to be seen as the leader of a successful

---

trip, a big one like this.'

'Then take it Al, 's all yours!'

'See no one in this country but Bonehead (Chris Bonington) can raise this sort of cash. If we pull this one off I'll be up there with him, big names. Never forgiven him for ditching me from the Everest trip.'

And then it all came out and I began to understand some of it. Al's story was that while on the Kongur expedition with Bonington, Tasker and Boardman, Al had persuaded an official of the Chinese Mountaineering Association to allow him permission to attempt the NE Ridge of Everest the following year. He told Bonington and then later turned the whole thing over to him because he was better able to manage the enterprise, but on the clear (but unwritten) understanding that Al would be a member of the team. Some months later Chris ditched him. Al was devastated, sulked for months and then, over a longer period, became embittered. And like all bitterness, it became acid eating at his soul and brought some darkness to the brightest light in Britain's climbing firmament. He would talk about it often and spend hours in wondering why and convince himself, and have us convinced, that it was Joe Tasker's doing, or, another day, another bitterness, Peter Boardman's.

I heard all this, for the first time, on the train from London to Sheffield. I was horrified. But then the intrigue, petty jealousies, and sordid politics of the upper echelons of the climbing world had always mystified me.

'Look Al this is all beyond me. You're the leader. I want nothing more to do with it—but I'd be grateful if you'd make that plain to everyone else, otherwise it's a bit embarassing. Stop pratting about, we've got a mountain to climb—we don't need molehills.'

'Your trouble JB, is that you're too honest.'

About that, he was certainly wrong.

* * *

On Sunday 20th April we all met at Rupert House for the last time and an orgy of packing ensued. Hargreaves had organised a tower block of robust cardboard boxes into which just about everything in Rupert House that didn't move was packed, banded, weighed and listed. The small range of hills of unpacked gear that ran from Al's office, through living room, dining room and into the kitchen was scarcely less of a range in packed cubic cardboard form. We worked late into the night until, with about twenty minutes of drinking time left, we shot down to the Byron to wet what was, for once, a pretty respectable thirst. Now Sheffield's climbers' drinking is programmed: Mondays it's one pub, Tuesdays another, and so on. Sundays is the Byron and that's where they were; all of them—and had been since several hours before. Al happened to comment that we had a deal of packing still to do and that was it. To a man, courtiers to the king's command, they equipped themselves with carryouts and paraded at Rupert House.

If there is anything more unhelpful than a drunk determined to be helpful it's thirty drunks with the same determination. People staggered this way and that, a load of beer in their bellies, a load of gear on their arms, a 'Where's this lot go?' on their lips. A shambles, but a shambles from which, somehow, emerged 70 tightly-packed, banded and labelled boxes of uniform colour and size. I'll never forget Al standing in the middle of his office while this frenetic industry milled about him, feet splayed in characteristic fashion, ten-to-two, arms flapping between resignation and despair, his face suffused by the dimming light of despond and uttering again, and again, 'Oh Christ, this is a whole new order of chaos.' For once, Al, who inhabited the farthest flung superlatives of the empire of hyperbole was not exaggerating; here indeed was a full tilt Miltonic chaos; not so much Paradise Lost as Paradise Packed—and almost certainly in the wrong box.

The next day the gear went by lorry to Heathrow and thence to Islamabad to await us. That it got that far was a small miracle of improvisation, luck and hope; a small miracle risen from a whole new order of chaos. That was one way of looking at it. Another, more realistic and therefore to us less attractive explanation was that the good offices of Jardine Matheson and Pakistan International Airways smoothly combined to make it so. These organisations were what Al called 'contacts', and contacts Al had in plenty, but since the most useful were always beyond his political pale no credit was extended.

A week later, the 28th April, the team, friends, girl friends and wives joined the directors of Fullers at the Master Robert, an hotel owned by the Brewery and conveniently situated between Heathrow and the Brewery Headquarters at Hammersmith. After a sumptuous dinner, Charles Williams, who with his faith, patience and quiet persistence had done more than anyone to convert K2 from an expensive dream into an affordable reality, gave a short, solid speech wishing us luck. Al was up in an instant with an eye-twinkling, quicksilver reply that was all Al at his mercurial best. It was an attractive contrast, but I sensed that the harmony in it was a fragile thing and wondered for how long Al could surefoot his tiptoeing along the point of balance between all the elements that now comprised the Fullers' K2 Expedition 86: the Brewery's legitimate commercial interests, publicity, the smaller but equally legitimate interest of lesser sponsors, the promises we'd blithely made, the idiosyncrasies of 11 fiercely independent team members and Al's own vaulting ambition—an ambition that ran on a high octane fuel but a fuel contaminated by the bitterness of the Everest misfire.

But, for the moment, all was well; Al conducted like Bernstein, balanced like Blondin.

OVERLEAF
Main picture: **Wide spaces on the Braldu river below Paiyu.**

Inset, top: **Crowding to cross the Braldu on the morning of the second day.**

Inset, middle: **Korophon: the sweep of the Braldu/Baltoro valley lies ahead.**

Inset, bottom: **Porters breakfasting at Concordia.**

The first wobble came some hours later when the team showed a greater enthusiasm for the fruits of Fullers' enterprise than the brewery had anticipated. The bar was under sustained and determined seige and its defenders, who had already conducted themselves in a manner well beyond the call of duty or job-description, looked ready to cut and run. Al, whose balance had temporarily tripped on a small mountain of Fullers' finest, was having trouble in restraining the zeal of his cohort and for an uncomfortable moment it looked as if the Fullers' K2 expedition might flounder somewhere along the Great West Road. Worse, it looked as if the bar might close which, to the twins, Al Burgess in particular, was a humiliation tantamount to the losing of colours in battle. Then Charles, level-headed as always, intervened with a peace settlement worthy of a Kissinger. He deposited several crates of beer on a table, raised the seige on the bar, set its beleaguered defenders free, bade us a good night and left us to it. This feat of consummate diplomacy had left Al's leadership untested, which was just as well since, comprehensively outflanked by Fullers in one guise or another, he could no longer stand.

The next day there was a press conference at the brewery headquarters. As we were driven there in the brewery double decker bus, I reflected that everyone ought to be allowed to be a VIP for a day, if only to see how ordinary it felt.

The team did not look well. Even Pyrrhus would have thought the battle the previous evening hard won. Al's flame spluttered briefly into a sparkle as he explained to the assembled press what we were about. But the sparkle wouldn't fire his main engine and he ended with a limp, 'and er, and that's it'—which was such a contrast to the feats of derring-do that he had outlined the evening before, that everyone, press, Fullers and the team, caught the humour of it and fell into laughter.

We took the same bus to Heathrow while the press returned to the booze—which of course is why they'd come in the first place.

*   *   *

And that's how it happened. How we got the team and money and kit to go and take a shot at the NW ridge of K2. Climbing the mountain might be easy by comparison.

Slouching Towards Base Camp

'All God's children need walking shoes.'

(Maya Angelou)

I couldn't think what we'd done to deserve our VIP status but whatever it was, the treatment endured to the door of the aircraft. A hostess, a Pakistani of charm and assurance, whisked us through the Heathrow jungle swinging us from bureaucratic creeper to bureaucratic creeper with the agility of Tarzan's Jane—though not before a lovely old cleaning lady, all mops and curlers, had accosted us.

'You lot that there K2 climbing expedition? Well then be careful. Every year I see some of you go out and every year not everyone comes back; you always seem to lose a few.' Then she added by way of a morale booster: 'Mind you, you always seem to be able to find some new ones, don't you?' We were cheered by her after-thought. She will since have been horrified by her own prescience.

On the plane someone handed me four sheets of paper that were headed 'Press Release: The Team'. It consisted of potted biographies that Al had cobbled together on his word processor from such fragments of autobiographical information as we had supplied, or that he already knew, or that he'd invented. It serves as a good introduction to the team:

PRESS RELEASE
The Team

AL ROUSE (age 34)

Born in Wallasey, Merseyside in 1951, Al went to Birkenhead School and Emmanuel College, Cambridge. Has climbed numerous first ascents in the Andes of Peru and Patagonia. First alpine-style ascent of Jannu and first ascent of Nuptse North Face, both with Brian Hall. First ascent of Mount Kongur, one of the highest unclimbed

Above: **K2 from Concordia (in July). The Abruzzi Spur runs down right.**

Below: **Porters readying to leave Concordia for the last day's march to Base Camp.**

peaks in China in 1981. Led expedition to West Ridge of Everest in winter. 1982 Ogre 2 expedition. 1983 climbed Broad Peak (27,000 ft), the world's twelfth highest mountain in pure alpine style. Attempted K2 in 1984 Pakistani-British K2 expedition with Chris Bonington. Works as equipment consultant, writer, lecturer. Has lectured in New Zealand, USA, France, and other countries. Now Vice President of The British Mountaineering Council. Considered to be Britain's leading young Himalayan mountaineer, having been to the summits of four peaks over 25,000 ft.

JOHN BARRY (age 34)
After becoming a Captain in the Marines, he left to become Director of Britain's National Centre for Mountaineering, Plas y Brenin. He is one of Britain's leading ice climbers and alpinists. He is married with two children, and lives in Llanrwst, North Wales. He wrote the book 'The Great Climbing Adventure' and has been on expeditions to Gauri Sankar in Nepal and Deborah in Alaska.

BRIAN HALL (age 34)
Born in Kendal in 1951, Brian became a leading alpinist and later expedition climber. He made a series of outstanding first ascents, such as Cerro Standhardt in Patagonia and the first alpine style ascent on the north face of Huascaran in Peru. He then went on to make one of the best climbs achieved by any nationality when he climbed Jannu (25,300ft) in alpine style with Al Rouse. In 1979 he made the first ascent on the very difficult North Face of Nuptse (25,850ft) in the Everest area. Along with team members Rouse, Porter, and the Burgess twins he attempted the West Ridge of Everest in winter. Married and lives in Hayfield underneath Kinder Scout.

DAVE WILKINSON (age 40)
A senior lecturer in mathematics at Birmingham Polytechnic he has remained an amateur climber. Nonetheless he had spent all of his free time in the mountains and is now one of Britain's most accomplished alpinists. He was educated at Hutton Grammar School near Preston and then gained an MSc at Manchester University. He is Britain's most experienced winter alpine climber, having achieved notable first ascents. He has been on five major Himalayan expeditions and in 1985 made the first ascent of Rimo 3, one of the highest unclimbed peaks left in the world.

JIM CURRAN (age 43)
Jim Curran is one of Britain's best known and most accomplished mountaineering film makers. He has twenty seven years climbing experience in Britain, the Alps, Peru and the Himalayas. His films, which have won numerous awards at international film festivals, include; 'Trango', 'The Bat', and most recently 'Kongur', a documentary of the first ascent of Mount Kongur in China with Chris Bonington and Al Rouse. He is at present Senior Lecturer in Foundation Art Studies at Bristol Polytechnic, though his home is in Sheffield. He wrote a book entitled 'Trango, the Nameless Tower', which tells the story of the first ascent of the most impressive rock spire in the Karakorum, which the climbers will pass en route to K2 this summer.

BEV HOLT (age 50)
He will take three months leave from his Anaesthetic consultant post. Recently

returned to the UK after seven years in Canada, with previous experience in Africa. Has specialist interest in high altitude respiratory problems, hypothermia and resuscitation. Has taken part in several expeditions and climbed extensively in many parts of the world from the Alps to the Andes. As Officer in Charge of RAF Mountain Units he developed an interest in rescue and evacuation which was later put to use in Africa and Canada. He lives in the Lake District with his wife and three children.

ALAN BURGESS (age 37)

He has been climbing for over 20 years. Born in Holmfirth, Yorkshire, after a grammar school education he completed a three year course in Physical Education at Chester College. He is now a Director of Alpine International, a guiding and trekking company. His expedition experience ranges from Alaska to Patagonia and includes 11 Himalayan expeditions, 5 of them in winter. He has climbed several times above 26,400 ft without oxygen, including an ascent of Dhaulagiri one of the ten highest mountains in the world. He has twice been on Everest.

ADRIAN BURGESS (age 37)

Al Burgess's identical twin brother with a similar climbing history. He is married to an American and lives in Colorado. (Or as Al quipped, 'as for Alan but can read and write'.)

JOHN PORTER (age 37)

Born in the United States, John Porter came to Britain to take a degree at Leeds University and has made his home in Britain ever since. He began climbing in his teens in the States and made a number of hard climbs in the New England Hills before graduating to the bigger faces of the Rockies. While at Leeds University he made numerous hard routes in the Alps, and in 1977 organised the first East-West expedition with the Poles during which six new faces were climbed in the Hindu Kush. Other expeditions include 1st ascent S. Face of Changabang, Peruvian Andes, Everest in winter, Annapurna, Tatra Traverse in winter, and Mt. Kenya. He works as an Economic Development Officer in local government.

JIM HARGREAVES (age 40)

Born in 1946 in London, educated at King Edward VI Grammar School, Totnes, Devon. Went to sea at 16. Joined the Army at 20, for ten years, (APTC). 1971 British Grand Canyon Expedition, 1972 British Army Expedition Mount Kenya, 1977 British Kayak Expedition to Cape Horn, 1982 Kayak Expedition to Chilean Andes. Currently a director of Wild Water in Harrogate.

PHIL BURKE (age 36)

Born in 1950 went to Stockport Grammar School. National Standard mile and cross country runner. Started climbing in 1968 and became one of Britain's top rock climbers. Made the first ascent of the Steep East Face of the Fortress in Patagonia and the first ascent of the East Face of Cerro Torre. He is also a leading caver, having descended the three deepest caves in the world. Now works in Civil Engineering, and is single.

I thought that Al's miscalculation of my age by seven years to be one of his happier errors: I was actually 41—but going on 34, according to Al. I was grateful to him for it.

The potted biographies were perhaps more significant for what they omitted—especially since *High* magazine had that same month printed a photograph of us captioned 'The Strongest Team' (we could have more accurately been described as The Fattest Team, or The Oldest Team).

For instance there was no mention of the fact that on my only two previous visits to the Himalayas I had failed to reach the top; that Phil Burke had never been above 6,000 metres; that the twins may have been on eleven Himalayan expeditions but that only on two of them had they reached the top; that Dave Wilkinson, although vastly experienced, was not at home on technically difficult ground, or that business concerns were superceding Brian Hall's mountaineering interests. But of course such warts are not good copy for attracting best publicity. It mattered little who believed what—as long as we didn't fool ourselves. I don't think we did.

Islamabad was hot, but not as hot and nowhere near as sticky as the Pakistan veterans in our team had led us to believe. At Airport Immigration we were confronted with a choice of three gates, one each for Pakistan Passports, British Passports and Foreign Passports. Bev, our most steadfast Brit abroad, strode towards the British Passports gate with confidence, a 'fit representative of the power that had thrown a girdle of humour and strong dealing round the world'. His own humour was tested to its limit when he was politely, but firmly, informed that he was a foreigner and that the sign on the gate referred to British Passport-owning Pakistanis. 'All part of life's rich pageant', I said as Bev returned puffing chuckled indignation through his beard, his prejudices setting fast in a slurry of half-hearted pomposity. After that we enjoyed a comparatively easy passage through customs and emerged from the airport entrance into the tinkling tinsel and plastic of this clamouring, cacophonous, teeming, urban East.

Barry Rundle, an engineer member of the Embassy staff and another of Al's contacts was there to rescue us, now limp from the accumulated effect of parties, press conferences, send-offs, travel and jet lag. He drove us to his bungalow in the diplomatic quarter of Islamabad where we showered, shaved and breakfasted. Afterwards he took us to his office, conveniently situated immediately behind the British Embassy Club swimming pool, where he allotted us a store of generous proportions and a desk. He was unaware of the tradition which decrees that expeditions are supposed to be organised on the back of cigarette packets. The desk and the Fullers' K2 Expedition never met again.

Later that day we were introduced to the members of the expatriate community who had volunteered to accommodate us during our stay in Islamabad. Jim Hargreaves, Jim Curran, Al Rouse and I were billeted with Shona Falconer, a First Secretary of the British Embassy. Her palatial bungalow was to become a refuge of tranquillity and calm in the hot and hectic days that followed. Shona's hospitality was tremendous. Food and beer alternated at alarming speed and in prodigious quantities. She had high expectations of a mountaineer's appetite and thirst and an exaggerated opinion of the elasticity of his belly. We were stretched.

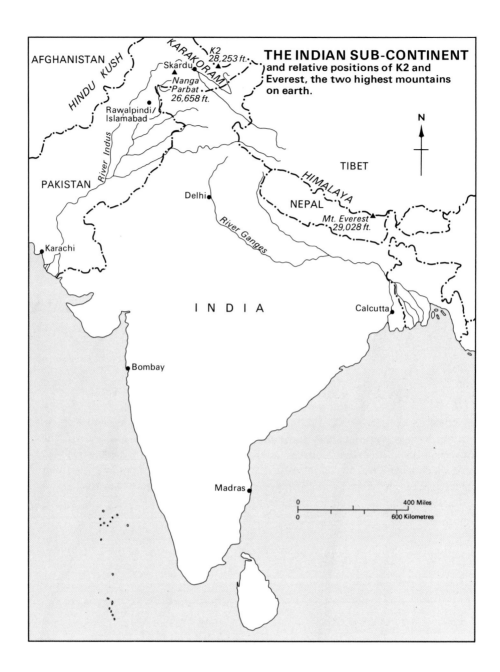

THE INDIAN SUB-CONTINENT and relative positions of K2 and Everest, the two highest mountains on earth.

(Although Pakistan is a fundamental Islamic republic where the sale or consumption of alcohol is prohibited to natives, foreigners are permitted to drink in the privacy of their homes or in certain authorised clubs such as those belonging to the Embassies.)

Islamabad is a purpose-built capital of concrete sterility; a manufactured capital for a manufactured nation. It is a geometric city. Geometric that is to Le

Corbusier and his disciples. To everyone else it was an algebraic shambles, especially for the poor taxi drivers whose lot it is to unravel the code that Corbusier, in the name of progress, has inflicted on a naturally haphazard world. Traditional names for places, areas and streets have been abandoned for addresses like House 1, Street 19, G Block or 482F, Sector G64. The result of all this logic is that no-one finds anything very easily.

We spent eight days in Islamabad. Incidents, vignettes, scraps of no particular importance, but nevertheless of interest, still come back easily even though I write this five months later and after they have been faded by hotter suns and greater, sadder toils:

. . . Hargreaves returns from 'Pindi where he's been shopping in the bazaars for *atta*, paraffin stoves, sack cloth, paper, dal, rice and sugar. He's candescent with the adventure of new things and new excitements. 'Bloody marvellous, bloody marvellous. They sell everything. Everything. You wouldn't believe what they sell. Everything. Bloody everything. Wish I'd had the missus with me.'

'Why, d'you wanna sell her?' quips Curran.

. . . Dinner Chez Shona who's holding forth on feminism in general and the lot of women in Pakistan in particular. I ask her if she might one day be an Ambassadress. To which she replies, transmitting one of those flesh-shrivelling gamma stares that feminists reserve for the frying of chauvinist pork, 'An Ambassadress is an Ambassador's wife. But yes I will be an Ambassador.' I dared not doubt it. Later she produced a copy of *What Women Want* by a feminist of some note apparently. It made mystifying reading.

. . . Meet an ex-marine acquaintance and his wife at the British Embassy Club who are quick to explain that they are only using the place because their own club's swimming pool is closed for repair. 'Well it's hardly the Officer Mess is it?' I am reminded of the arid, debilitating snobbery, admittedly a disappearing disease, that I gladly left behind when I reluctantly left the Marines ten years before.

. . . We are dining at the British Embassy Club when Phil returns from a shopping trip to 'Pindi in company with Nazir Sabir. Nazir, who has been to the top of K2, and who modestly describes his part in that expedition as very small when clearly it was fairly big, is a local travel agent and long time friend. Phil brings Nazir to our table. There is much uncomfortable shifting of feet and a couple of club members look anxious. After an awkward minute Nazir flees. We are filled with righteous indignation (and genuine remorse) that our friend should be excluded from a club in his own land because he was of that land. Our righteousness is soon punctured, our indignation deflated, when we learn that he is excluded by the laws of Islam from a place where alcohol is sold. The club members were anxious because they saw the implications of such transgression. In our ignorance we had cried racism too soon. Now we felt wretched for the embarrassment our carelessness had wrought—and not only to Nazir.

. . . There's a press conference at the Embassy. Shona has it well organised: top table, chairs, tea, coffee, small eats—and all the big newspapers invited, for K2 is big news. The questions begin. 'You have radios from Plessey?' (We do—but how did they know?) Do we realise that Plessey have strong links with South Africa? No we didn't says Al truthfully. Had we done so we wouldn't have brought them he adds untruthfully. I am tempted to ask what South Africa and K2 have to do with each other but say nothing. Tempted too to point out that there's a Plessey office right here in Islamabad and that the Pakistan Government happily deals with them. The questions continue. 'I see that you are sponsored by a brewery.' Al's on guard. 'Do you have any beer with you?' 'No' says Al truthfully. 'We thought it would be wrong to bring alcohol to Pakistan; we respect your laws and customs' says Al, not quite so truthfully.

Afterwards a reporter collars me. He used to work for the *Sunday Times*. He was used to Fleet Street ways. 'You could have brought beer' he tells me. 'There is a system of exemption.' He loves lager himself.

The whole thing is a disaster. We have hopelessly underestimated their intelligence, their sophistication. We had been arrogant; perhaps racist too. They were steps ahead. Maybe streets. They took the tea and eats, swallowed insincerity with grace and charm and that night earnestly lucubrated over their presses while we drank smugly at the club. Next day they nailed us. The press reports were unenthusiastic. It was no more than we deserved.

. . . We're licking our wounds. Jim Curran says it could be worse. He recalls a post-expedition press conference at which the climbers reported that they had failed because of frost-bite. This was reported next day in the English-speaking Pakistani papers as frog bite. The day after an Urdu issue proclaimed 'Expedition attacked by Mountain Frogs'.

. . . Entry in my diary. *6th May*. 'Al a scatterbrained genius but hopeless at organising. Doesn't brief collectively. Accountancy a shambles. Porters' wages have been increased by 25% by government decree. Al does a complicated chart to compute wages. Complications caused by fact that some porters' loads are food for other porters which, when consumed, frees them to be sent home. Al's a mathematician—a Cambridge mathematician. Mathematics is the language of logic. Al says it's logical. It baffles me. Al produces the Budget Plan. The 5th Revision says we're in easy street, plenty of money. The 6th Revision said we were broke.

. . . I'm tasked with depositing the Helicopter Bond (a cash deposit that ensures that we pay for a helicopter rescue if need be—a precautionary measure introduced after a British team were so rescued and then left the country without paying. No other nation need deposit a bond: only Britain has earned this stigma.

I imagine it's an easy job, depositing $4,000 US with the National Bank. There's a form. The Ministry of Tourism stamp it. The bank refuse it. The form is incorrect. I return to the ministry who insist that the form is correct. The bank are unimpressed, politely unimpressed, with this news. The ministry, in their turn, are unperturbed, politely unperturbed, by the bank's news. I try again. And again. Then I ask the ministry to phone the bank to ask what exactly is unsatisfactory but the telephone isn't working. I go to the bank. Their sympathy fans my frustration but they are air-conditioned: it's a cooler place than the ministry not to get cross in: a cooler place to wait, to do business. I make it my base: this could be a protracted transaction. At last I persuade the bank to try phoning the ministry again. Ah! All is clear. I need only to return to the ministry, collect the right form, bring it to the bank and they will be happy to take my $4,000 US. At the ministry the Minister himself scrutinizes the form that I have carried back and forth umpteen times these last four hours. He is expressionless as he opens a drawer and without looking withdraws a rubber stamp. I glance over his desk to see that it is one of dozens. He adds his stamp to the collection that already adorn the form, sighs as if the effort has been enormous, pushes the form to me and offers me a cup of tea. The bank are delighted though they hardly glance at the maze of stamped ink, and anyway this new imprint is as camouflaged as a pattern in a test for colour blindness. Would I be paying the $4,000 US in dollars or pounds sterling? Pounds sterling. That was a pity. No matter; quick calculation; that will be £2,714. I only have £2,700. I'll come back tomorrow.

. . . Al and I go to meet the Liaison Officer. (Every expedition is obliged to employ an L.O. They are usually officers of the Pakistan Army and their job is to advise, to assist and to ensure that foreigners stick to the rules.) Some expeditions are blessed with one. Some are burdened. In the *Index for Terms and Conditions for Grant of Permission to Mountaineering Expedition Parties for climbing Peaks in Pakistan* issued by the Tourism Division of Pakistan, it states at *Section IV Liaison Officer (L.O.):*

14. A party shall include in the expedition, as its member, at least one L.O. to be detailed by the Government of Pakistan.
15. A party shall pay for his food, accommodation and transport from Rawalpindi/Islamabad to mountains and back to Rawalpindi/Islamabad from the date he reports to a leader till the date a party returns to Rawalpindi/Islamabad and is de-briefed.
16. During the stay of a party at Rawalpindi/Islamabad a L.O. shall, from the date of reporting, normally share food, transport and accommodation with it. In case accommodation in the premises occupied by the party is not available or is not catered for, a party shall arrange for it in a hotel not more than 3 kilo metres from the premises in which it is staying. Rent of a room so hired shall not exceed Rs. 60/ per day. According to this arrangement a L.O. shall share food with a party.

A further seven clauses take care of the L.O.'s food and accommodation requirements.

Our L.O. is Agha Hussein. Agha, he tells us enigmatically, is pronounced the French way. He is a Lieutenant of Signals and directly descended, so he tells us, from Allah. He has a half-handsome, half-querulous face and a fine sense of his own rank and importance. I don't take to him, nor he to me, but he likes Hindus, Sikhs, Russians and Negroes less. He assures us of the superiority of Pakistan over India, pointing out that in the Ran of Kutch War they had fought to the last man. He is very hurt when, ill at ease with such introductory exhortations, I suggest that the last man was only last because he was the slowest. He protests. I

55

say that Rushdie agrees with me. But Rushdie is an Indian and is not to be trusted. It is a bad start.

. . . A French team also bound for K2—the Barrards, as I later discover—leave their entire expedition budget in a taxi. It is never recovered—though somehow and astonishingly their expedition recovers. What a taxi driver made of a gift from Allah of umpteen thousands of francs is a delight to conject.

. . . We are packing in Barry Rundle's PSA shed. Packing, unpacking, repacking. Hargreaves packs chocolate to one climber's specification ('good stuff, chocolate'); unpacks it at another's directive ('chocolate's no good, it melts'). Repacks it at the instigation of a third ('chocolate's good, full of calories'). Karabiners suffer a worse fate. Jim assumes, not unreasonably, that 8,500 metres of mountain will consume a fair quantity and packs the lot. They are unpacked by a climber who thinks he knows that 8,500 metres of this mountain will consume only a handful. Result: chocolate but no krabs. We have six or seven would-be loadmasters, one poor packer. But we're getting there! *Atta,* sugar, rice— spillables—are packed into a tightly woven bag, then into a jute sack, and maybe into another. Inner bags are tied, the outer bag stitched and numbered with paint: B60–B131, loads for Base Camp; AB1–AB59, loads for Advance Base; K1–K18, kitchen loads; W1 and X131, aberrations; W 01 an oversight; 1–60 standard loads; 206, 207, 208, loads that no-one was ever to be sure about.

. . . Someone says that the food had been well organised. John Porter disagrees, 'I can assure you it hasn't, I organised it myself.' That was something no-one cared to dispute: it was hard to take issue with so confident a self-denouncement.

. . . Discover one of Al's lists. Al is famous for them:

TO DO

AR	*1*	*Helicopter Bond*
AR, JB, BH	*2*	*Meet LO*
JH	*3*	*Address postcards*
JB, AB, AB	*4*	*Pack loads of 25kg*
	5	*Customs 9am Saturday*
	6	*Hire lorry & Minibus for journey to Skardu*
	7	*Sort out freightage of ITN news back to U.K.*
	8	*Make postal arrangements for exped.*
	9	*Hire staff (?)*
	10	*Make return reservations*
	11	*Buy fuel*
	12	*Buy fuel containers (not necessarily in this order!)*
	13	*Buy base camp cooking gear*
	14	*Buy sunglasses/shoes etc. for porters*
	15	*Sew on badges*
	16	*Buy food*
	17	*Check on Skardu flights*
	18	*Change money*

JB	19	*Buy sacs*
	20	*Insure 210 porters*
	21	*Sleeping bag liners*
	22	*Vehicle for tomorrow*
	23	*Buy sacs*

. . . Budget. 8th Revision. The expedition is broke. We all chip in £400. Some chip in more.

At last after eight days of small successes, bigger frustrations, petty arguments and larger reconciliations; of baggage, bagging, bundling, barter, buying, bingeing, bravura, braggadoccio, bullshit, bathing, boozing, grand-boeufing, bitching, beefing and beginning again; at last we were as ready for the off as we ever were likely to be.

We'd hired a bus to take us to Skardu and a fine bright painted thing it was too.

The plan was to load the gear and afterwards to crush on as many of the team as could find room. The remainder would fly direct to Skardu on the first flight on which seats were available. Flights from Islamabad to Skardu take about an hour and are actually cheaper—thanks to a state subsidy—than the bus fare.

The road journey along the Karakoram Highway (the KKH) takes between 18 and 36 hours depending on a number of inter-relating but often irreconcilable factors such as the driver's ability to function when asleep, the passengers' nerve and collective bladder capacity, the number of mud slides to be negotiated, how frequently the span of the road exceeds the span of the wheels, and, of course, what duration of journey it was that Allah willed, or indeed, whether he willed it at all.

Anyone who has ever estimated volume by eye would have immediately realised that there wasn't room either on or in the bus for our gear, let alone any climbers. We all saw it. Al himself agreed, the driver too and the team of coolies that Barry Rundle had assigned to the loading. And having agreed that the thing was impossible by a margin too great for any intervention by Allah to influence, we stood back fatalistically to let the lads begin. Fortunately Allah is not constrained by the laws of physics and, into a smaller volume, he allowed a larger volume packed. There's no explanation for it, but that's what happened. The rest went onto the roof, higher and wider again than the laws of equilibrium said was possible. But it was done.

The driver, justly proud of his charge, polished the bonnet, the only remaining visible flank of what had once been a garish multi-coloured bus and resisted all pressures to hurry until he'd shone it to a fine burnish. Then he mounted the driver's seat with some panache and bade us enter. We had counted six seats spare at the front (the remainder were taken with the kit) and so John Porter, Jim Hargreaves, Jim Curran, Agha, whose services were thought to be needed along the way, and I were detailed 'by road'. In addition there was Aftab, our cook who we'd recruited in Rawalpindi. At his interview for selection to this prestigious post (something of a formality since there was no opposition) he had answered a question on whether a townie such as he would make the walk to Base Camp with,

'If you can why shouldn't I?' It was half-insolence, half-pride. Unfortunately, Aftab proved to be better at repartee than either walking or cooking.

The rest of the team were designated 'by air, tomorrow am' and departed in barely concealed relief towards the club bar and another binge. The five of us (Aftab was already installed) made as if to enter the bus, only to find that there had been an error: for into the five remaining seats we had to squash seven passengers.

The driver, Durvaish Ali, had acquired a conductor, Mustapha, though to what purpose was not apparent. The entire bus being ours by hire, there were no tickets to issue, nor, as far as I could see, any other duties conductorial. That made it passengers 6 for seats 5. But there was also the owner of the bus and he too was Skardu bound. 7 for 5. And from the shadows, as the engine burst into life and a mild flame or two, 2 more essential crewmen materialised. One, it was explained, via Agha, was a short-stay passenger who would only be with us a night, as far as Abbottabad. He would ride the roof. The other? He was an engineer and a Skardu man but would sit the door which he did, knees to nose, for 480 dusty, fume-filled, pot-holed kilometres.

A double ding on a bell announced the off and the old bus pulled steadily away. A bell, had we heard a bell? Indeed we had, though for whom it tolled Mustapha never said, hunched as he was half on Durvaish's shoulder and half in his lap.

A party spirit prevailed even in the midst of such discomfort.

'I'm firmly switched into expedition mode now,' Curran said, 'whenever I close my eyes my thoughts are exclusively of sex.'

For so long as Allah willed it we drove into the northern Punjab night, climbing steadily from the plain towards the foothills of the North-West Frontier Province and the Northern Areas. Names melted into history, names still with the ring of adventure about them, names given more in hope than confidence, as if things might yet change, as if today's Areas might tomorrow be another cease-fire line.

Allah willed it as far as Abbottabad, where with Mustapha lolling across Durvaish and Durvaish asleep across the wheel we thought it imprudent to press an infidel's luck further. Agha explained to the crew that we were to be here until 6 am—it was already past midnight. Durvaish turned a key unlocking a sudden silence that swept in behind the raucous diesel's retreat. The contrast was marked, almost unnerving for Abbottabad seemed, at that hour, a spectral place; black, pitch black and not a soul nor sound but for some distant desultory dogbarks that made more sinister the silences between—silences inhabited by Deev, Asura, Rakshasa, Iridpur, Siddha, Yaksha, Gandharva, Vivyadhora, Asvamukka; ghosts of an Eastern night.

We wandered along the road and in two hundred metres found the Springfield Hotel, a name the very incongruity of which broke the spell that had bound us. A chowkidar materialised out of the darkness, showed us to a room and then, just as we were gratefully throwing ourselves on anything horizontal, announced that we were too many for that room. We assured him that as far as we were concerned that was no inconvenience, but he insisted: this was a three-bedded room and we were six—Agha and Aftab being of our party. 'But we'll sleep on the settee, cushions, the floor, anything', we pleaded. 'A 3-bedded room sleeps 3 people; 3

beds, 3 people', the chowkidar patiently explained. 'If more want to sleep you will need another room, OK?'

'OK, give us another room.'

'All rooms full.'

'Look mate'—Hargreaves had decided it was time that his version of diplomacy was brought to bear. 'Look mate in Bradford you lot sleep thirty to a room so what's the big deal with six?'

'3 beds only 3 persons.'

'Look mate . . . OK. Three of us'll have to sleep on the verandah.' For some reason that was acceptable and our fastidiously numerate chowkidar slid off into the darkness and troubled us no further. Seconds later the three from the balcony slipped into the room and onto the floor.

'That fooled the bugger.'

But the next morning we were handed a bill for six; some games you can only hope to draw.

We ground on toward the dawn, still climbing steadily and now leaving behind the savannah woodland of the Islamabad plains for cedar, birch and pine. After a few hours Agha brought us to a Public Works Department rest-house where he ordered breakfast of eggs, paratha and tea for all. We took it on the lawn in the warm morning sun, green fertile acres all about, and relaxed in a pleasant breathing space between the yesterday of Islamabad and the tomorrow of K2; forgot for a short while the debts we'd left behind, ignored the price we knew would come; the cost could catch us when it might for here was breakfast and all that mattered then.

'I've got a bit of a tummy bug', Curran said.

'Plenty of room for it,' Hargreaves replied, convulsed at his own wit.

We rattled onwards—interminable dusty hours of grabbed sleep, brief minutes of desultory conversation, and silences of two kinds: one sullen, fretting, careworn and laded with apprehension; the other bobbing carefree and lighted with hope; it depended on whose metaphysics were up for introspection.

Our bus was unable to exceed 20 mph thanks to its enormous burden and the way being always slightly uphill. We were happy about that. Twenty miles per hour is quite fast enough to be hitting anything. (The question of whether in Pakistan they drive on left or right is purely academic—for they go left, right or middle; whichever takes their fancy or has most to recommend it.)

. . . A Coca Cola advert urged us to 'Have a Cock'.

. . . A road sign bade us 'Relax on the KKH. Goodbye. Becare. Full'.

. . . Another warned. 'The Icy Finger of Death Points at the Speed King.'

. . . And yet another 'Don't nag darling, I'm driving'. Feminism and Islam have yet to collide.

Besham is a foul town: fetid, ugly, dirty and dank. On Agha's recommendation we stopped there for lunch. He ordered tea which never came and a little later curry, and a little later curry again. Nothing happened, though in this same space half the population of Besham had arrived ravenous and left replete. Agha was embarrassed that an Officer of Signals could command so little respect. Perhaps his Urdu confused them. He smiled apologetically and said that he'd try Punjabi—which he did—not that we were able to appreciate the difference. When half-a-dozen other tongues met with the same indifference, Hargreaves, our second 'gigantic, red and merry, and fit representative of that power which had thrown a girdle of humour and strong dealing round the world', was on his feet and ordering a whole new repast in the simplest of Anglo-Saxon. Curries appeared in no time, and the long forgotten tea too.

'Just goes to show that English is the world language.' With Hargreaves on the end of the tongue it was certainly a living language.

'This morning I had the worst dose of shits I've ever had,' Curran announced, adding, a little ruefully, as a tablecloth of flies was swept temporarily aside to make room for chipped enamel pots of greyish dripping curry, 'that is until tonight'. But appearance belied taste: it was delicious—if deadly—and in no time at all Curran, face full of the stuff, was holding forth as if there were no tonight; it was like being addressed by an animated plate of rogan josh.

We too left replete. Deeper into Besham, Mustapha swung through the door and disappeared skywards. Fifteen minutes later and Besham just behind us, he reappeared—from above—and took up his position on Durvaish's lap once more. Agha explained that he'd been riding shotgun to stop the townsfolk jumping on the bus from behind and jettisoning our cargo. Mustapha was to earn his ride in the next few hours for a succession of Beshams followed, sufficient to give the impression of an under-world—and indeed we were descending for a while.

But before too long we climbed back into the sunshine, and into clean air, cedars and a wider road, an opening space.

That evening we came to Chilas. The immense gorge that the KKH had been tortuously following all afternoon gave way to an expanse of alluvial plain and a dry land of semi-desert. Wood and wattle houses gave way to clay-walled, square-cut huts, and trees gave way to shrub as green surrendered to brown, mud to dust: not yet the full-blown desert of Baltistan but getting there, getting higher.

Just beyond Chilas we found a Shangri-La, 'a' because this name is given to any number of hotels throughout Pakistan. It was a pleasant spot, a Shangri-La indeed compared to the Beshams of this world. This Shangri-La was a modern motel and part of the Ministry of Tourism's drive to generate a tourist industry in Pakistan and it seemed to us to be a step in the right direction without conceding too much to western hedonism. Hargreaves thought a bigger step would be to abolish, or at least suspend, Islam and get some alcohol brewing—and, purely from a commercial standpoint, he's probably right; the self-inflicted rigours of Islam on top of the naturally inflicted rigours of the climate hereabouts make Pakistan rather less of a main attraction than, say, Ibiza, Goa or even Kathmandu.

We ate curry—nowhere near as fine as Besham's—and collapsed abed in small, white-walled motel rooms. Porter worried that we should not have stayed there. 'Too expensive?', I wondered (which by local standards it was). 'No, prolonging the agony of the break from civilisation.'

. . . A brochure intended as lure for tourists assured us that Baltistan (within the bounds of which we now lay) was a 'non-violent culture and a crime-free society. A high fence has been erected around the hotel for your protection.' I'm not sure which information was the most reassuring.

We slept the sleep of the innocent and rose at six to an intoxicating morning freshness, open places, a caressing breeze, sunlight that was not strained and new hopes. John may have been right to fret over the prolonging of the agony but in the dawn of this unadulterated day I felt for the first time that I had sloughed off the langours of leaving parties, jet-lag and Islamabad. We breakfasted on a verandah overlooking a series of natural terraces that descended to the Indus wide and slow here, as if resting between the tumults of gorges above and below. Beyond and behind were dusty hills, and beyond and behind them, more hills and somewhere beyond and behind again mountains—the biggest on this earth. And the morning sun warmed this earth; this soul too. It was good to be here, to be alive, Shangri-La or not.

Two Europeans approached. They were English, worked for the *New York Times* on whose behalf they were based in Peking—whence they had travelled by the KKH (now opened into China) via the Khunjerab Pass. When they discovered where we were bound they asked, in that ingenious way of non-mountaineers what was the most important quality in a mountaineer. Three of us answered off-handedly and in quick, too quick, sucession: Curran said, 'bullshit'; I, 'luck'; and Porter, 'stupidity'. None of our answers was very truthful and I wonder what we think of them now. One of the reporters said that they had put the same question to an American team who were approaching K2 from the Chinese side (to try the North Ridge) and had received in reply a fullsome discourse on the metaphysics of mountaineering. The Americans' views, they said, had generally been 'cleaner'. We drove off wondering what they meant by that. Possibly it says more about the differences between American and British people than it does about mountaineering.

Not long after that Shangri-La Bunji, the KKH divides. The major part continues northward to Gilgit town along the Gilgit river, past Rakaposhi Mountain, and after Gilgit to Karimabad, Hunza and over the Khanjerab Pass (4,572m) and into Chinese Sinkiang. The minor, but more spectacular part, swings east and follows a now ferocious Indus 100 kilometres to Skardu. Soon after the split the Skardu road enters a gorge which has been cleft in rock, hewn from hillside and though not as dizzying as the road from Chamba to Brahmaur or even the one up to La Barade, it is a considerable path, an impressive feat of engineering. All along there are villages clinging to the banks, little patches of green optimism, stamps tenaciously clinging to the most unlikely envelopes: a life of hanging on.

I could hardly concede that life was worth this effort, but then I didn't live there. Agha would point at them as we rumbled through, or more often, under, and tell us that 'Brigands and other bad types' were in the habit of swooping on these villages and raping the girls and carrying them off—which information was invariably met with a chorus of decadent western scepticism.

Our patent irreverence notwithstanding, the stories of rape and pillage multiplied with miles and altitude. If our problem was decadence Agha's was lack of it. Perhaps the purity of fundamentalist theory breeds perversion in practice. Perhaps minds and bodies were not equipped for such unnatural burdens. Certainly Agha, for all his professed, and I think, genuine, horror at our views on sex, women, marriage and girl friends, was possessed by an obsession with things rapine.

About mid-day we came to a level place where there were no immediate hills for brigands to descend from and where a series of bicoloured signs in simple geometric patterns bearing codes like 'Eng Coy HQ', 'HQ and Sigs Pett' and 'Officers Mess', and straight lines of white-washed stones, signalled the presence of a Pakistan Army in some permanence. Agha urged us towards an especially dismal looking shack, smartened himself and followed the arrow of the Officers Mess signpost. We had delicious tea, nan and dal and stretched and relaxed in the dry warmth of the sun at 2,000 metres. Agha returned an hour later announcing that his morale had been considerably boosted and that in the next war 'those bloody Hindiwallahs will get a proper thrashing'.

Not long afterwards we stopped again. Dervaish said something to Mustapha who leapt from the door, returning a split second later and shaking his head. We had a puncture. The crew set about replacing the wheel (which, without a jack, looked like a job that was going to call for some ingenuity), while Curran hoisted his mighty Scoopic camera and tripod a hundred feet up the hillside for what he called some 'footage'. As far as I could see the art of film-making consisted of pointing the camera at some obviously interesting feature, and then—and this was clearly the artistic bit—poring over the top of it with an expression wrought of pain and concentration, eyes squinting, lips drawn tight, one hand chin-stroking, the other backside-scratching for as many seconds as breath can be held, before collapsing, either from hypoxia or the sheer artistic torture of it all—I'm still not sure which. Curran said that film-making was all in the editing; that a monkey could shoot the things. 'And you're about to prove it', one of us said. It was an unfortunate metaphor. A man of Curran's experience is rarely caught with his guard so low.

The boys were struggling with the wheel when two fiercely-painted trucks came careering around the corner above us, driven as if bent on discovering the fullest extent of Allah's will. As one they skidded to a halt opposite us and perilously close to an edge beyond which there was nothing for a thousand feet and then only a seething Indus. From four flung doors erupted a piratical crew; Agha's brigands perhaps? I hoped that they would confine themselves to pillage. They were swaggering, buccaneering and handsome, their leader strikingly so with fine chiselled Caucasian features, a straight nose, proud lips, oil-fired eyes and a mane of thick, black, shiny hair. He exuded the easy confidence of a man who knows he's a cut above the rest, a natural leader and unafraid, unsuspicious; he could be friendly towards anyone he chose. A great grin showed he had chosen us; there would be no pillage. When these buccaneers saw the flat tyre that our crew were struggling with they went to it with a laugh and a shout and the co-ordinated panache of a well drilled field-gun team. One produced a jack, another positioned it with a flying tackle, a third positively hefted the bus skywards and the leader looked on, a slightly darker Errol Flyn to the shoulders, a ragamuffin to the ankles; his was a face that arrested glances. The spare wheel was on in a minute and with more gay shouts they bounded back aboard their chariots. These were covered in hand-painted scenes of war, warriors and other fierce things, all depicted in that simplistic way of fairground rides. They gunned the running engines and roared off with a wave, flashing brigand smiles, and the elan of an imperial guard. Agha told us that they were Afghans free-trading the half of Asia; latter-day privateers. I was impressed. It was easy to see why we had had such a hard time between Kabul and Kandahar. Poor Russians, someone said. No bomb that ever burst shatters that sort of crystal spirit.

Hargreaves produced a crate of beer, illicit we thought, and extra tasty for it. There was sufficient for four cans each. We decided to ration ourselves to one. And then another and—four cans apiece later we were ready for anything they could serve up from Kabul to Kandahar and a sizeable chunk of the Russian Army too. Just then a police road-block stopped us and while Agha stepped down to negotiate we piled out to invade a roadside volley ball game. We were good humouredly accommodated into one team, and soundly thrashed.

Al was waiting round the next corner. He had intended to fly with the others but had encountered some last-minute hassles which delayed him and so he had jumped on one of the curious Suzuki two-stroke minivans that buzz up and down the KKH like angry bees. Somehow, somewhere along the way he'd slipped passed us without either party noticing. And here he stood athwart the KKH, feet at ten-to-two and a wide smile. He declined our invitation to join the cramped bus and we met again an hour later in Skardu.

Skardu: threshold of the greatest mountains of this world and chief town of Baltistan,.a great splash of colour—greens, reds and ochres—in an alluvial saucer with a 3,000-metre lip. We entered through a lowering of the lip on the western side and drove the last ten kilometres along a sandy plain, past the airport and into Naya Bazaar, a single street of small box-like shops. The breadth of panorama, the wide sky, elegant poplars, white-capped mountains and pewter evening light all combined to make a fitting climax to our journey. Skardu was a good place to come to.

> Little known and little studied, Baltistan is a land of endings and beginnings. Here the Tibetan culture has reached its westernmost point although Islam replaced Bhuddism more than 500 years ago. The Balti language bears the same kind of resemblance to modern-day Tibetan that Chaucer's language does to contemporary English. The people are of both Caucasian and Mongolian stock, and among the various isolated valleys that comprise Baltistan, people of some highly dissimilar ethnic strains reside in adjoining houses—a mixture of Islam, Tibetan-speaking people living in villages that edge on the world's most impenetrable mountain mass.

Culturally and geographically, Baltistan is probably part of Kashmir but when Kashmir was divided by the same accident of history that severed a piece of the

Punjab from India in 1947, Baltistan formally became part of the new Nation of West Pakistan (from Urdu—*Pak* meaning 'pure': *istan* meaning 'land': Land of the Pure.) while Ladakh remained in India. Until the road was cut along the Indus to Skardu, Baltistan remained practically isolated from the remainder of Pakistan for to the north lay the vast Karakoram; to the east, Kashmir, a political barrier; and to the south and west the trackless waste of the Deosai Plains of which Alistair Crowley, in 1929 wrote:

> In front of us lay the Deosai, an absolutely treeless wilderness of comparatively level country framed by minor peaks. It gives a unique impression of desolation. I have never seen its equal in this respect elsewhere.

We drove to the K2 motel at the far end of town where we found the other half of the team ensconced in the dining room watching a luminous pop video that was all bare dancing legs and posturing rock musicians. The video tape was the proud possession of the motel's manager who was always ready to emphasise that he was a Hunza rather than a Balti. Certainly by Skardu standards he was urbane, and joined by his wife and daughters, all girls of great beauty and reputedly princesses of Hunza, he watched the video with the sophisticated detachment that might only be expected of westerners inured by years of overexposure. But these westerners were glued agog, and a positive embarrassment to Ahga who could only bring himself to watch this titillating decadence through spread fingers. The manager, always careful to expel all his staff and any other locals before these showings, was mortified to spot Aftab amongst us; both were betrayed by that mixture of embarrassment and awkwardness that the collision of cultures, religions and societies often brings.

The two teams swapped stories, each striving for maximum emolument from minimal anecdote. We made an epic of our two days on the road; they wove a technicoloured embroidery of a flight around Nanga Parbat (and indeed we were envious).

That night, before turning in I noted in my diary: 'There is a larger hope in Pakistan than in India; more vibrant, and a greater willingness to help fellow travellers.' The cultural claustrophobia of Islam notwithstanding I was enjoying Pakistan.

We all spent the next day, the 10th May, sorting kit in a final attempt to pack everything into 25-kilogram loads for the porters for, despite that night of a 'whole new order of chaos' at Rupert House and the eight days of equal chaos in Islamabad, there was still plenty to pack and sort. We worked on the lawn before the solid stone-built motel with scales, cardboard boxes, hessian, needle and thread, rope wire and paint, battling with suggestion, counter-suggestion, opinion, second opinion and opposite opinion, order, counter order, disorder, levity and lack of it, patience and impatience, banter, badinage, argument and accord until everything the expedition owned was a bundle of some shape or form, and designated (or was it re-designated?) with a daubing of red or white, W or B or AB. (Ws were loads to be consumed on the walk-in; Bs were destined for Base Camp, ABs for Advance Base.) The last destination was nothing much more

Above: **Social intercourse at Base Camp. A group of Australians and the British Chogolisa team are visiting. From the left: Abdul, Bev and Wilkie, with Jim Curran in yellow.**

Below: **An avalanche sweeps from Broad Peak—as seen from Base Camp.** (Photo: Jim Curran)

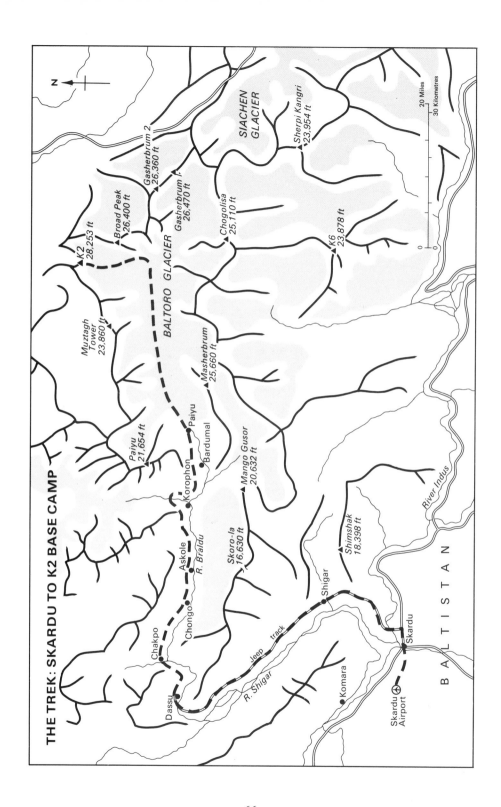

THE TREK: SKARDU TO K2 BASE CAMP

N

K2
28,253 ft

Broad Peak
26,400 ft

Gasherbrum 2
26,360 ft

Gasherbrum 1
26,470 ft

SIACHEN GLACIER

Sherpi Kangri
23,954 ft

Chogolisa
25,110 ft

K6
23,878 ft

BALTORO GLACIER

Muztagh Tower
23,860 ft

Masherbrum
25,660 ft

Paiyu
21,654 ft

Paiyu

Bardumal

Korophon

Mango Gusor
20,632 ft

Askole
R. Braldu

Skoro-la
16,630 ft

Shimshak
18,398 ft

River Indus

Chongo

Shigar

Chakpo

Dassu

Jeep track

R. Shigar

Komara

Skardu Airport

Skardu

B A L T I S T A N

20 Miles
30 Kilometres

0
0

than an uncertain dot on the whimsical map of Al's mind. We knew only that it was a long way from Base to the beginning of the NW Ridge so that an Advance Base, or, as Al had once described it to Fullers, a brew tent, would likely be needed somewhere.

There followed two days of packing, of last minute shopping, of sight-seeing of trying to open windows into this Islamic republic; of glimpses within; and of deeper glimpses of one another.

Some images of Skardu:

. . . Hargreaves goes shopping for porridge which we have unnaccountably neglected to bring.

'You have porridge?' he asks at a general store.

'Yes. You have black boots?'

'Black boots? Porridge?'

'Yes boot porridge. You want black?'

. . . I am wryly amused to find that, as the expedition's Karrimor rep, I'm the only one who doesn't have a Karrimat for the walk-in—but that Aftab has two.

. . . My morning job is to count the money. It's not as easy as you'd think. At last I can state with near certainty that we have 299,207 rupees, more or less, of which 21,907 are in notes of 1 rupee denomination—give or take . . .

. . . The motel manager sees Aftab in daylight for the first time and is horrified. Aftab is a slight, pock-marked townie and is forever producing a photograph of himself in a white suit with hair smarmed down.

'What are you trying to do to him?' the manager asks. 'He's a townie. You'll kill him long before Base Camp. Your L.O. too is a weakling. He will also never make it. Bloody lowlanders.'

Hunzas are very snooty. We employ Abdul Rahman as a second cook. He's a local lad and strong as an ox.

. . . Agha announces his intention to go to the summit of K2. His wife has said he must.

. . . The local cinema advertises two films: 'Samson and Delilah Wallah' and 'Mr. Navaronne's Guns'.

. . . The World Service of the BBC tells us that Liverpool have won the FA Cup 3–1. I wonder if Kath and Joseph got to Wembley as they had been hoping.

. . . Al explains that the small insurance policy he has taken out on behalf of the expedition specifically excludes roped climbing. It was suggested that if anyone fell survivors should untie as quickly as possible.

Overleaf: **Our early 'pedestrian' approach to Camp One.**

. . . Al holds a briefing, allots tasks. I'm to be the loadmaster and responsible for counting the loads out and counting them in at the day's end. I make 210 tickets. The plan is to issue one on collection of each load, to be returned with the load at the end of the day's march. Someone says that if my system works it will be a miracle. There was to be no miracle.

. . . We are to leave on 12 May. Five tractors and five trailers are to take all the kit to Dassu from where it'll be carried by porters.

. . . Meet a wizened old hand in the bazaar who greets us with a leg-pulling 'Ah my rulers.' He'd been in the British Army in Singapore during the war. He seemed to have survived the horrors of Changi prisoner-of-war camp unscathed; his sense of humour was more than intact and his eyes sparkled with wit and good spirits. To me his persiflage was a signal that he liked us; still liked the British—which considering what his loyalty had cost him earlier was an interesting thing. There must have been more to the Empire than is now fashionable to admit; and not all of it bad.

. . . Hundreds of the K2 postcards that we had brought from England do the rounds for 11 signatures. They are posted. Each reads 'Best wishes from K2 Base Camp.' It is, after all, the thought that counts. Every Fullers pub is sent one, and one goes too to everyone that we can remember helping us in some way no matter how small. It is a tedious business addressing several hundred postcards and affixing twice that many stamps; stamps that have no stick and have to be glued; a small labour though measured against all the help that had been so willingly given.

. . . K2 is everywhere. It is slept in K2 motels, smoked in K2 cigarettes, drunk from bottles of K2 fizz, and eaten in K2 restaurants.

. . . The British team bound for Gasherbrum IV arrive at the motel. Their leader, Dai Lampart (Do or Dai), a lad of prodigious energy and piratical appearance, harangues us for being so slow to get moving. He too is set to leave for Dassu on the morrow. A day less in Skardu than ourselves.

. . . Al is worried about overcrowding campsites and persuades him to rest a day longer in Skardu so that they remain a day behind us. Bribes him actually. We pay their motel bill for the extra night; the price of inefficiency—the wages of too many cooks.

. . . Dai asks if we have an altimeter spare that he can borrow. Hargreaves finds one with the line, 'You might as well have this one, it's no use to us. Only works up to 8,000 metres'.

. . . Liliane and Maurice Barrard turn up. They with Michel Parmentier and Wanda Rutkiewicz (a Pole), are the French K2 team headed for the Abruzzi Spur, the SE Ridge by which the mountain was first climbed by Italians in 1954 after an epic struggle which broke Bonatti's heart, though not his will. The French tell us that Renato Casarotto is already a week ahead of us. With him are his wife and and L.O. He is intent on a solo ascent of the unclimbed SW Ridge, Messner's 'magic line'.

. . . Curran frets about the weight of his walk-in load. With good reason. He needs to carry the same as the rest plus a Scoopic 35mm camera and a solid-looking tripod. I'm glad only to be a climber.

. . . Ramadan begins. We are advised not to wear shorts into the town, but like much second-hand advice its quality is suspect. In Islamabad a European had warned us not to shop in 'Pindi in shorts but when I mentioned this to Nazir Sabir he thought it nonsense to suggest that our bared legs would cause offence. It was interesting to see what credence we attached to any statement on almost any subject by a local. Anyone, so long as he was a Pakistani, was assumed to know the answer to any question we put to him, so long as it could be listed under the general heading of Pakistan. The answers were never doubted, never subjected to the least curiosity—and this in a land where the words 'I'm sorry I don't know' seemed not to exist in any of its languages. So that the very same people who would automatically pour scorn on any statement made by a member of the British Government, say, would readily accept the daftest assertion from the lips of a 'local'. The equivalent might be an educated Pakistani asking a British butcher some arcane question on our constitutional history. I found this lack of intellectual curiosity—the automatic believing and disbelieving curious,—perhaps more than that.

. . . Hargreaves has three bottles of whisky, the tastier for their being outlawed. One is sacrificed to the greater god of bullshit; a second is devoured by the genies of the first. The third is declared sacrosanct—just in time—and spirits give way to smoke. Rouse is on fine form; theory tumbles after theory, superlatives climb on superlatives. Inconsistencies seem to possess him at times like these, but he never compromises, and pursues instead, the logic of several incompatible opinions to absurd ends, relishing their incongruity. His thoughts are only at ease in extremes. The twins are in fine form too: Aid, streaked blond Californian sixties hair and greek god, has been honing up on Zen Bhuddism. He tries some on us. Hargreaves, a man of primary colours with no half tones in his register, considers Aid's gentle utterances for a second before denouncing them bollocks. Which sums up the general opinion. Aid persists with a bit more half-baked undigested theory on the meaning of life itself, until, somewhere after midnight the whisky, great truth drug and enemy of Zen, pulls out a story from his pre-Bhuddist past—a past not yet lost in the mists of time.

OVERLEAF
Main picture: **Wilkie and Al Burgess work in poor weather on the slopes between Camps One and Two.**

Inset, top: **Camp One, the NW Ridge behind. Our route lies up the snow slopes immediately above the yellow and brown tent.**

Inset, bottom: **The twins skiing 'at a suppressed dog trot' in a white-out.**

Aid had taken a taxi somewhere in Peru. At the destination he and the taxi driver got out and standing on the roadside negotiated the price. At least negotiated was the word Aid used for a form of commercial intercourse that owed more to Ghengis Khan than Siddartha. The gist of the story was that a Peruvian taxi driver had expressed dissatisfaction with Aid's settlement of the fare and that Aid brought the transaction to an early conclusion by kicking him in the throat. When we evinced surprise that a practising card-carrying Zen Buddhist could kick someone in the throat Aid helped us over this philosophical hurdle by explaining that it wasn't all that difficult, 'cos he was only a little fella, four-foot-six at most.' A helpful elucidation. That was the sort of Zen that Hargreaves could understand and he fell about in his conversion. The taxi driver story had Rouse, recovering from his most recent theory, all alight with 'the definitive Twins Story':

'At this bloody party Aid and I are over one side of the room chatting up a couple of birds when we hear this kerfuffle and I look across the other side and there's Al with his fingers up this bloke's nose and this bloke's head under his arm and he's battering this bloke's head against the bloody wall. And Aid looks up and sees all this and puts his beer down and moves in to help: "Heyup, our kid's in trouble".'

We'd all heard the story umpteen times before but that didn't spoil it in the least; it gathered timing, power and effect with every telling.

Too late, and protesting too much methinks, Aid objected to Rouse's biographical badinage and embarked on some new Bhuddist tack but, as any child will tell any mum or dad, war stories are the best stories and Siddartha's peregrinations had nothing on the pillage that the twins wrought with a little help from a Rouse unfettered by mere fact. Hargreaves, not a raconteur greatly shackled by the truth himself, and of a sudden not to be out-recounted either, was off his belly and onto his feet with deeds psychopathic of his own. Hargreaves always told his tales standing up: otherwise he couldn't get sufficient leverage into the hooks, crosses and uppercuts that punctuated even his most pastoral yarns. He had developed an interesting, if ultimately wearing, method of emphasis. Some raconteurs emphasise by employing superlatives or by raising their voices, or by deft timing, or by some animation or other. In this Hargreaves had a problem: he spoke always at fuller volume than any other human who ever uttered a word, he already inhabited superlatives and in any case, when he spoke he thrashed about as if simultaneously engaging a Joe Louis, a Rocky Marciano and a Raging Bull La Motta, but each from different corners of the ring of his yarn. I have seen furniture made matchwood at a muted rendering of one of his mildest misadventures. So for emphasis Hargreaves said everything twice, and since emphasis and the man were inseparable, you always got two stories for the price of one—concurrently—whether you liked it or not.

Fida had travelled on the previous day's tractors and had already assembled three hundred or so candidates for the two hundred porter jobs. Our sirdar knew the trek to K2 well from fourteen previous expeditions to that area and he knew most of the cohort paraded before him too. He selected the best two hundred. This was survival of the fittest unstrained: the lame were sent packing without ceremony or sympathy; midgets and idiots too (and there was a share of both) and then the crooks, cheats, troublemakers and whingers. Fida ruthlessly weeded them all out and announced himself satisfied with the remainder. To these he issued the kit that we had provided as required by *Mountaineering Rules and Regulations Edition 1983,* issued by the Ministry of Culture, Sports & Tourism for the Government of Pakistan. 'Annexure D, Scale of Equipment for Low Altitude Porters' gives these instructions:

S. No.	Details of Items of Kit & Equipment Required	Quantity	Remarks
1.	Gas/Petrol/Oil Stove (depending on altitude)	1 number (for 8 persons)	
2.	Tarpulin/Top [sic] (4 to 4 metres size maximum) with nylon chords [sic]	1 number (for 8 persons)	
3.	Ordinary rain coat/plastic sheets of appropriate size for cover against rain	1 per person	

Hargreaves, Base Camp Manager and quartermaster general, had unearthed a job lot of raincoats in a down-town 'Pindi bazaar—and secured the lot: two hundred raincoats at 2 rupees apiece (about 10 pence). The job lot embraced the full sartorial scale for rainwear from the nastiest plastic to Third-Man trenchcoats to spiv Italian numbers to best Burberry. Fida issued without favour but a certain amount of redistribution followed his issue as the biggest bagged the Burberrys and the runts skulked away with placcy macs. I wondered why the last were unpopular—they were surely the lightest and most weather-proof—until I saw that on receipt of their mac each porter made straight way to the local haberdasher there to trade his acquisition for cash or kind—and Burberrys fetched more cash and bigger kind. It occurred to me that since there was hardly a ready market for two hundred pieces of rainwear in Dassu, the greater part of this merchandise would find its way to Skardu, perhaps even 'Pindi where some future Hargreaves would complete the commercial circle.

The rest of the kit issue consisted of a pair of stockings per man—Pakistan army surplus, ex-'Pindi (via Hargreaves again), and 15 rupees in lieu of a pair of shoes. Rouse forever told us that on a previous trip his expedition had equipped the porters with training shoes only to see them removed and carried in hand on the roughest ground so that feet, rather than smart new shoes, bore the wear and tear.

Overleaf: **The author on the 'arete' between Camps One and Two.**
(Photo: Aid. Burgess)

We also paid each porter 15 rupees a day in lieu of their regulation food ration listed thus:

ANNEXURE 'G'
SCALE OF RATIONS PER HEAD FOR LOW ALTITUDE PORTERS

1.	Atta (wheat flour)	22 ozs per day
2.	Ghee (cooking oil)	2.5 ozs per day
3.	Sugar	2 ozs per day
4.	Tea	$^1/_2$ oz per day
5.	Milk	2 ozs per day (fresh/tinned)
6.	Salt	$^1/_2$ oz per day
7.	Dal Chana (fried)	2 ozs per day
8.	Dal (pulses)	1 oz per day
9.	Cigarettes	10 sticks per day
10.	Match box	1 per week
11.	Meat	$3^1/_2$ ozs per day
12.	Onions dried	$^1/_4$ oz per day
13.	Condiment powder	$^1/_4$ oz per day

Other regulations in the same document regarding the porters included:

VII. WAGES OF PORTERS AND TRANSPORT HIRE CHARGES:

40. Wages for hiring porters, animal and mechanical transport shall be communicated along with the formal permission letter.

41. Payment of wages to porters shall be made in the following manner:-
(a) Porters engaged for 7 days or less shall be paid 50% of the daily wages for the said period on the day they are engaged. The remaining 50% shall be paid on the day they are discharged.
(b) Porters engaged for a period of more than 7 days shall be paid 50% of the daily wages for a week on the day they are engaged. The other half shall be paid at the end of the said week. Thereafter payment shall be made on weekly basis. In case a period falls short of a week then full payment shall be made for the said period on the day they are discharged.

42. In addition to daily wages, a party shall provide to a low altitude porter free rations as per Annexure 'G' or money in lieu of rations, as fixed by the Government from the day he is engaged till the day he is discharged.

43. Similarly, free rations shall be provided to a high altitude porter as per Annexure 'H' from the day he goes above 5,000 metres till the day he returns to the said 5,000 metres. He shall, however, be provided with free rations as per Annexure 'G' or money in lieu of ration up to a height of 5,000 metres.

44. Except in the case of sickness/injury and subject to paras 56 and 57 no wages shall be paid to a porter for a day on which he does not work. If, however, a party wants to have a rest day then a porter shall be paid full wages etc.

45. Similarly because of forced halts and bad weather days a party shall pay to a porter full daily wages and rations (or ration money in lieu thereof). Decision of a leader about 'march' on such days shall be final. If, however, a L.O. feels that

*the weather is too bad to march, he will ask the leader to halt the party. If,
however, a leader disagrees with the advice of L.O. he shall give him in writing
the reasons for such disagreement.*

*46.   A porter marching with a party for more than seven days shall be allowed every
seventh day as holiday with full daily wages etc.*

For their part, the porters had to undertake to abide by the terms, promise
neither to desert nor to insist on an increase in the wages during the march, and to
'serve the party diligently and faithfully'.

I had, on Al's instructions, made over two hundred photocopies of Annexure
'J' as this undertaking was called. They may still be found at Dassu Inspection
Bungalow where we were staying, unsigned, un-thumb-printed, proof that even in
Pakistan expediency sometimes triumphs over bureaucracy. We'd gone through
pretty conscientious motions and Agha seemed satisfied that sufficient gestures
had been made and enough ado done to sustain his self importance for the
moment. So I forgot them.

We had learnt in Islamabad that the government had awarded the porters a
25% wage increase that very spring. This made a nasty mess of Al's budget, the
more so since porters' wages were already by far the biggest single item in that
budget. For their toil to Base Camp a porter would earn from us about 1,000
rupees, more than they might otherwise earn in a year, rather less than most of us
would accept for a single day of like work. The moral sums were conflicting and
confusing: it was simpler to stick to the monetary arithmetic.

By late afternoon we had the 210 loads sorted into neat lines ready for
allocation the next morning. I had readied my load tickets and drawn up a chart
to check the loads against. Rouse had out-bouldered us all on some climbing
problems he'd created on the walls of the bungalow; Bev had held a clinic, treating
in the main whitlows and children's coughs and had photographed and admired
half the goitres in the village; Hargreaves fussed about the kitchen and Porter
fussed about the food (for which he had responsibility) and we all ate and turned
in anyhow on floor, mattressless beds, and a settee. I fell asleep under a
glass-covered picture frame that showed the Inspection Bungalow rules. The rules
were quaintly stated in exquisite, old-fashioned English and woven into the rules
and threaded between the lines there was history.

Dassu to Base Camp 13th – 22nd May

We were up at 5.30 am on the 13th for a breakfast of paratthas, eggs and tea. The
porters fell to at 6. They were a raggle taggle lot mostly dressed in rags that were
once woollen chemise and trousers. Some had coats of sorts, a few the coats that
we had given, but for most the only additional protection, day or night, was a thin
woollen blanket which with their few other belongings—pot and food—they
carried on top of our 25-kilogram loads, the whole suspended from a single cord
of woven goat-hair over either shoulder. The same method is used in Kashmir and
areas of Himachal Pradesh in India. It is a primitive and hideously uncomfortable

Above: **Skiing just before the site of Advance Base. The West Ridge of K2 is on the skiers' right.**

Below: **A skier above Advance Base. The NW Ridge rises above him in profile. The pinnacles that stopped the American team in 1978 are to be seen clearly on the left. Above the pinnacles is a notch: the point at which we gained the crest of the ridge from the slopes immediately below.**

way to carry anything but the slightest load and it amazed me that a people who make a profession of carrying have not yet developed a more comfortable way, nor even an ergonomically more efficient method. A few, it is true, had fashioned crude frames from Y-forked boughs which they positioned between load and back for support and which they called rucksacks. Our porters were all from surrounding valleys and all Baltis. These are Caucasian people though some displayed a Mongolian influence in eye or cheek bone. They were mostly handsome to my European eye with fine faces, rich black hair and spare but strong frames. A few were especially handsome; about the same number especially ugly. The former were also the tallest, strongest and most intelligent—the leaders; the latter were stunted (some under 5 feet), the weakest and moronic. Bev said that these phenomena were predictable symptoms of inbreeding and that for every ten halfwits a genius would be thrown up. That the genius should also be blessed with the limbs of an olympic 1500-metre runner and the looks of a film star seemed hardly fair. Rouse said that he'd noticed the same when teaching which seemed a surprising thing for a socialist to say and an even more surprising thing for Rouse to say; it was the first work he'd ever confessed to. Certainly Marx would have had a hard time sustaining the environmental versus genetic bit of his theory in Baltistan.

But the Baltis were the least morbid of peoples who had accepted the gift of life without question; not for them the metaphysical introspection that beset western people. I found it hard to imagine any of them contemplating suicide—yet for them death was no grief—just as I found it equally hard to imagine any westerner who had not, at some despond, contemplated suicide. And yet for us death is a great grief. Nor was the gift of life in Baltistan as attractively packaged as our own yet they harbour no grudge against nature or Allah or whatever it was that condemned them to this harsh place. In the weeks that we were together I grew fond of them, though nothing as lofty as T.E. Lawrence's fondness for his Arab comrades: 'We were fond together, because of the sweep of the open places, the taste of the wide winds, the sunlight, and the hopes in which we worked'. No, it could hardly be expected that a Balti lugging 25 kilos of white man's burden for about £4 a day could be wrought up in our hopes. But there was some of that, some of Lawrence's eloquent sentiment, washing between us. What else explains a fondness that some of us felt towards the porters and they evidently towards some of us?

Reduced to itinerary, the march from Dassu to K2 Base Camp looked daily something like this:

Customary daily stints		Miles	Height gain (feet)		
Dassu	– Chakpo	12	8150	–	8600
Chakpo	– Chango	9½	8600	–	9400
Chango	– Askole	5½	9400	–	9750
Askole	– Karophan	7½	9750	–	10400
Karophan	– Bardumal	5½	10400	–	10750
Bardumal	– Paiyu	9½	10750	–	11050

Paiyu	–	Lilligo	6	11050	–	12190
Lilligo	–	Urdukas	$7^1/2$	12190	–	13160
Urdukas	–	Biange	$5^1/2$	13160	–	13600
Biange	–	Gore	6	13600	–	14300
Gore	–	Concordia	$5^1/2$	14300	–	14900
Concordia	–	Base Camp	$11^1/2$	14900	–	16750

Miles = 91.5   Height gain = 8600

But this walk is not so easily tamed: it's a walk on the wild side and no easy options—'as hard as anything I have come across which is not actually climbing'. Joe Tasker said that, and he'd done a bit. I felt that we were poised, one foot lifted in anticipation, a half-step from the start of a trek that would lead to the throne of the greatest mountain kingdom on earth: into the Karakoram.

'The Great Himalayan Range consists in reality of a series of ranges together forming a great arc whose outer side faces due south. To the north lies the boundless table-land of Tibet, to the south the depression of the Indus and the Ganges. At its two extremities the series of ranges falls away and curves southwards, forming in the east the mountains of Burma, in the west the hills of Baluchistan. On this side, however, almost adjoining the northern extremity of the Himalaya proper, is an enormous corrugation in the earth's surface containing a chain of exceedingly high mountains, commonly called the Karakoram, after its best-known and most important pass, the Karakoram Pass. The word karakoram signifies in Tibetan "black" (kara) "gravel or earth covered with detritus" (korum); and from its initial letter are derived the abbreviations K1, K2, K3 etc, which have been adopted by the Indian Topographical Office as a means of identifying a very numerous series of peaks without local names. Whether the Karakoram constitutes a system of mountains in itself or whether it forms an integral part of the Himalaya is not very clear. But since the geographical nomenclature of the great mountain ranges of the world is for the most part conventional it is usual to regard the Karakoram as one of the great orographical units of the Himalayan chain, occupying a position comparable to that of the Bernese Alps vis-à-vis the Alpine system. The Karakoram is, moreover, the northern most portion of the Himalaya, its latitude being roughly the same as that of Gibraltar.' (Ardito Desio)

I kept a diary along the way which brings a more accurate and honest account than I could summon now, even though there were days when I could find no leisure to see the beauty which sometimes accosted us at corner, or brow, or prospect; nor any energy at the day's end to record sensation. There were other days when awe at what I had seen paralysed sensation and pen alike; though I always tried to scribble a sketch.

13th May Raining; a dreich drizzle; cool. Set out at 8-ish by a rough jeep track (some jeep!). The Braldu river is unseasonably low which allows us to cross to the left (east) bank, and an easier trail. No sign yet of the 'searing heat' the veterans of this passage had forecast.

Curran and camera took off ahead of the most of us so that he could film-ambush as we approached. He takes the high road, the right bank and several unnecessary thousands of feet of misery, been this way before, knew the way, waits in vain, then in anger. The left-hand bankers take lunch just outside a village typical of the area. From a distance they look like one of those line drawings that architects use to mislead planning committees, clients and maybe, who knows, themselves: lots of low flat artily unstraight lines between elegant clusters of impossibly slim and tall poplars: the proportions look too good to be true: Corbusier in reverse. But here, unlike the drawing board, they are true: and there's no-one to fool.

Rouse holds forth on the art of bullshitting which he says is knowing how far to stretch the elastic of credulity before it breaks. He's concerned that Burke strains the tension a twang too far. Refers to an earlier Burke essay where he'd shredded our collective elastic with some tale about the sighting, at the age of fourteen, of a UFO, after which, reporting to the local police station, he'd been made to sign the 'Official Secrets Act'. (The secret's out, Phil and I confidently await prosecution).

'Bad that', Al said—but not about the veracity. 'I mean lying's fine, but being disbelieved leaves you stranded. You gotta stop earlier. Otherwise there's no skill and you have either to confess or stick to your guns. Never lie beyond the point of total improbability.'

Later Phil told some new, and only slightly less improbable story. Al, grandmaster and judge, considered it for a moment and said, 'That's probably good enough to pass for the truth on this expedition. In other words you're lying through your teeth.' Al at his best. Phil laughed too, though not much. After all he was a professional northerner who mustn't be seen to be enjoying life too hugely in Britain's divided society, the iniquities of which he was the walking, talking incarnation. Phil was the expedition's chief, but not only, proponent of the conspiratorial theory of government; that is that once in power a Conservative government sets about making life as difficult as possible for all those living not much north of Watford. Phil wore the grief of these downtrodden millions personally in a haunted expression that women found irresistible. What he could never forgive was that he'd been forcibly propelled into the ranks of solid middle class with a salary about twice the national average and company car to boot; and he disguised this betrayal of his origins and his own accursed upward mobility with ever hollowed cheeks and ever anguished visage. And all the women in the land wanted to fatten him. Phil had been deprived physically too, coming north of the Watford-to-nowhere-in-particular line. Because of this he could only run Cram, Coe, Ovett et al to within a second or two of their best times. There was no telling what he might have done with another bowl of tripe a day and a lighter pair of clogs. And of the estimation of his speed over the mile there was no doubt: Phil himself told us—daily.

Plod on through villages and patches of green that spring wherever there's available water—which isn't often. The Braldu roars through like an express train, stops for nothing and feeds nothing but its own volition. Our porters seem cheerful, friendly, honest. I'm impressed with the way they help one another over difficult bridges.

John Porter advises a well-known importer of outdoor equipment on such things as boots and rucksacks. On his feet he has a pair of their latest boots, product of the best advice and latest technology. He is crippled by blisters. Some others with the same boots are equally crippled. They have some advice for him. It isn't polite.

Between them they share enough blisters to skin an army. They excruciate the last few kilometres to the campsite. The rest of us trip lightly along on *schadenfreude*. Descend steeply into the Braldu Gorge, a mile of rock and sand desert deep, cross a tremulous bridge on shuffling feet, too tremulous at 50 metres up to step out, across a terrible slit-eyed rock chasm through which runs tumultuous water, across to a levelling of sand and grass on the far bank and a trickle of water; the first campsite.

The Baltis arrive in cheerful bunches and set about collecting grass, brushwood and dung for their evening fires and brew up on the blackest pots with great efficiency: tea and a sort of 'field' or crude heavyweight chapatti. Curran's crew drifts in (Bev, Hargreaves and Hall had trod the high route too) unfilmed and unfunny. I tick the loads in as they arrive. By pm all are in except AB5 (Advance Base 5), which I seem not to have ticked out that morning either.

14th May Away by 5.30 under a clear sky. No sign of the elusive AB5 and wonder did it ever exist? Through the Braldu Gorge on a low level; tottering boulders overhead, sometimes literally so; foaming brown Braldu snatching at our feet. But not as bad as the stories tell it; they have it a real frightener whereas in reality it is just not the safest place, though one is left with the distinct impression that, at best, the Braldu Gorge is but a temporary arrangement. Funny how so few phenomena are quite as big, bad or ugly as their reputations. Hargreaves emerges from the Braldu very gay and all of an animation: as if the boulders and the threat of their percussion had stimulated his intellection. 'Did you see that and this?' he cries to half of Baltistan. At the village of Chango the world opens up wide again, and there's fields and trees before the next desert.

It's hot: searingly hot. We rest under Chango's shady trees. The porters trundle in, set down their loads, look set for the night here. There's some excitement between a larger and a smaller faction, Fida Hussein refereeing. Watching, it becomes clear that the majority want to stay the night at Chango, a minority to press on to Askole, their home. Fida confirms it. Most of us are for staying but Rouse is for pressing on, and wanders off down the path leaving 200 squabbling porters and a divided team. I run after him and tell him that most of the porters are for staying. He replies 'I didn't know you could speak Balti'. I consider throttling him but it's hot and I'm tired. A mutinous crew and a mutinous team plod on. 'There's plenty of water between Chango and Askole' Al has said. There's none—though that's hardly Al's fault. The blisters on the advisor and his advised are increasing in acreage; the sun is overhead and hot and dizzying; the way dry, we dryer; Curran is filmless, the team near open mutiny, morale invisible. Arrive Askole dehydrated; not a bead of sweat between us. Park in a dusty yard that may once have been a field, on the edge of town. Drink and drink and gradually we top up and cheer up. Some banter creeps into the conversation—a good sign. To bed in good spirits at 8.30 having all agreed that we should keep the days shorter rather than longer. Al talks into the night about reaching Base Camp in 7 days if we keep on at this speed. It seems he's in a hurry but it's not clear why.

15th May Woken at 2.30 by hideous wailing of prayers. Try hard to remember that this cacophony is ethnic and these days, therefore, a good thing. I can't remember if I convinced myself but woken again by a similar din at 4.30 in a second test of ethnic tolerance. I'm some way from being converted to Islam.

At breakfast Curran turns on Rouse, 'If we don't start walking traditional stages I'm leaving now'. A bit of a bombshell. Jim is worried that he's shooting no film.

As I quit our camping ground the village school is holding an alfresco assembly in a corner of the field and young boys—only boys are educated—are singing a harmony in clear, pure, choirboy voices. At the gate a mother is scooping water from a stream to dampen and comb her son's hair; straightens his cap and fastens his top shirt button before lifting him over the stile and sending him off to school with a pat—like any mum the world over. It was both a moving and a heartening incident: moving, I suppose, because I have a son of a similar age whose hair, cap and buttons have wills of their own, and heartening because it seemed to demonstrate that maternal instinct transcends frontier, creed, race and any other boundary that man might draw across his progress.

Askole is run by a colourful old crook called Hadji Mhadi and run with a feudal fist. The man, a sort of Islamic Godfather, extorts something for everything and even charges the porters 10 rupees each for the privilege of passing through his village. Askole may be seen by various eyes: Rouse dismissed it with the obvious cloacal pun; Allessandro Gogna, a leading Italian mountaineer saw it as:

> The last habitable refuge in a valley dotted with oases, oases which through centuries of effort have been wrenched from the desert. You can honestly say that we now find ourselves at the very end of the earth. The extreme poverty, the dirt, the sickness, the intermarriage have all contributed in dragging the people down to a near-animal existence. The houses are of clay and stones with scanty wooden framework; the roofs of mud, topped with thorny bundles of brushwood. Women with children in their arms stand outside; animals go in and out through the doors. And over everything, the dust and dirt, fleas and lice . . . It is not long before a crocodile of patients queue up, moaning in front of our doctor. There is a woman who has given birth to dead twins and now suffers from pneumonia; a man unable to urinate. People with infections, tuberculosis. I notice that some of us keep our eyes averted.'

But to me, the alarming dirge forgotten, and intoxicated with this morning's freshness, the place seemed green, vigorous, wide and wonderful; I walked sun-dappled avenues of noble poplars; wondered at the intricacy and science of a system of irrigation channels that threaded this pastoral margin; took pleasure in sweet hellos from cheeky, dirty-nosed children; watched industrious farmers and yak-drawn ploughs and hoes drawn on chains by men and women as they turned their stony fields to tilth; admired well planned crop rotation; and thought it a goodish morning to be alive and Askole a goodish place to be alive in. Bev Holt will have yet a different version; he was chased from the village by a group of irate women for aiming his camera at one of them. Bev had owned the apparatus but a week and had been full of early enthusiasm, much of which (and particularly his interest in portraiture) now evaporated. 'Ugly cow anyhow', he panted ungallantly, the unrepentant Englishman to the last stitch of his lion tamer's suit as Curran had christened Bev's safari-like ensemble.

A little outside the village we came upon the purest of mountain streams and washed head and body. Later we bathed in hot sulphur springs. Curran filmed the while calling for more genitalia. 'It's OK on Channel 4 you know.' Well there's only so much a man can do and nothing on offer that day was likely to offend other than the most optimistic viewer. We held breaths and sucked in bellies and tried to be Davids for our Rodin but none had the lines for it and Curran soon turned his lens exclusively on the twins who were doing a fair impersonation of Romulus and Remus in a higher pool.

'I'll do a second take on the way out when you're all thinner,' said the fattest. Hargreaves, second fattest, dragged himself from the warm green water and lay like a beached whale, drying in the strong sun.

Jolly along an hour or two more in company with a yak that the boys are driving to dinner, when we meet Aid greek-godding in the sunshine. He tells that there has been a change of plan and that we are now going further than Al, who was nowhere to be seen, had agreed to. Porter, now in a position to advise on blisters as no-one in history, is angry. We are all disturbed, more by the uncertainty than the possibility. Porter's blisters moan a lot; we all moan a little. K2 looks safe. A mile later we meet Al and there are some angry words with almost everyone getting his oar in. Brian, ever the level head, and with a wealth of common sense, explains that the stages are arbitrary in the first place and change from year to year according to conditions—but fails to convince anyone with his diplomacy. Al says it is all Fida's doing. There's a choice of ways; one involves crossing the snout of the Biafo glacier, the other fording the Braldu, comparatively tame here, but getting angrier with the afternoon melt from the glaciers above. Most of the porters and half the team head for the tip of the Biafo. Phil shouts at Curran 'now look what you've done', which confuses everyone, and the rest of the team and a few of the porters make to ford the torrent. I strip off my pants to keep them dry, link arms with Al Burgess and together we stumble across. The current is strong and the bed uncertain; it's excitement enough. Hargreaves joins with Brian and is nearly over when Wilkie stumbles and is swept away. Hargreaves, no mean paddler before he was a whale, reads water as well as the *Beano*, grabs at Wilkie and hauls him out. A good effort. The water is almost literally freezing: a swimmer would not last long. On the far bank Agha, who has been carried over by a brace of porters takes enormous offence at my naked loins; his offence, I might add, being indirectly proportional after that icy wade, to its object.

But all this little commotion has boosted spirits and we bumble on to Karophon, along breakneck moraine, still in company with the yak who is having a hard time slouching to his place of execution.

We arrive at Karophon, a pleasant and bushy place at about 2.30 pm. It's been an easy day after all. As we relax in the sun, there's much badinage, a re-emergence of good humour, and Al promising easy short days all round. The team's repaired but it's worrying to see how easily we are punctured.

Agha regales us on the virtues of Islam, is puzzled that we do not contest its superiority over Christianity and then is horrified to discover that none of us profess to believing in any god.

'How do you think you arrived in this world?' he asks. He receives a number of replies varying from Porter's cultivated treatise to Hargreave's no-gynaecology-spared blow-by-blow account. Agha was appalled.

The ox is brutally slain, after the halal fashion (from which I walk away), and apportioned to two hundred porters in brutally unequal portions; the biggest to the biggest, the smallest to smallest.

'SOF' says Hargreaves.

'SOF?'

'Survival of the fittest', and slips a couple of tins more than Porter has authorised into our evening stew. 'Fattest too.'

Curran comes over and, referring to this morning's little contretemps with Al, says 'S'pose I'm in the book now'. There it is Jim.

And so we went along.

16th May Bardumal: a dusty flat, not far from the Braldu. Al vomits half the night. Bev administers his patent cure, codeine and bacteria by the shovel. I spot a porter apparently drinking in the evening view (which is stupendous): wonder if appreciation of scenery is an educated or a natural response. Our filter pumps can't cope with the Braldu and are clogging badly, which had me scribbling home:

'The taste of the Braldu! This ferocious river, comparatively meek in spring, impatiently awaiting the Baltoro's summer melt to slake its thirst, may be as all good scientists will assuredly avow, merely H_2O, like all the other water in the world. But there's more to life than facts, and more to water than chemical formulae; and more to the Braldu than water. It is not so much that it serves as a sewer to a dozen villages that dot and cling to its bank; nor that the roar of its torrent is mighty, though that it is . . . it's the silt; silt so fine that it runs rings round—or rather through—the finest filter we could cobble—a foot square of finest cotton sheet. A mug of Braldu began battleship grey, and finished, filtered, as grey as a battleship, not a shade, not a nuance, lighter. This water supports a suspension so fine that only our Katadyn water purifying pumps, guaranteed to knock dead at a stroke all trace of typhoid, dysentry, cholera, colibacillosis, amebiosis, giardiais and bilharsiosis (the label that advertises these claims adds *etc* for good measure) could render the solution clear. Even then the ceramic filter which did the job clogged impenetrably after the passage of only a litre and needed to be vigorously scrubbed before filtering could be resumed.

A story goes that the Hadji Mhadi of Askole, the headman of the last habitation that Concordia-bound travellers encounter, sells bottles of the stuff to passing trekkers as the 'Hadji Mahdi Elixir', surest laxative in all Islam! Apocryphal of course. Nevertheless, he needn't be so modest! Another tale tells of a British climber who imported a bottle of Braldu and kept it a year on his shelf, undusted, unmolested and 365 days later the silt remained as happily suspended as the day it was plucked from its plunge toward the Indus. And not one grain of that silt had found its way to the bottom of the bottle. Something else, Braldu water!'

17th May, Paiyu Another easy day. Paiyu is a frail wisp of a wood, the last trees on this earth, clinging—but just—to a barren hillside, 500 feet above the Braldu. The hillside sweeps on, regularly angled, so that the eye may follow its line, to twenty thousand feet and more; here are intimations of big hills. This wood, the wisp of it, is fed by a sickly dish-water trickle that, slipping between garbage, is dammed by cans. Every year the trees are ravaged by a thousand fuel-gathering porters to provide fire for a week on the Baltoro glacier, carrying for those who prize mountains above a lower world. The place is fetid with the wafted stench of effluent and human excrement: Paiyu is paying a high price for its last trees and too soon it will have paid in full and will pay no more. (Pakistan's regulations say that mountaineering expeditions must supply porters with a stove between eight. Expedition economics say that the porters are given the cheapest stoves that satisfy the regulations. Stomachs say that it is more efficient to cook on natural fuel, on dung or 'shilang' and on wood. So bits of Paiyu are carried as far as Base Camp on the tops of loads to be sacrificed nightly.)

The Duke of Abruzzi passed this way with a mighty throng and levelled himself a number of platforms in this very hillside. They accommodate tents to this day, though tents of a geometry the good Duke would scarcely recognise. There's a crude subterranean hut of the same vintage too, which has sheltered more porters than he could have imagined.

The Franco-Polish team breeze in: Maurice and Liliane Barrard, Michel Parmentier and Wanda, and 40 porters. They were hoping to push on tomorrow but a vociferous strike persuades them to grant the regulation rest day.

We rest a day too. It gives us a day's acclimatization and the porters a chance to bake sufficient chapattis for the five days to Base Camp. A few of them are paid off—we have eaten the food, or burnt the fuel they were carrying. This happens at the end of every day. Rouse calls it an exponential curve which means nothing to me but it is apparently the basis of his calculation of the porter wage bill.

The rest day is marred by the production of coffee in lieu of tea for breakfast. I show Hargreaves a passage in *Other Men's Flowers:* 'I have always charted some decline in English character from the time when coffee replaced tea on the breakfast table', to which he replies 'bollocks, I prefer coffee'. A second and greater disaster: there is no porridge, not just for today—never. We haven't brought any. I'm mortified and the morning is cold.

It snows that night but the porters, most of them with nothing more than a rag blanket between them and the stars, show no sign of being cold. They're a hardy crew. Our earlier grumbling compares shamefully: they bear our luxuries with a grin, we grin only in luxury.

'The speed of the walk-in should be set by the slowest man', the slowest man announced.

'No, it should be set by the average man', Rouse contended.

'And then what happens to the slowest?' someone else asked.

'Hey Jim' (Hargreaves) 'we should be eating the Kit-Kats on the walk-in, they're useless on the hill, they melt.'

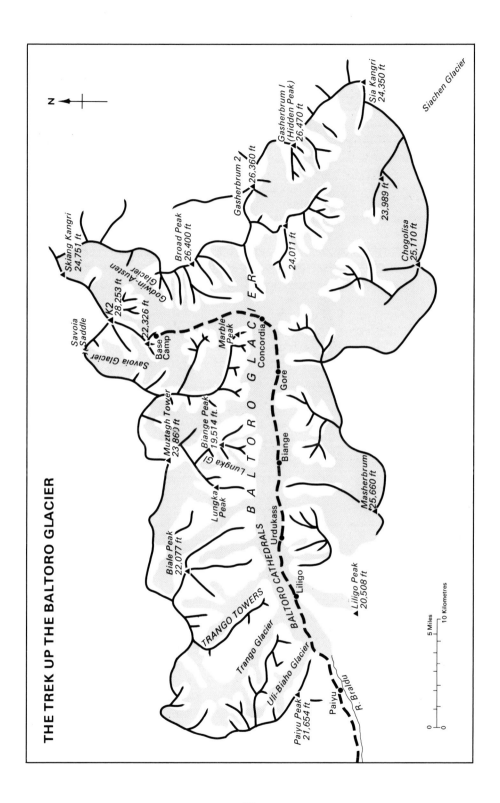

THE TREK UP THE BALTORO GLACIER

N

Siachen Glacier

Sia Kangri
24,350 ft

Gasherbrum I
(Hidden Peak)
26,470 ft

Gasherbrum 2
26,360 ft

23,989 ft

24,011 ft

Chogolisa
25,110 ft

Broad Peak
26,400 ft

Skiang Kangri
24,751 ft

Godwin-Austen
Glacier

K2
28,253 ft

22,326 ft

Savoia
Saddle

Base
Camp

Savoia Glacier

BALTORO GLACIER

Marble
Peak

Concordia

Gore

Muztagh Tower
23,860 ft

Biange Peak
19,514 ft.

Lungka Gl

Biange

Masherbrum
25,660 ft

Lungka
Peak

Biale Peak
22,077 ft

Urdukass

TRANGO TOWERS

BALTORO CATHEDRALS

Liligo

Liligo Peak
20,508 ft

Trango Glacier

Uli-Biaho Glacier

Paiyu Peak
21,654 ft

Paiyu

R. Braldu

0   5 Miles

0   10 Kilometres

'Hey Jim, we should be saving the Kit-Kats, they're great hill food.'

Someone said three words that stops the expedition in its tracks as we realise, as one, that this is the first time that they've been uttered. The words were 'I don't know'. They were never spoken again. Bev pulls fifteen Balti teeth, his anaesthetic reinforced by a Burgess neck lock. It's a medieval sight but there's no shortage of patients. Agha says, 'tooth pulling is harder than leg-pulling!'

A group of porters pass through on their way down from an earlier expedition. There is much embracing and sharing of tea and chapattis. At least porter camaraderie is strong.

Bev has the BBC world service on. Iran and Iraq are still knocking the blazes out of one another; Pakistan has shot down an Afghani aircraft flown by a Soviet pilot. Reagan has had £35 thousand million cut from his defence budget; it's all a world away.

Do or Dai's Gasherbrum team storms in, having overtaken us by a day since Skardu. One of their number, an irredeemably dour Scot, asks why our team is so fat. And we thought we were getting thinner. Curran is certainly doing his best, he's getting thinner by the retch.

The next day is cold and snowy as we take to the Baltoro glacier but there are fleet views of architectural wonder to compensate: of Paiyu Peak, of the Trango Towers, of the Baltoro Cathedrals; arches, buttresses, walls, roofs that would be decried artistic licence if any artist ever risked such things. Fleet views as I say, titillating, tantalizing, 'now you sees me now you don't' flashes; subliminal suggestion. It was very frustrating to be continually reminded that just across there is the most gobsmacking mountain scenery in the world when that scenery insisted on a discreet purdah behind a veil of mists and clouds and showers and storms. Then Lilligo—a terraced morraine, a balcony with some view. Above a huge wall of loose conglomerate rose a hundred feet or more, and immediately under it the porters camp, bang in the path of a thousand boulders should Allah will it—which, that night at any rate, he didn't. We infidels site our tents at the balcony's edge, as far from Allah's temptation as possible. A porter lugs by an enormous bough, and there's not so much as a bush for miles. Now there's foraging. Maybe it was the last of Paiyu wood.

The porters, tarpaulins strung low against the cold and the softly falling snow, sang down the night; sang in open-throated chorus and rousing harmonies that brought a surge to our spirits, and tingle to flesh; song that seemed to swell in those scant bivouacs and shore them with substance, and growing too big, burst, unstrained, into the naked air and fled our darkness to be welcomed and whispered in the silences of stars. I wandered, camp-fire to camp-fire, drawn by smiling eyes and friendly glances and saw allegiance in a hundred handsome firelit faces. At La Scala Pavarotti has stirred a thousand souls with a single silver voice, and at Cardiff Arms Park the Welsh, with a single silver song, all the souls in a nation: but the Baltis did it better and sang that cold night warm; but then their house is Baltoro Cathedral, their pitch Baltoro Park.

When they stopped and the night was dragged over Lilligo I returned to my tent to find Hargreaves already there and in a wakeful semi-slumber through which, and from about half way down his sleeping bag, he mumbled, 'what was that fucking awful noise?' James Hargreaves: no half-tones, man of primary colours.

At Urdukas, over a huge moraine, there are more of the Duke's platforms, flattened from a steep hillside and set between fine ochre granite boulders and, unlikely in this desert of rock and ice, patches of green. Dave discovers an offwidth which is 5C until I get up when its 'bog standard gritstone 5A'. Whatever the grade, it's a mightly pant at 4,000 metres. There's also a boulder problem which it seems no-one can hack until, 30 minutes after the rest of us have found other diversions, a triumphal whoop tells the Karakoram that Al is up it.

Confusion at Biange; to camp or not to camp. Not to camp; and on to Gore amid arguments and under snow showers. And past a hint of Gasherbrum IV and the mighty Muztagh Tower. But no filming for Curran, this weather, this pace. Curran has been assigned a porter, Ghulam, to help him lug his filming paraphernalia. Ghulam is the product of the healthiest and happiest collection of genes in the whole of Baltistan—tall, lean, loose-limbed, bright and Hollywood handsome. The Sheffield boys reckon he'd cause the right kind of race riot 'down the Porters Arms, Friday night'. But what impressed me most was that, having reached Gore a while or two before Jim, he dumped his considerable load and returned down the glacier to give Jim a hand—unbidden.

Rouse has a climbing plan that he puts to individuals as he happens upon them along the way.

'Eight's a bit too many clambering over the mountain all at once. What do you think? We'll split into two teams of four and go like that.'

I could see the practical sense in the scheme but voiced a misgiving about the wisdom of creating two teams when we had yet to weld as one. I said so. Al replied that he had had no management experience but saw it purely as a question of arithmetic. I didn't think it so easy a sum.

From the mists a Pakistani Army signal corporal materialises. He operates a telephone here at Gore, just he and a mate; between them the front line in the Indo-Pakistan argument about who owns this bit of the universe. But then, who wouldn't own it given half a chance?

Agha pulls the hugest rank in history on the feckless signaller. Not only is he, Agha Hussein, a captain, but he is directly descended from Mohammed, the man himself. The corporal is beside himself in reverence and takes Agha into the cardboard hut that serves as home, fortification and telephone exchange, evicting his front line comrade to make room for the prophet's son. Next morning Agha looks better fed and rested than for some time and for the second and last time, declares his morale to have been 'considerably boosted'.

The porters were into the snow shin deep in their trainers all the way up to Concordia. It's well below zero and some have no socks, having either sold or saved those that we issued. That evening, clearing the snow from the rocks they crowd fondly, many to one tarpaulin and share what comingling heat their thin bodies can generate. Nor is Allah invoked that night, too cold for him too, apparently. Fida does his book-keeping under a tarpaulin that Hargreaves calls the kitchen; two more porters are sent down the curve back to Askole or Dassu or beyond.

Hargreaves cooks against all odds which are: a blowing storm; 4,500 metres of

91

thin air; a heated argument between Porter and Hall about food which simmers long enough to brown into heated agreement; conflicting advice from too many cooks; Abdul, whose sea-level energy no longer conceals subterranean cooking skills; Aftab who looks as if he's left his lungs in 'Pindi where he's certainly left his heart and whose menus are rather less exotic than those so confidently advertised at more equable altitude; and Agha, whose continuing demands for waiter service are flying sparks around the smoking tip of the *maitre d's* notoriously short and flammable fuse. But his broth was not spoiled and we ate well.

* * *

The weather was foul all night. From famed Concordia, so called in 1891 by William Conway because the mighty confluence of glaciers reminded him of Place de la Concorde in Paris, there was not a hint of anything that might have inspired Sir Francis Younghusband to write:

> We had just turned a corner which brought into view, on the left hand, a peak of appalling height. The mountain filled the whole end of the valley, with nothing to draw the attention from it. Its lines were ideally proportioned and perfectly balanced, and its powerful architectural design was adequate to its majesty without being heavy. The scale was too vast, for one to receive at once an impression of the whole.

Or moved Ardito Desio to recall:

> The view of the Baltoro is breathtaking and fascinating in the extreme. From such a vantage point the glacier appears as a colossal, I would say monstrous, river of ice that fills the valley as the sea fills a fiord. It is the image of what our great alpine valleys must have looked like during the Ice Age. In the background rises the pyramid of K2, while at the sides can be seen those other colossi of the Karakorum, Broad Peak, and the four Gasherbrums with their satellites.

But we saw none of it; not a hint until the next morning. Then we saw it. The sort of belief-suspending panorama that had had Younghusband all agog and: 'saying emphatically to myself and to the universe at large: Oh yes! Oh yes! this really is splendid! How splendid! How splendid!' And that now had Hargreaves equally agog and saying to himself and to the universe at large, 'Fuck me'. No half-tone man remember. On Jim's invitation, for it was invitation as well as it was execration, confession, astonishment, enthusiasm, declaration—and it was all those things—on Jim's invitation, I scrambled from the tent to see for myself. An hour later I tried to record the sensations in a letter to Fullers:

We arrived at Concordia, the junction of two of this Earth's greatest glaciers, the Godwin Austen and the Baltoro, on 21st May. And from this throne of Mountain Gods could be seen—nothing; a pea-souper prevailed. Jim Curran, maker of films and one-liners, who with our atmosphere daily and progressively rarifying, would have cheerfully exchanged all the oxygen under our sun for a half-decent view of anything, and whose mood, as his art surrendered to the mists, might be best described as determinedly despondent, quipped through a grimace, 'who put the Con in Concordia?' The mists lost the laugh too.

But the next morning a great skylight had opened in the roof of the world, and there, joining Heaven to the unspotted Earth and filling all the space for an infinity on either side, were mountains we thought existed only in dreams; mountains that would have sent Michelangelo home to think again; mountains that said that there was somewhere a Greater Sculptor than them all; mountains that make mock of time and place; moments of arrested grace; simply the greatest collection of mountains anywhere. Ask me why men climb and I'll answer—go to Concordia. If that fails to explain, everything will.

Al Rouse and Aid had left early to break a trail through the new snow on the last leg of this journey, and to site Base Camp. I was glad to be spared this bout of breaking trail, though it may have been less arduous than I feared—last night's snow lay only a few inches deep on an older crust, and in any case twenty or thirty porters had just returned that way from an expedition which had been a day or two ahead of us. What with my attempts to record sensation and the lingering awesomeness of the panorama that punctuated my every footfall with an upward gaze, I was soon at the back of a train two hundred strong with a wide well-trodden trough to follow. I strolled along with Curran who was airing much of the good humour and instantaneous wit that made him such good company. The weather was clear and he could film to his heart's content. And did. To such extent that he forgot the fatigue and altitude that had ailed him this last week and regaled the entire journey, Concordia to the foot of K2 with tales of the utmost irreverence on subjects as diverse as being 'the other man' to an expedition doctor of his acquaintance who he claimed had once announced, 'there are two types of illness: those we can cure, and those we can't. In both cases our role is peripheral.' Jim was one of those fortunate people who could find humour in everything, even, indeed sometimes especially, in his own misfortune. His fund of anecdotes seemed to be inexhaustible and of infinite variety—as distinct from Al's which were infinitely variable. Nor did Jim's wit discriminate: there was a seam of humour to be mined in every human circumstance and he excused no-one. 'I can't imagine how awful it must be to be fucked by me,' he had once confessed. Once you've said that, all else is fair game. And so it would be, 'Hey Jim, tell us the one about . . .' and Jim, needing no second incitement would launch, lip licking into some classic that at the hundreth telling still had the humour of the first and still bore some resemblance to it.

After a while Ghulam, Jim's caddy, found it impossible to maintain our waddling snail's pace and shot off toward K2 as if in the final strait of an Olympic 1,500 metres race, toting the greater part of Jim's film equipment.

'No more filming today, Jim.' But, for once he was delighted to be done with it: this day was too fine to be taken second hand through a lens; it was a day to be taken neat. The sun got up and now we fermented again, the sun's heat bouncing with interest off a dazzling snow. It was hot; that special mountain heat that has its own smell, drawn by the sun from a barren waste of snow and rock: a noisy heat too for it buzzes as if the sun is boiling it. You get it in the Alps in the afternoon. It starts earlier here, that's all. I thought of the lavender of the first day but try as I might the imagination couldn't sniff it; or any smell else; olfactories were going to be idle this summer.

A little later we passed Agha, his morale considerably dented, slumped on a rock at the side of the trail.

'I'm too hot and cannot go on.' He was up to his ears in bright, canary-yellow fibre pile.

'Take your jacket off.' It was obvious but necessary advice.

'But how will I carry it?'

'Give it here, I'll put it in my sack.'

He rose but his morale was not considerably boosted.

Not much later we found Aftab in a similar state and gathered him up too and cajoled and coaxed him to Base Camp. All this while the quite unbelievable bulk of K2 stood immediately before us dwarfing the 8,000 metres of Broad Peak and the Gasherbrums with imperious ease. It's something when, having craned your neck to the summit of Broad Peak, you have to crane again to accommodate the top of K2. We were in a world of new proportions. It would take some time for the mind to acclimatize: the lungs would take a lot longer.

We dallied and we strolled, dazzled alternately by sun and snow and scene. This was the Godwin-Austen glacier. Henry Haversham Godwin-Austen was the first European, possibly the first of any race, to advance along the Baltoro Glacier when, in 1861, he reached a point about fourteen miles above its snout. From a vantage on top of a hill of moraine he spotted K2. The name K2 had already been allocated in 1856 by Captain T.G. Montgomerie, an officer of the British Survey of India who had seen 'a cluster of high peaks' from a distance of over 100 miles. He named them as he numbered them in his survey, K1, K2, K3 etc, the K signifying Karakoram. For a while the mountain was known in Europe as Mount Godwin-Austen and then as Chogori (Big Mountain) as a rumour that the Baltis had already a name for it gained ground. But neither name endured and today K2 is still, and universally, K2: in Pakistan as elsewhere.

We dallied and we strolled, dazzled alternately by sun and snow and scene, but no matter where we looked, our eyes would always be drawn back to feast on K2; the mountain would not be escaped. We were pinioned in its gaze; transfixed somewhere in that tight squeeze between awe and despair and fear and courage. The sub-conscious self gave little squirts of hope, squirts which seeped into the conscious self, drop by drop, so that by the time I reached Base Camp I wallowed in a pool of hope so transcendent that all earlier ambition had drowned in its depth. After a surprisingly easy four or five hours, we brought up the rear of our column to the site that Al had selected for Base Camp. It was set hard against the very foot of the mountain on a shelf of moraine, perhaps thirty feet off the glacier itself. It was flatish, stony and barren, and separated from the usual site of Base Camps on this side of K2 by a half mile of convoluted seracs. Behind, a wide gully led for a thousand metres to a monstrous hanging ice cliff, itself a hundred metres high. The gully looked a lethal conduit for the million tons of ice that surely tumbled off the ice cliff from time to time; but Al's purblinded eye of faith said no and that, in any case, all would be pulverised to dust long before it tumbled this far. We wanted to believe him so we did. Immediately to the eastern flank of our site rose a number of rocky pinnacles thirty metres high. One bore a cross and half a dozen beaten tin plaques. This was Mario Puchoz's grave and Art Gilkey's tomb, and cemetery for uncertain numbers more. For now it was but a sombre reminder that the stakes in the game we had come to play were high; later, when its business was brisk, it cast a haunting shadow over our little encampment; a longer and a darker shadow than was healthy to live in. Beyond and over three thousand metres above all this stood K2.

It was mid-day. Fida Hussein had gathered all the porters for pay parade. A load was breached and, to the wide-eyed disbelief of the lad who had carried it there, hundreds of thousands of rupees were taken from it. I wondered how he felt surrendering 250,000 rupees in return for 1,000. But whatever fantasy of flight he now wished he had taken, it was now indeed just fantasy; the twins, operating a sort of two-man high-altitude securior system, had had him covered the twelve days. He wouldn't have got far. Nevertheless, in his injured ignorance, he managed to look like the man who broke the bank at Monte Carlo only to be told that it was all a mistake, but not to worry, here was a consolation. Fida's accounting was a wonder of the book-keeping art—or is it a science? He knew who had done what and for how long, who had carried over-the-odds loads and who therefore was owed what. He'd call a name, a number of days, and a sum. Al double checked, thumbed out the appropriate notes and handed them over: a king's ransom by local standards, a good week on the dole by ours. The remunerated porter would grin his gratitude before scuttling off towards Askole and places far beyond, hurrying to get as far as the remainder of the day allowed. We asked Fida to select twelve of the fittest to make one more carry from here to where we planned to place an Advance Base at about 5,500 metres on the Savoia Glacier.

The bill for 200 porters for the walk-in was £10,000 from a budget that was beginning to look like £40,000. The sums shocked me; it was a lot of money to spend on a climb. Someone pointed out that Bonington's 1978 K2 Expedition cost £60,000 and employed 300 porters in order to bring fewer climbers to the same place. I felt a bit better.

By early afternoon the walk-in was over. The first 150-kilometre step had been taken, a tiny step compared to the tens of thousands of steps that we hoped would carry us the remaining 3,500 metres of this journey. But I felt there was a degree less optimism than should have been on the start line of so great an opportunity, so big an enterprise, and even allowing for the way, and the weather, and the intertwining idiosyncrasies of eleven fiercely independent climbers, the step was not as well taken as it might have been. And that was a worry.

But the heck, we had slouched it to Base Camp and this was a wonderful place to be.

95

Matterhorns Too Few

'Play for more than you can afford to lose, and you will learn the game.'

(W.S. Churchill, presumably having won)

'Stuff this for a game of soldiers.'

(J. Hargreaves, about to lose)

'In outline it resembles the Matterhorn yet it would take no less than 41 Matterhorns to assemble the amount of rock from which K2 is constructed.'

(Wilhelm Bittorf)

It is not entirely indolence. I have tried for waking nights and sleepy days to untangle this climb; untangle the physics of it—who did what and when; untangle the emotions of it—who reacted to what and why; untangle all the other tangles of mind and memory, fact and fiction, interest and disinterest—and all the interdependent whos, wheres, whens, whys and hows. But I can't shake it out cleanly into new narrative. So there's my diary, a small thing, written with no purpose other than to record something which was likely to prove unique in my own experience. It admits as much of the truth as I dare admit to myself; it tells no lies beyond the lies that I have told to myself. Even so, as a record it has manifest weaknesses.

We operated, for the most part, in two teams and often separated by several miles of mountain. No diary could span the two: mine makes no great attempt to. Some expeditions, those of Bonington in particular, have a system under which all a team's diaries are surrendered—usually to the leader—on conclusion. Sometimes the arrangement is formalised by contract. Whatever the merits of such a system (and accuracy, objectivity and even-handedness will be claimed as some of them), a casualty is surely the truth—not the sturdiest of soldiers at the best of times and unlikely to survive intact the threat of another's eyes—let alone the possibility of publication. So I have not seen other records (though I solicited contributions from all and John Porter's and Wilkie's retrospective accounts are

Facing page: **Wilkie trips through 'Death Rattle Gulch'.** (Photo: Al Rouse)

quoted verbatim) and this will not be a history; rather it is the story of the climb as I saw it.

This is of course a weakness, this single testimony. For example, our team was riven by argument, dissent, disloyalty and pettiness. Not all were equally guilty. I accept at least an eighth of the blame—there were eight climbers—but it may be that another judge would award a larger proportion. I cannot know for certain; but I do not intend to strive any harder, or longer, for a greater share.

Another weakness is the memory. Mine is feeble at the best of times. It grew feebler still at altitude. This should not have mattered since, on all but a few days, I made my entry that same evening. Not even the feeblest memory can fail to summon a past that is only a few hours old. What amazes me now is that, reading though the record for the first time since our return, I have no remembrance of many of the events that I have recorded. Forgetfulness? Healing? (in which case some wounds will be re-opened in the telling). I don't know. But things must have happened the way I tell them or they wouldn't be in my diary. Or would they?

But for all a diary's weaknesses—fallible, subjective, selective, unreliable—it does have the merit of comparative simplicity. There is simply no time or energy to work up great pretensions or to invoke tracts from the Old Egyptian Book of the Dead or to cull wilfully obscure aphorisms from seventeenth-century Urdu poets, unknown Red Indians or the book of Zen, which makes it, if not more honest than the massaged memory, more short. The only licence I have taken is to correct poor grammar and smooth out my abbreviated notes that would otherwise have been unintelligible to a third party; inconsistencies in the usage of feet and metres I have left as I wrote them.

First though, take a look at the drawing of K2 and you'll see something of the size and geography of the problem ahead for us. Our Base Camp was 10 kilometres and 750 metres from the start of the NW Ridge at 5,800 metres. For the most part those were ten straightforward kilometres up the Savoia Glacier but the entrance to the Savoia was gained by way of an ice fall. This was a risky journey not so much from the tottering ice of the fall itself but more from avalanche and rock fall from Angelus, footstool to K2, between whose legs the path from Base Camp to the Savoia Glacier necessarily ran. In the end we ran the Angelus gauntlet so often that we became blasé about it, though to begin we gave it caution. After all one of Messner's porters had been killed here in 1979. Later we were to find that porter's hand—just that—a hand which is now part of Bev's personal medical museum.

Bonington's 1978 Expedition to the West Ridge of K2 had made their Base at the foot of that ridge, 300 metres higher than our own Base and about three kilometres above the Ice Fall. We had decided against basing ourselves in the same spot for two reasons. The first was that medical men who know about these things—and they are few—claim that the human body does not go on acclimatizing to altitude above about 5,000 metres; rather, above that height, the body deteriorates. We felt that rests at 5,000-metre Base Camp might not be rests at all, and that an extra 4 kilometres and 100 metres was a price worth paying if it meant recovery—especially since we had brought skis to make the upward trip easier and the downward trip a doddle—(provided you could ski and

K2: PLAN OF AREA

Savoia Pass Camp 2
N.W. Ridge
Abruzzi Spur
Camp 1
K2
Godwin-Austen Glacier
Angelus
Advance Base
The Strip
Savoia Glacier
Broad Peak
Base Camp
Ski Park
Concordia

--- line taken by British 1986 Expedition

Ice Fall excluded). A second difficulty was that there were few porters who were willing to carry beyond our present site. You could hardly blame them. They were woefully ill-shod for a trek in deep snow on a high glacier, and they all knew that one of their profession had been killed going there in 1979. The financial reward attracted only eight—which was about as many as we could afford anyway. So we kept the eight volunteers for two carries which got the bulk of the kit that was destined for the hill to the bottom of the West Ridge, at 5,300 metres our Advance Base. They would go no further and sprinted for home on completion of the second carry.

Now porterless, our immediate task was to carry the remaining gear to Advance Base and to establish it as a comfortable 'rest-stop'. From there we had

Overleaf: **On the crest of the NW Ridge at about 23,000 feet. A Karakoram panorama to the south includes the Muztagh Tower (23,860 feet) and Gasherbrum (25,660 feet).**

to gradually carry or haul (we had brought kids' plastic toboggans along for the purpose) our ordinance to the foot of the NW Ridge—a further 5¹/2 kilometres. An American team had tried this route in 1975 starting at the Savoia Pass, the very toe of the NW Ridge. It was the purist, but not the most practical, of lines and very soon they floundered in a maze of pinnacles at 6,500 metres. A big Polish expedition had later (1982) avoided these pinnacles by climbing up easy snow slopes into a cwm on the Southern (Savoia) side of the NW Ridge. From this cwm the ridge proper was gained at a point above the pinnacles by 1,000 metres of comparatively direct and only moderately difficult mixed climbing. This led them to a shoulder and at 7,000 metres a terrace that led easily around to the North and Chinese side of the mountain. From the shoulder the NW Ridge runs more or less directly but not particularly distinctly—it blends too readily into the N Face—to the top of the mountain. Our plan was to follow the line taken by the Poles unless we saw something better along the way. As it turned out we followed the Poles fairly faithfully.

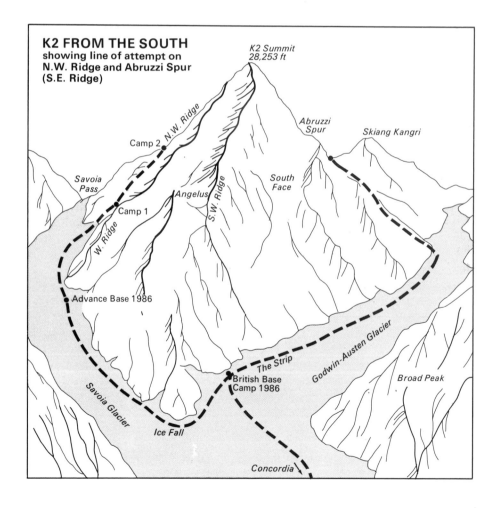

K2 FROM THE SOUTH
showing line of attempt on
**N.W. Ridge and Abruzzi Spur
(S.E. Ridge)**

K2 Summit
28,253 ft

N.W. Ridge

Camp 2

Abruzzi Spur

Skiang Kangri

Savoia Pass

Angelus

S.W. Ridge

South Face

Camp 1

W. Ridge

Advance Base 1986

The Strip

British Base Camp 1986

Godwin-Austen Glacier

Broad Peak

Savoia Glacier

Ice Fall

Concordia

Beyond Advance Base then, we planned a Camp 1 at about 6,000 metres in the cwm under the south side of the NW Ridge. From Advance Base this involved an easy-angled—though by no means easy—lunged-ski to the foot of a 40-degree snow slope, too steep for skiers of the arboreal arrest, from where a plod and jumar—once we had fixed the rope—led, in 200 metres to a Death Rattle Gulch between seracs and thence to the cwm and Camp 1. The views were spectacular, the ambience awesome.

In all, the time spent on the mountain, once we had reached Base Camp, was just over two months, and the diary extracts begin with Al-B (Al Burgess as opposed to Al Rouse who here will appear as Al-R) and I setting up Base Camp.

First Week: 23rd May—29th May

23rd May pm Al-B and I erect a monster North Face dome tent, a marvel of geometry, that defeats our attempts to mis-erect and stands in no time 8 feet high and 15 across; dining room, conference room, room enough for all. Later Abdul and I wander in search of water. I dig desultorily and find none. Abdul digs with purpose and unsnows a reservoir. He's going to be a handy lad.

There is still no hint from Al-R about what is to happen tomorrow. I wish he'd get a pencil and bit of paper, forget that he can play ten games of chess simultaneously without need of a chess board and give us a good old-fashioned briefing.

That evening Wanda Rutkiewicz, part of the French team (with Liliane and Maurice Barrard and Michel Parmentier) visits. She is well known to Al-B and John through their visits to Poland. Wanda was already the first woman to climb Everest and says she hopes to be the first woman to the top of K2—in company with Liliane presumably. They are booked on the Abruzzi (SE) Ridge. She looks ferociously fit, dauntingly determined.

It's cold that night, − 18°C inside my tent.

May 24th (Base Camp—an admin day). Spend hours making flat spots of the stones on which to pitch our tents. One man per tent: each has his shut place. Phil christens his area 'Abruzzi Close'.

Al-R denies the porters the use of spare tents and boots, which is unnecessary and unfair. We could lend them a mountain of gear, instead of which it lies stacked in boxes doing nothing, and many of us have two of everything. Al-R holds a briefing of sorts at last, a desultory affair: We are to split into two:

Team A: Al Rouse, Aid, Phil, John Porter
Team B: Al Burgess, Brian, Dave Wilkinson, J.B.

So now there are two K2 teams. That may be a harsh judgement but I wonder: a. Why we've been split—control would seem to be harder, not easier.

Overleaf: **The Abruzzi Spur: Camp 1, looking SE towards Chogolisa.**

b. If it's not flexible in the exchange of personalities who don't get on.
c. When do teams re-join?

The arrangement might work if Al-R was able to place himself equally and fairly between the two teams, a foot in each, bestriding, balancing, adjusting and fine-tuning. But arithmetic doesn't allow. And having opted for division he must necessarily place both feet in one team. It will be difficult for him not to put his heart there too.

This was my view at the time. I have not revised it since. There were other opinions of the plan. John Porter has written since:

Al and I became paired almost at the beginning of the trip. Al's plan was to divide the climbers into two teams of four, and within those groups to split the obvious partnerships. The idea was a good one, but like many of Al's plans, it created its own problems. On the one hand we were supposed to be democratic. On the other, we all looked to Al to tell us what to do to prevent total anarchy. Inevitably, deals were hatched within the groups. Al's plan was to get everyone to work with everyone else, to avoid a situation where someone would fall behind early on, thereby losing their own mental grasp, and the team's belief, in that person's ability to get up. That had happened on Everest in winter to Al, and to other members. The core of the Everest team was here now on K2. It was a difficult and subtle plan to implement among a team of hardened individuals. Perhaps it would have worked had the weather been good, but it was doomed when the bad days began to outnumber the good after only a week in Base. Competition went beyond the telling of jokes, and Al was perhaps more susceptible than anyone else to competition.

Al-R makes no provision for a 'loadmaster'. As a leader, his is an inept performance. He admits that he wants the commercial benefits of being leader but is unwilling to take the responsibilities that go with it—mainly the reduction in his chances of making the summit. Overheard him say that he'd prefer to go alpine style and abandon the expedition.

May 25th (Base Camp). The A-Team go up to site Advance Base. Found an easy route through the Ice Fall to about 17,500 ft. They took the 8 porters. The B-Team remained at Base and fixed ski bindings, sorted loads etc, Al-R's team returned about 11.30 am reporting no particular problems. Porters complain of wet feet in their sawn-off wellies. They said they aren't going tomorrow—the first move in a wage negotiation. We argued at dinner about the wisdom of giving them some gear. I stated my belief. Some of the others are less forthcoming: it would spoil them; it's what they are used to; it's their own rules.

Al had a story. Once he'd been given some tents by a well-known manufacturer: this particular model was called the 'Hurricane'. One night a couple of them blew down in nothing much worse than a mild gale. Al complained to the maker that the name 'Hurricane' overstated the tents' performance—a breach of trades description perhaps. 'Nonsense,' the maker replied, 'you don't expect Mars Bars to come from outer space.'

May 26th (Base Camp–Advance Base–Base Camp). B-Team away 5 am with 8 porters—now kitted out with boots and other spare gear. (One has my spare double boots.) We carry very light sacs. Easy going. A couple of fixed ropes through the Ice Fall. Gentle rise. Terrific views of the top of wedge of Gasherbrum IV. Going well which pleases me. Brian ill—tummy—and turns back after an hour. Al-B storms on at a suppressed dog trot with the porters. Dave and I stroll behind roped together. Porters in good crack. Arrive Advance Base, which has been sited near bottom of W Ridge, at 9.00. Stunning views of W face of K2. Could see the site of Nick Escourt's accident in 1978. Dumped loads under a tarpaulin and sprinted down—foolishly unroped. Porters at least should have been roped, for which carelessness Al-R properly chides us.

Al-R criticises us for not carrying bigger loads. This angers me. There are no clear instructions, no communication, no direction; no leadership. Later I apologise though still not sure what future plan is. Will ask Al tonight. Fix more ski bindings and help Jim Hargreaves—real Goth—with his. Jim Curran still ill-ish so no filming yet. (These two Jims will appear as Jim-H and Jim-C from now on).

May 27th (Admin in Base Camp). Write a report and send it to Anthony Smee to do with it what he likes. Last day for letters—write 3 or 4. Ghulam shoots off with them. His turn-around time is likely to be 2 weeks. Sort kit: adjust bindings, make prussik tapes, stick gaiters to boots, pack sac.

Jim-H holds forth at lunch on subjects as diverse as classical music, art, sex, opera and ballet. He knows more about one than the rest of us put together. Good evening meal. Agha stuns us by producing the answer to an English word puzzle that none of the rest of us could get. I note that he never says 'please' or 'thank you' and wonder if such words exist in Urdu.

A-Team set off at dawnish for Advance Base with heavy loads. Jim-H succeeds in contacting them with a number of radio calls. Then they go out of sight around the corner, and out of radio contact too. Jim-H has plans for an automatic re-broadcasting link to reach around corners. He can't raise a spark on his HF set and frets and puzzles. Brian, our Mr Fix-It, thinks the polarity is wrong and re-charges the batteries correctly by means of the solar panels. And it works. Jim-H may get through to the UK tomorrow provided L.O. is laid low—such transmissions are outlawed by the Pakistani authorities.

May 28th (A-Team carry and fix toward proposed site of Camp 1. B-Team, Base Camp to Advance Base with loads). We set out about 7am with heavyish sacs, skis and the last minute addition of a 4-lb bag of sugar.

Jim-L has gone ahead to film us en-route and does so—very successfully. Al B goes off like a rocket. Brian and Wilkie follow. Bev and Jim-H set off later still but some stone-fall sends them scuttling back.

We continue, Al-B forging ahead. Very hot. I suffer from heat on steeper bits. Feet hurt—wet and slightly blistered. Ankles rub on heel hinge. Reach Advance Base about 11am. Phil, John, Aid have already returned from their work on the

---

Overleaf: **Al Burgess on the 'Dome' above Camp Two on the north side of K2. China lies behind (Sinkiang).**

route to Camp 1. Phil is feeling ill—has had to drop his load half way and feels badly about it.

Advance Base looks good. Brew lots of liquid—lots. Slight headache. Snows quite heavily in the afternoon. Al-R says they got off late. Failed to reach the site of Camp 1 by a few rope lengths because the snow is soft. Avalanche threat. John and Aid were knocked over in a small snow slide.

We all muck in sorting loads for tomorrow's carry. Big argument about how much we carry—I'm in a tent writing this and listening. Argument rages back and forth; leave it to individuals; standardise at 20 kilograms, at 15 kilograms then; let people carry what they can.

Phil is perking up. Al-B and I share a tent. MSR stoves need some maintenance. More gas stoves than we know what to do with. Slight headache, may go back on Diamox. Feet bit sore. Otherwise fine. Tomorrow's plan—all 8 of us to carry load to site of Camp 1. Then Al-R's team may go down to Base while the B-Team carries Advance Base to Camp 1 for two more days. Hill food seems excellent.

Al-B has managed to put his boots on the wrong feet despite having marked them conspicuously L and R!

May 29th (Both teams carry to Site of Camp 1). Off early after tea and Granola. Al-R's team away 1 hour ahead of us. Slept fairly well. Took paracetamol, Diamox and steroids for headache—it didn't stand a chance. A beautifully clear but cold ($-15°$) morning. Al-B away first as usual. He and I are using sleds. They work very well for towing gear on flatish ground. Fairly easy, rhythmical pull to the bottom of the slope that leads to Camp 1. Brian and Wilkie arrive later. Sun hits us as we prepare to jumar. The other 4 can be seen at work on the slope finishing yesterday's fixing and humping loads. We carry about 20 kilograms. The snow on slope is soft and the steps are ill-formed—and a long way apart for my short legs. Hellish hot in sun. Catch Al-B and Phil as they wait for John and Al-R to fix the last of the ropes. Arrive on plateau where Camp 1 is to be sited in a cwm below the NW Ridge. Follow an alley through some tottering seracs and deep snow. Al-B and I humping John's sac between us (John had dumped it on the slope because he was carrying and fixing ropes above). Exhausting. Stomp out platform, erect a tent and stock it full of gear, ropes, food and hardware—it seems an impressive amount.

This is Camp 1—20,000 feet. Not bad in 6 days after arriving at Base. Hand round what drinks we have left. Twins going well. Rest of us quite tired, Phil especially so.

Then down the fixed ropes trying, as Brian had exhorted, not to disturb the 'up' steps. I bum-slide the last 200 feet.

Wonderful swoop of a ski back to Advance Base in no more than 15 minutes. Brews. Doss. Hot. Prepare loads for tomorrow.

Al-R's team continues to Base Camp. We are to carry 2 days more, then to Base for swop over.

Second Week: May 30th–5th June

May 30th (Advance Base–Camp 1). Wake to snow heavy on tent. Delayed start.

Leave at 7. Weather not good but at least cool. Slope up to Camp 1 has snowed-up so no steps. Al-B well ahead even though he is breaking trail. But at least he says he finds it exhausting—as I do, even with his steps to follow. It's good to be able to lie back on the ropes and rest. Spared the sun for the most part. Wilkie arrives when I'm about three-quarters up the slope. Al-B goes down and takes half of Wilkie's load for second trip up—a good effort. The serac alley—Death Rattle Gulch—doesn't look any more inviting today.

Great ski down again. It had been hard to convince Al-R of value of skis and toboggans but they are both working well, so far. Wilkie arrives Advance Base as we are into second brew. I'm tired.

Stunning view of West Face of K2.

Then cool. Another trip up tomorrow—weather allowing. Running out of things to take.

May 31st (Advance Base–Camp 1–Base Camp). Snowing again—lightly. Away at 7 am with full loads. Kept up with Al-B this time though he was cruising—he says. Wilkie still behind—but not so far. Feel as if I'm getting fit(ter).

Pick up some rope and a tent from a dump at the foot of the fixed ropes and hump up to Camp 1. Serac still threatening; nor am I inspired by snow conditions on slope. Al-B breaks new trail—another superhuman effort. Great ski to Advance Base. Stop to pick up personal kit and onto Base Camp. Tea waiting when we arrive at 1.30. Great to lie in sun to rest. Notice that a big radio ariel has been erected. 'Thereby hangs a tale' says Jim-H who has been caught attempting an illicit transmission. Agha confronts us that night: 'Some of you don't like me', he states. Complains about our farting in the dining tent and my nakedness in a stream crossing on the walk-in. The cultural/religious/social gap seems well nigh unbridgable. Sleep well.

June 1st (Rest day). Tea in bed thanks to Abdul. A-Team up the hill with radio relay link which they position and it works. Aid carrying a huge solar panel to power it. Wash some kit. Bullshit breakfast.

Visit American camp. They are ill. They are attempting the unclimbed SW Ridge: Messner's 'Magic Line'. An Italian, Renato Casarotto, is attempting the same route, solo.

'What pills shall I take Doc?' one of them asks their doctor.

'What have you got?' he replies.

They all look half our age; maybe they are. They are sponsored by a sun cream company—and they have no sun cream. Nor we any to spare them.

6 pm. Jim-H gets through on radio to Advance Base. A-Team ask us to bring washing-up liquid, Mars Bars, Brillo pads and toffees.

Doughnuts for lunch. Kebabs for dinner. Jim-C in better spirits.

Overleaf, left: **The author on the slopes above Camp One.**
(Photo: Dave Wilkinson)

Overleaf, right: **A climber on the 'arete' above Camp One.**
(Photo: Dave Wilkinson)

Brian's knee is not good—is thinking of returning home if there's not some improvement soon. Or may help Jim-C with the film. (Brian's knee has been troubling him since he had damaged it in a skiing accident a week before we left Britain).

Al-R has asked me to talk to Jim-C. He is worried that Jim is also thinking of going home.

Try Anthony Burgess's *Kingdom of the Wicked*. Heavy going so swap to John le Carré. Wonder for the umpteenth time what it's like at 8,000 metres. Agha shocked when he learns that we use pee bottles in tents when at altitude to avoid struggling out of our sleeping bags. Asks about prostitution and adultery. Al-B shocks him with stories of N. American decadence.

I shave—for some reason—and take a bird-bath for better reason.

Snowing and wind this afternoon.

June 2nd (Base Camp). Another day of dossing. Some sun but also snow. Radio report from Al-R and the A-Team says they are going up with 'heavy loads' to Camp 1. An element of competition? Stick 'Fullers' labels on anything that doesn't move. Try to adjust downsuit. Tinker with gear.

Enormous avalanche off Broad Peak—quite staggering. It sweeps half across the Godwin-Austen glacier.

Jim-C very ill—spewing all night. He is not well. Brian has bronchitis. A very cold night.

June 3rd (Base Camp). Beautiful sunny day. Sunbathing and body maintenance. My legs are already shedding scales of dead skin. Tend ankle wounds: doctor boots. Radio link to Camp 1 working well. We shoot advertising photos; Fullers, British Wool, Plessey, Sunpak, etc. Brian energetic about all this with his large format camera—a professional.

Finish *Spy That Came in from The Cold*. Ravens get very excited when I inadvertently release a storm of down from a hole in a downsuit, which I try to fix with Copydex—a real botch.

Base Camp stoves are going on the blink at an alarming rate. Radio call, pm, tells us that the A-Team have beaten a track across the cwm to the start of the slope that leads up to the crest of the NW Ridge but that they are unable to fix because of avalanches all around.

* * *

Looking ahead . . . the route from Camp 1 upwards lay first across a gently rising plateau—the floor of an enormous cwm in which we were dots on a vast landscape. It was about a mile to the bottom of the face where the Poles had fixed ropes in 1982 and which we now intended to re-fix. From the foot of the face to the crest of the NW Ridge was about 750 metres of mainly snow slope, though some of the ground was mixed. The Poles had said that it was about the same order of difficulty as the Swiss Route on the North Face of the Courtes. It seemed easier than that to me. When completed, this route joined the NW Ridge just above the pinnacles that had halted the Americans in 1975. It was easy to see how they had been brought to a halt: they'd have been going up and down them forever. In fact, at the point at which we gained the NW Ridge, it was not ridge at all, but a broad shoulder that on its northern side led directly onto a vast shelf that ran more or less continuously across that entire northern flank of K2, across to the N Ridge, a mile away.

This was China. From here were grand views of Kashgar and far, far beyond; endless dreamy views, browner than our white, snow-bound southern side. There was acres of room for tents.

A second gigantic avalanche roars off Broad Peak. And another from seracs on Angelus—which appears to have cut across our route to Advance Base. Recall serac debris lying across our ski tracks below Advance Base the other day which hadn't been there on earlier ascents.

Afternoon radio call says that A-Team intend to fix tomorrow and next day. We decided that we will go up the day after tomorrow.

Good evening meal. Not as cold as last night.

Jim-H completes a stock-take and concludes that we have plenty of food at Base Camp but not much variety. No porridge, jam, marmalade, syrup, puddings or custard. Eric Clapton a firm favourite on tape. I do not make myself popular when I accidentally press both the 'record' and 'play' buttons and erase half of 'Lay down Sally'.

June 4th (Base Camp). Morning radio: cold but they will try to fix. They are still in their pits at 7 am. We tell them of our plan. Al-R fusses that we won't carry heavy enough loads—which is mildly irritating—and I think stems from a conversation between Al-B and Al-R a few days earlier, about how much individuals should carry   Al-B mentions how selfless he found some previous army expeditions that he had worked with and notes Italian K2 rule of not making known the summit pair—even after the event.

Some dangers in this A and B-Team system. Al-R must exercise much greater care in what he says and how he says it. Bev frets that John has gone through (or lost) 3 or 4 first aid kits.

Leisurely breakfast. Will all go up to Advance Base tomorrow including Jim-C, Jim-H, and Bev. Then maybe the 3 of us will go on to Camp 1 the same day—depending on whether the A-Team are to quit it tomorrow pm or not. Don't know what we'd do without radios. A large German team (I think) arrives. That makes five K2 teams this side so far this year. There is also a second US team on the north side, climbing the North Ridge from China. A Korean team and an alleged 1,500 porters are yet to arrive.

June 5th (Base Camp). Snows heavily all night. Woke up suffocating. Neither candle or lighter will light. Open tent to breathe air.

Still snowing heavily at 5.30 am. Decide against going up. Radio call at 7 am—the others seem surprised at our decision. Al-B says sharply 'we'll discuss it when you return—out!'

Overleaf: **The Abruzzi Spur looking down on Camp One. The Godwin-Austen Glacier lies below.**

Snows heavily 'till 11 am. Others return to Base at about 12.00. Phil comes first looking tired and drawn. A discussion ensues. It becomes clear that we have two very different perspectives of the same thing. It surprises me to hear that we have been down 5 days. Check in my diary—and we have! It does seem a bit idle. Then I remember that the reason we didn't go up yesterday (4th) was that we couldn't see the point of two teams doing nothing at Camp 1—but it becomes clear that the A-Team have fixed 1,000 feet of rope—a good effort in the circumstances. Phil was buried in a snow flurry. There were avalanches. They describe conditions as 'marginal'. Their programme must have looked like this:

Day 1 Base to Advance Base (1st May).

Day 2 AB to C1 with loads (2nd May).

Day 3 Hot, sunny, avalanches, no fixing. (3rd May). Very cold in morning, Aid says.

Day 4 Fixing in poor weather (4th May).

Day 5 Some more fixing, then back to Base (5th May).

Eventually we resolve our differences. We are to go up tomorrow. American team visits. Friendly. All crowd into our dining tent. Aftab makes green tea. They have brought some honey to swap for tins of salmon.

Third Week: 6th June–12th June

6 June (Base Camp to Advance Base and Camp 1). All ended amicably yesterday. Drank tea in big tent 'til 7.30 last night. I was ribbed again for my belief in law and order. Al said that laws were originally made about property and are designed to maintain the status quo (didn't say of what period). Also claimed that rich people were never breathalysed. Phil always agrees. What crap! As a life-long kicker against the idiots it amuses me to find myself defending the establishment. Up at 5.30 off at 7. Three of B-Team with Jim-C (Brian is resting his knee). I carry Jim's tripod. Jim carries his cameras, films, super 8s. He moves very slowly with this heavy load. We 3 have medium sacs. Good névé but doesn't last for long—sun up by 9 and very hot. Jim decides to go back. He is coughing and does not look well poor chap. He must be despondent.

We continue. I think Jim will try again tomorrow with Bev and Jim-H.

Hot ski to Advance Base. Damn ski comes off 3 times. Reach AB at 11.15 am. Adjust binding. Brew. Collect food, stores, stoves, support film and personal kit. Rest an hour then on towards ropes. 2 hrs to bottom. Hot and snow is heavy—as are sacs now. 2 sledges work well except for the last traverse. Al-B reaches ropes ahead of us and breaks trail again to Camp 1. I rest until Wilkie arrives. He is tired—so am I. I set off up—he follows, having ditched some gear which can be collected later. My marker wands slip from my sac. Wilkie picks them up. Flog up to Camp 1. Al-B has soup and his 'elixir' waiting. The 'elixir' is a ferocious compound of garlic, chilli, pepper and onion; a concoction that he stirs into all his meals giving everything a uniformly blast-furnace taste. Al-B claims it was good for all mountain illnesses. It might have been true: it was difficult to see how anything could survive it. Drink, drink, drink. Wilkie arrives 50 mins later—tired but cheerful. Snowing hard.

7th June (Camp 1, break new ground, back to Camp 1). Started brewing at 4.30. (Wilkie too tired to come with us today—remains in camp tidying etc.) Away by 6 am breaking a new trail in new snow all the way to foot of face: a MILE. Hard work. May try snowshoes on this bit tomorrow. Nordic skis would have been a boon. Al-B going like a train as usual. Rise of about 500 feet to 'schrund. Steep jumar over it and then jumar about another 350 feet to a traverse line. Neither of us like the soft slab snow, though it was difficult to be certain about its danger—but there are signs of slab avalanche all around. After a while we decide to turn back. Abseil down and stomp back to Camp 1—our tracks are already filled in.

Hard work all day. Both very tired when we reached Camp 1—I especially so. Need liquid. Left some gear—pegs, nuts etc.—at our high point. Snoozed pm—but too hot in tents for comfort.

It is now 6 pm and we are wondering what to do about the 7 pm radio call and tomorrow—it is snowing heavily.

Slight headache this pm, now gone, probably thanks to liquid. Eerie slash of bright light over K2 summit—dark satanic clouds and this strange light boring through. Tried some super 8 filming today but forgot the battery pack. Wilkie seems to have recovered.

Weather a worry. If it snows like this every day then regaining our high point will always be exhausting—and possibly dangerous. Wind and snow not a good combination.

Fail to get through on radio for second night running.

8th June (Camp 1). Wake at 4. There is a lot of new snow, although the weather is fine—and cold. Al-B says it was snowing at 2 am when he got up for a pee. Decide new snow is dangerous and to delay for a day. Re-awake at 7. Raging thirst and dry throat. Brew. Fail again on radio.

It really would be useful to be able to get through. Will make a more determined attempt tonight and tell others to bring more snow shoes. Just breaking trail to the foot of the route every morning is exhausting and it will be hard to make progress with loads unless a broken trail remains—or unless snowshoes make a discernable difference.

Set up Karrimats black side up which produces water for as long as the sun lasts. Very hot by 10.00 am. We drape a silver foil sheet over our tent which makes it cooler.

Dig out tent, clean stoves, site shit pit and generally tidy up. It starts snowing heavily again at about 2 pm. Hope that it doesn't last—we'd like to leave very early tomorrow—say 4, and get some new ground in. Books available at Camp 1 are: *Athabasca* – A. Maclean, *The Haj* – Leon Uris; *The Nehrus and The Ghandis* – Tariq Ali. One of Al-R's dafter statements was that radio communications were a double-edged weapon. Perhaps he meant they were an incomplete weapon

---

Overleaf: **Camp Two on the Abruzzi Spur (just below House's Chimney) looking south towards Concordia.**

especially when half-heartedly used. Here we are having been unable to raise Base Camp for days and wondering what are their intentions and having no idea when they are coming up. Communications are vital.

Got through on radio—I had moved about a bit and Jim-H says a day's sun may have charged the solar panels. A-Team are coming up to Advance Base tomorrow. I tell them of our plan which is to climb as high as we can tomorrow and then to descend for a rest the day after that. Al-R baulked at the bit about our returning to Base but I can't see what else we can do. Anyway we can discuss it at AB day after tomorrow when we meet there.

9th June (Camp 1, break new ground, Camp 1). Up at 2.30 am. Brew efficiently—two mugs each and enough for a water bottle to take with us. Away by 4 am. I can't get snow shoes over my boots so Al-B uses them—to good effect. Al is going to trail break so he is not carrying anything—and going like a train. I have a light load. Wilkie is going to pick up Phil's sac if we can find it (Phil left it at the foot of the fixed ropes some days earlier) but it has been buried in the snow avalanching off the slope up to the N.W. Ridge. It contains 5 ropes and bits and pieces. Wilkie and I make heavy going of the stomp—it seems this snow will never consolidate.

Al-B finds Phil's sac—well buried. Al-B leads. I follow carrying 3 ropes and Wilkie carrying 5. It's breaking trail three deep, all the way and desperately hard work. If it was névé it wouldn't be half so bad. Jog up to A-Team high point—only a little beyond yesterday's foray. Then hard going all day. Signs of Polish rope. Anchors not easy to find. Up to a beautiful snow arete from where way to crest of NW ridge is clear. We admire fantastic scenery, drink water—1 litre between 3 doesn't last long—and descend trying not to spoil upward steps. But it is nearly impossible. I try to film. Fierce spindrift blows. Flurries are the order of the day, even though the sun shines for most of it. Though never hot while climbing—duvet, two pairs gloves, cold feet. But as soon as we descend to the basin—3.30-ish—it is baking hot and we feel very tired. Walking back is almost as bad as up except that it is slightly downhill. Al-B confesses himself tired—which pleases me. Can't imagine what it's like at 28,000 feet. Reached about 22,500 today. Reckon there is 5 or 600 to go to the crest of the NW Ridge plus some traversing. Wandering back we ponder what we should do tomorrow: another rope fix is out of the question—we are too tired. We fancy going down early to fetch a load from AB to C1. We suspect Al-R doesn't want us to go to Advance Base. Fact is that we will get a better rest there. We'll have to wait 'till 7 pm, radio call to see.

In all a good day with a satisfying height gain and arresting scenery. 3 brews straight off when we get in. I can hear Wilkie grunting happily in next tent. Get through on radio to Advance Base where the A-Team are spending the night on the way up. Our plan is OK'd.

10th June (Camp 1 to Advance Base to Base Camp). Woke at about 6 am to perfect weather outside; minus 20 degrees C inside. Wash up, tidy up. Leave most of our personal gear in sacs and set off with minimum gear in a bulky stuff bag. Our steps to the foot of the face are still in place and frozen hard—for the first time this trip—which should shorten the journey up by half, as long as they remain intact.

Death Rattle Gulch was more ominous than ever. You have to duck to get through. Must get a photo before it collapses.

Pound down the slope to meet others at bottom. Phil is in the lead, looking fit and much less drawn than the last time I saw him. Said he felt great, 'running fit'. It was good to see. He asked us to make sure that some letters he had left in his diary in his tent were given to Ghulam—who was expected to return that day.

Al-R was sitting on his sac by the ski dump looking tired. He said things with the L.O. were better. Stressed they had big loads and that they were going up to Camp 1 for at least 10 days. Brian was going home.

(We seem to have a childish, silly, but real split; are they deliberately goading us about the weight of the loads or are we over sensitive?). Aid arrives with a huge load in a green sled, dragging ropes behind that had fallen off and in his usual implacable humour. John arrives with a grump on. My attempts to humour him fail miserably. His parting remark as we ski off is 'see you in a week'. Al says quickly 'no 4 days'. Was this a snide remark or an innocent and unimportant miscalculation? Whatever, it certainly annoyed Al-B and me. Ski to Advance Base in 5 mins—superb conditions and empty sleds banging behind—where to my delight we find Jim-C. He is full of beans and has come up alone that morning. Good to see him well, hearty at last, and looking fit and slim. Al-B and I enact a skiing shot for him. We cruise on down to the Ice Fall, making a slight detour to check the radio relay box of tricks, to see if we can spot why it hasn't been working very well. There seems to be nothing wrong with it. Ski on down to the Ice Fall. It's a great way to travel. Wilkie comes behind with Brian's kit from Advance Base. Arrive Base Camp about 12.00. Sun shining but wind cold. Wash in solar shower. Jim-H certainly not getting on with L.O. who has Abdul trimming his moustache and beard at the click of his fingers.

Great meal. Radio contact at 7 pm to both Jim-C at Advance Base and the team at Camp 1. We're told from Camp 1 that we've left our sacs up there—'How are you going to carry up your kit?' More hassle, more insult. Is it silly for us to be offended? I just don't know.

Windy night and weather deteriorating again. Ghulam arrived at noon from Skardu with 23 kilos of spuds, 2 kilos of tomatoes and mail. Jim-H has perfected curry making. We were visited this afternoon by Julie Tullis and Kurt Diemberger; as well as a contingent from the Italian '8,000-m Challenge Expedition' and some of the Americans.

11th June (Base Camp). Snowing heavily. Lose myself in Eric Clapton and *'Other Men's Flowers'*. The L.O. is beginning to look wild eyed. He has gone visiting for the day.

OVERLEAF
Main picture: **Storm clouds gather on Broad Peak.**

Inset: **Lonely Al returning from the Strip.**

123

7 am Radio: A-Team has fixed 800 feet of rope, a good effort in conditions. They say they are 4 rope lengths short of NW Ridge. Brian packs, readying to leave with Ghulam on his second mail run.

12th June (Base Camp). Brian delays departure at 5 am: it has been snowing all night. Heavy wet snow. Eventually he leaves about lunchtime. I am sorry to see him go. Ghulam has wrapped his feet in poly bags to try to keep them dry. Sit in tent all morning talking about art! Lunch. Visited Americans to try to scrounge more snow shoes. No joy but had a cup of tea and some goodies. Great supper.

It snowed all morning. BBC World Service tells us that Bob Geldof has been knighted. 7 pm call to the A-Team who say that they 'spent all day in their tents staying alive'.

We plan to go up tomorrow—late to avoid sun.

That evening Jim-H amuses us with stories which are based, with no great deference to the facts, on his experiences of running a filling station in Snowdonia. The L.O. asks what 'rock me' means in 'Rock Me Amadeus' (a pop song that one of us had on tape). We find it difficult to explain exactly how it translates. (To unlock a society look at its untranslatable words.) Some refuse to travel across linguistic frontiers—as Salman Rushdie explains to me that night in *Shame*.

Fourth week: 13th June–19th June

13th June (Base Camp, Advance Base). It snows most of the day. Manage to scrounge a pair of snow shoes off US team after all. Tooled up after lunch for Advance Base—eventually left at 4 pm. Snowed heavily at 3 pm for 1 hour. Pleasant ski up to Advance Base $2^1/2$ hours. Al-B breaking trail; madness to stop him!

Jim-H has been in great story-telling form. Radio contact at 7 pm from Advance Base to Camp 1 but not to Base. A-Team's programme for last few days has been:

Day 1 BC to AB.

Day 2 AB to C1.

Day 3 Fix in bad weather about 8 ropes—a very good effort—to within 4 rope lengths of Col on the crest of the NW Ridge (c 23,000 feet).

Day 4 Bad weather, tent bound.

Day 5 Bad weather, tent bound.

On radio they said that they were coming down to Advance Base tomorrow (14th) to do a carry to Camp 1 before returning to Base Camp. Want us to continue to Camp 1 and remain there. But our idea is to get all seven of us at Camp 1 to make an impression on the mountain. K2 is lucent in a lovely evening light.

14th June (Advance Base to Camp 1). Up at 5.30—should have been earlier. Brew. Breakfast. We are digging stores from the snow when when the A-Team arrive from Camp 1 in drabs. Monster discussion: cross words between the twins. A pity. Finally we agree that all will carry a load to Camp 1 where B-Team will remain while the A-Team descend to Base Camp.

Leave Advance Base late after brews, and suffer in desperate heat all the way to the bottom of the ropes. I need a rest every 100 yds. Others suffering too. The jug up the ropes is misery. A wet snow slide and an ice fall from overhanging rocks spur me on a bit. All in all a ballbender. Arrive exhausted. Lots of brews courtesy of Al-B, who has arrived well ahead as usual. Aid has broken trail all day—in both directions. I curse the sun which shows no sign of having heard. Hope I can rehydrate by tomorrow. John tells me that there is a feeling in the A-Team that Al-B is not pulling his weight. I stress that this is not the case and that he has done much more work that either Wilkie or myself. Aid later apologizes to me at bottom of fixed rope (for being cross with his twin brother) in a very pleasant way. He says 'got to keep pushing, we're a small team for this route.' Al-R, Phil and John all have encouraging remarks as they pass us on their way down to Base to rest. Al-R said he too was close to collapse in heat; Phil too. Lesson: avoid mid-day snow basins!

(So what happened to the 10 days that the A-Team had stressed they were intending to spend at Camp 1? After only 3 days at Camp 1—1 of work, 2 of storm—they are (sensibly) scurrying back. If Camp 1 is such a good place why aren't they staying up? Al-R scoffs at medical evidence of malabsorption and non-acclimatization above 20,000 feet—says his own empirical evidence suggests otherwise. Why then after 2 days of lying on his back is he going down? These questions, churlish though they are, occur at moments between wake and sleep.)

15th June (Camp 1, attempt new ground, Camp 1). Awake at 3 am, slightly later than intended. Seems to take longer to get organised, despite having pre-melted a pot of water last night. Now frozen, of course, but in theory still faster than melting snow. We are lethargic. The weather looks good. Stars. Though there are clouds threatening. Al-B says he did not sleep at all well.

Very thirsty. 3 brews and cereal. On with snowshoes and off at about 5 am. Have only been going about 20 mins when Wilkie stops, announces he is shattered and is returning. I think I can force my way to top of ropes and fix 4 or so but Al-B is also tired. Now snowing—wild, and a thundering wind. Looked to be wilder still above 22,000 feet. We follow Wilkie to Camp 1 about ten minutes after he has turned back. Sleep for a few hours. Read *Shame* back to front. Fry in tent which seems to find heat where there is no sun. (Alternative energy people should investigate.)

Note: to date, weather has not been very kind to us. Two days' consecutive good weather so far at most. It would make a big difference if our footsteps on the fixed ropes would stay in.

Phil says he was terrified the day he and Aid fixed across a gully. Spindrift, cold. Aid talking of taking 200-feet slides as par for this course, can hardly have bolstered his confidence.

16th June (Camp 1, bad weather) Radio call last night—Al-R suggested that we went down today if weather was bad. But we prefer to stay up at least another day now we are here. Wake at 2 am. Snowing hard—and that wind too. Doss all day. Snows all day. I would love to get onto that ridge. Not sure how long it is worth continuing like this at Camp 1. The toss-up is: do you have someone waiting to pounce when weather turns good, or do you have everyone resting properly lower down? Would take a day of sun now anyway to make snow safe. Avalanches all night; like express trains. Dig out tents. There has been a lot of

snow. Finish *Shame*.

Begin *The Nehrus and The Ghandis* and *The Book of Laughter and Forgetting* (Milor Kundera)—both have forewords by Salman Rushdie. Worry about money of all things in all places. Miss my boys. Hope tomorrow we can either go up—or down.

There's a shortage of pots. £40,000 and not enough billies! Suspect we have left them in Sheffield in Wilkie's preference for tower stoves—which do not work well—even with extra holes drilled. Have had to send to Skardu for some more. Expensive pots they will be.

Skardu shopping list: Porridge, Pots

'Surprise us with something nice', Jim-H says to Brian. Ghulam will bring it back.

17th June (Camp 1, bad weather). Woke at 2 am but since it was still snowing, though only lightly now, we decide to give this new weather a day to clear things. Snooze on. Radio at 8. Jim-H tells us that the A-Team are coming up tomorrow. We doss. Dossing is getting dull. Look out of the tent door to see Wilkie filling his snow bag—an old polythene rope bag depicting Edlinger finger-hanging on sunny rock somewhere in the South of France—climbing is a broad church. Snowing heavily again by mid afternoon. *Must* give the hill a go tomorrow. It's an unreal world; a tent at 20,000 feet and about 3 forays outside in 3 days. Irony: I spent 7 years teaching people not to venture out for 48 hours after heavy snowfall. Here we discount it completely saying, 'Oh the sun will burn it off' or 'the slope is too steep to collect'.

18th June (Camp 1, break new ground, Camp 1). Awake at 2 am (having decided to give it one last chance). Weather good. Away and determined to get to ridge. Snow shoes work well across plateau and up to the foot of the 'schrund. Beyond that new snow makes step-kicking hard work—thigh deep in places. I wilt when the sun hits me but when it later clouds over I feel fine—get stronger as the day wears on. From A-Team's high point we fix up a subsidiary couloir to within a rope length (I think and hope) of the col. Wilkie doing all the leading and going well. At 4.30 we decide to abseil down. Try to avoid upward staircase. From our high point I saw figures at Camp 1 (and ski tracks on the Savoia) which means that the others have come up. Get back to Camp 1 at about 6 pm. New tents and all A-Team; we are tired out but very pleased to have got that day in—as were the others. John and Phil have only 3 weeks left which explains why John feels bad about missed climbing days. Brew, but not enough. Half a meal. Sleep on 2 pills. Slight headache.

John Porter summarises this period, the 1st – 17th June, from the A-Team's perspective:

Facing page: **Al Rouse on his 'leader's day' on steep ground high above Camp Two at about 24,000 feet on the North Face of K2.** (Photo: John Porter)

From Camp 1 it took another three weeks to reach the ridge proper and to establish Camp 2 at 6,700 metres. These were frustrating weeks. First Al Burgess's team went to stay in Camp 1 but returned after a few days with no progress. Brian Hall left the expedition with a damaged knee ligament. Al and I managed to get some ropes out, climbing in appalling weather even by Scottish standards, pushing five ropes a day up dangerous slopes that hissed and shuddered with coulées. It was never possible to climb for more than one day at a time. We snatched a few hours in between storms and spent the rest of the time lying in the tents talking Al's favourite and least favourite topics: climbing, business, science and women. When we realized we were eating more than we were earning by staying high, it was back to Base, or drop down to AB to bring up a load. We spent more time high than in Base. For some reason both Al and I were sick in Base, and felt better on the mountain. The inactivity at Base seemed more depressing than on the mountain where you could at least sense the state of the weather higher up. On one sortie on the slopes above Camp 1 Phil arrived a bit late at the bottom of the ropes. Aid, Al and I watched him start up, a thousand feet beneath, only to be engulfed in a massive powder slide touched off by the fall of increasingly heavy snow. A white blanket filled the sky and Phil was lost in it. When it cleared, a small dot was seen descending back toward Camp 1. The avalanche had carried him several hundred feet then spat him out at the bottom. We put up another rope, then tensely made our own way back.

In the middle of June the weather briefly improved. Our team was in Base on the morning of the 17th when we awoke to a still, bright sky. We set off for Camp 1 knowing that Al Burgess's threesome would be making the most of it and might reach the ridge that day. We were not long in Camp 1 when JB, Al and then Wilkie arrived. The strained feelings that had been growing between the teams dissolved in a thanksgiving of progress and the prospect of good weather. A quiet evening spread across the massive west buttress of K2, seemingly for the first time in an eternity.

19th June (Camp 1). A-Team leave at 4. Sounds as if the weather is not good. But they go anyway. We awake at 8 am, to a perfect day. Going to be a hot day. We haven't decided on what to do so ask Jim-H for another radio schedule at 10. Brew. Decide to stay and carry to Camp 2 tomorrow. Time is getting short, begin to wish that I had my SLR camera up here. The views yesterday during clear patches were breathtaking—literally. Dry kit. Rehydrate for tomorrow. I think I'll start very early to avoid sun for as long as possible. Wish I had some white gear. Apparently Scotty (Doug Scott) uses white. 'Not all his ideas are potty,' Al-R says. I'll be interested to see how I/we go tomorrow. We've now been at 20,000 feet for 5 nights. Jim-C has come up to Advance Base alone and is today wandering about on his todd which we find worrying—he should not have to be alone on that glacier. The A-Team brought up a story of a big avalanche at Base Camp. Apparently it knocked over 2 tents including the dining tent. American doctor saw it from his camp, safely half a mile away, and said to himself, 'Holy shit, bye, bye, Brits'. Then came round to see if there were any survivors. John heard it coming, decided it was as well to die in comfort and remained in pit. Jim-H legged it barefoot and naked in the night looking for cover. A-Team return. Change of plan.

Al-B and Aid to go up tomorrow to stay one night at Camp 2 and fix next day before returning. Wilkie and I to carry to Camp 2. The rest to rest—they are tired after today's carry to the Col, which was one rope length above our point but they had to traverse for 3. Not sure why. Will see tomorrow. Phil finds sun a problem. Big discussion on who should rest when—teams have now merged but logistics (pans, cups etc) complicated—as are sleeping bags. We want to leave two sleeping bags at Camp 2 but if we do there are not enough for everyone to sleep at Camp 1—should that be the need. Weather looks good for a spell and in three weeks we could be at the top and John and Phil back for their jobs. Difficult to say. Aid going very well. Al-B too. The rest about the same. Al-B a bit worried about sleeping at 23,000 feet so soon.

John Porter recalls the 19th June:

We were up at 4 am the next morning. I had melted snow the night before, and was able to lie back and settle my aching head while the stuttering blue flames heated the pan. Al and I were half way up the ropes when it became fully light. We carried good-sized loads now that we were fit. I was always amazed how much Al would carry. I dropped my sack at the high point to take the lead. One pitch brought me to the ridge, but only to discover a knife edge with a view vertically down to Sinkiang. I descended and then traversed several pitches across ice gulleys and around towers before we landed on a broad col. Al was in great spirits. We looked up at the jumbled buttresses above that in profile had appeared a ridge. While Al explored, I descended to bring up my load, passing Aid and Phil on the way up. The others descended past me as I panted back up to the col. I stayed for an hour, climbing to a small rock tower from where I could look back down the route in the blinding afternoon sun. I watched the others diminish downward until they were lost in the harsh black and white world below.

Fifth Week: 20th June–26th June

20th June (Camp 1, Camp 2, Camp 1). Away by 5. Cold. Steps in good condition which makes the jumaring easier than before. Sun doesn't hit till last few hundred feet (I'm now wearing a white home-made chemise). Good to see Al-R and Aid at Camp 2 which is sited on a large terrace. Above it the NW Face looms another 5,000 feet to the summit. The NW Ridge and the NW Face are indistinguishable. Over to the left we can see the North Ridge which is being attempted from China by a second American team.

We can see nothing of them, then we hear a female voice—Catherine? (Catherine Freer, a friend who was part of the American team). Then we saw a figure in red—only one—a mile away. Strangely pleasing to see. Spied out our route ahead. Hung around for 2 hours then went down. Hot—hard to concentrate, clip into short end of fixed rope and come within 6 inches of abseiling off the end. Drop a glove—but watch it fall to glacier where I retrieve it. Abseil anchor comes out and drops me 10 feet. Must be more careful: concentrate. The flog back across the cwm to Camp 1 is hard work enough though it is gently downhill. The snow is soft now and the sun's rays come from every direction, reflecting—with percentage it seems—the great white walls and floor that imprison this basin. There is no escape. *This* is fermenting. I strike a rhythm to some words of Robert Frost that enter my dizzied mind from somewhere in that buzzing silence.

'The woods are lovely, dark and deep,
But I have promises to keep
And miles to go before I sleep,
And miles to go before I sleep.'

'Miles to go and promises to keep; miles to go and promises to keep, miles to go . . .' They give me rhythm those musical words and on them I ride to Camp 1. I recall a passage from *Seven Pillars* too (which I have since checked for accuracy and found my memory better on this than other things):

His body plodded on mechanically, while his reasonable mind left him, and from without looked down critically upon him, wondering what that futile lumber did and why. Sometimes these selves would converse in the void and then madness was very near.

As I reached Camp 1, Porter stuck his head out the tent. I said, 'The woods are lovely, dark and deep, But I have promises to keep . . .'
And straightway he began it:

'Whose woods these are I think I know,
His house is in the village though;
He will not see me stopping here
To watch his woods fill up with snow.'

He finished it too, word perfect as far as I could tell. There is poetry in the soul of a man who can run off four verses of Robert Frost at 20,000 feet.

Arrive Camp 1 to find Jim-C. He's in great form. Says all is not well at Base Camp between Agha and Jim-H. Wilkie goes down for Base Camp as I arrive. I procrastinate. To go down or to carry again? I decide to carry again tomorrow although I'm feeling tired. Phil, Al-R and John also carrying. Then Al-R and John to stay at Camp 2. Phil and I to go down along with twins who are at Camp 2 and will try to move higher tomorrow before descending. Get the twins very clearly on radio at 5. All's well. Jim-C says being the cameraman is like being the female climber: every modest achievement is greeted with chorus of 'well done'.

21st June (Camp 1, Camp 2, Base Camp). Alone in tent (Al-B is at Camp 2). Slept well. Woken at 3 by Al-R. Set off with Al-R, John and Phil. Carrying 5 ropes. Tired at first but grow stronger. Al-R coughing and retching but as always pushing himself. He is hoarse and doesn't look well. Phil going well. John too. Reach Col about 8. Still cool. Phil descends immediately. I sit about. Watch twins who are fixing just above the tent—clearly didn't start till late—no need; not hot up here even in sun. They are fixing to top of a snow dome which we hope will lead to bottom of central couloir on N Face. Al-R I think, favours a buttress to the right but the rest of us think the couloir looks easier and more direct. Al-R and John settle in tent. I acclimatise for an hour or so then go down. Very hot, balling crampons, rest on arete. Plod into Camp 1 at 21,200 feet. Tired from heat. Chat to Jim-C and Phil. Twins arrive 1 hour later and unexpectedly early having fixed 4 ropes. Apparently John said to them 'Is that it?' and conspicuously announced 'we'll take 10 ropes tomorrow!' Al-B goes down to Base Camp. I hang around delaying mainly because I'm tired. Brew (thanks to Jim-C) and eventually leave about 3 pm with toothbrush. Death Rattle Gulch has a crevasse, the slope below has avalanched, wet and horrible; but the ski to Advance Base is great. Check tents, pick up a sleeping bag and stove and gas cylinders for Yanks (to swap for snow shoes). Ski on. Snow ploughing when a crevasse opens! Close skis and just get over. Bev has been up glacier without skis to see if Jim-C is OK. He had not been heard of on radio and was known to be wandering on glacier on his own. Bev herring-boned for 4 km but found no Jim. Good effort. Interesting skiing but avalanches and sun have changed the map. Arrive Base Camp at 4 pm. Tea from Aftab. Lovely tea Aftab, lovely boy Aftab. Bad news. Two of US SW Pillar team (John Smolich and Alan Pennington) have been avalanched and killed. One body recovered. Rotten luck. Wanda came over a few days before to borrow a tent, gave Aid 2 potatoes in exchange, thinking he was his twin (with whom she shared a romantic interlude in Poland some years ago). Now came to collect her dues—a tent—so she didn't have to share with Maurice. They may reach summit today via the Abruzzi. Glacier rumbling: creaking, slipping, sliding towards Skardu.

22nd June (Base Camp). Agha combing hair in preparation for a visit to The Strip. The Major always inspects him. Watch teams on Broad Peak. Wonderful day, not a cloud. Jim-H bronzes as he reveals row in A-Team. He says that Al-R lost his temper and declared that he didn't want to be the leader in the first place.

We were idling a hot day to restfulness when, about mid-morning we became aware that a number of folk were gathering at Puchoz Grave. Puchoz Grave is the name given to a pinnacle that rises immediately behind the Abruzzi Close area of our camp. Here, under stones, lay the body of Mario Puchoz, a casualty of Dessio's 1954 Italian Expedition which made the first ascent of K2 via the Abruzzi Spur. Since then more bodies have been buried there. This pinnacle has become K2's cemetery. Now were come the Americans to bury the recovered body of Alan Pennington. A sleeping bag served office for a winding sheet. Slowly and quietly folk from half a dozen expeditions, all based on The Strip, gathered for the service. Pall bearers struggled up the rocky slope to a grave as apt to climber as is the sea to sailor. We weren't quite sure what to do. We had no warning, no invitation. We turned off the boogie box and sat around in awkward sun bathing half-nakedness. Then, simultaneously it struck Bev and me that funerals need no invitation—at least not this one. And if we weren't quick we were going to miss it, for here was the body now. Bev was already respectably attired in his 'lion tamers' suit. He climbed up to the service. I grabbed a T-shirt and followed, wondering whether there was some etiquette that said that funerals should not be attended in bare legs. The scramble made us both puff most unceremoniously at the grave side as we stood with a score of mountaineers from a dozen nations. The Italians had brought flowers; flowers from Italy for just such a purpose! Was that planning or pessimism? I need not have worried about bare legs. There were powder blue booties, snow white breeches and ten-gallon hats—it was a colourful occasion.

The body was fed into a sarcophagus that lay under a cairn bearing the name plates of the seven or eight that already lay there. An American made a dignified little speech rounding off with a Mallory quotation to the effect that we eat and make money to live—not the other way around. It was a quotation equal to the occasion. A second American, Chelsea, their Base Camp Manager, said something plain, sensible and suitable too. Everyone was holding up well. Then their doctor spoke. He got three words into his bit and broke down, and brought a few others down with him too. But it was a fine funeral, if a funeral can be fine, and K2 is as good a headstone as any parish slate. The assembly dispersed and scrambled each to their own shut place, to their own shut questioning: why? what for? and all the rest of these unanswerable things.

In the afternoon we visited the American Camp. We strolled across the intervening mile of Godwin Austen Glacier to the strip of it which ran below the S Face of K2 where all the other Base Camps were sited. They lay in line. The whole looked like a film set of some medieval tournament bedecked with flag, pennant and pageant. This was The Strip. The ground between our camp and The Strip was referred to variously, as the English Channel or La Manche, depending on ethnicity. I doubt that any of us were very clear why we were visiting, only that it seemed right that we should.

They were taking stock: deciding whether to quit; counting cash, sorting the dead's belongings: making a tin-top plaque.

'Hey how old was Allen? I wanna put his age here.'

'39' someone said, reading from a passport.

'39! Really. That old. I'm surprised he got so high.'

Macabre humour though it may seem now, it made us laugh at the time. Walking back across the English Channel we looked up at the scar of the avalanche that had swept the two Americans away. It was acres square and yards deep. A stone, a single stone that had fallen from high on the SW pillar had triggered it. The first stone of that day's sun; and that and a hundred other coincidences of time and place had turned it to tragedy. We scratched our heads and searched for something sensible to say and said only daft things and drew only daft conclusions, avoiding the only one that mattered which was that climbing is dangerous, and that games that are dangerous sometimes end in death.

The Americans quit soon after. I would have done the same. Later someone noted that one of the Americans had been buried with his camera and in it a film. The day before he'd been photographing Mario Puchoz's grave. I followed the macabre logic of that for as far as I dared which wasn't far. It was too much like gazing into yonder stars. That night a fullish moon rolled round the southern flank of Broad Peak and bathed the Baltoro in a pale lustre; sight to stir any soul. Such a moon must surely illuminate the whole world.

23rd June (Base Camp). Sunny. Some high cloud has cleared. 9 am radio call from Camp 2. Aid and Phil are there already. Weather poor when they started out but clearing. Al-R and John up the hill above Camp 2 and fixing. Yesterday they fixed 1,500 feet of rope to about 24,000 feet. A real leader's day and a fine effort. Radio call from Aid says that Al-R has said they need a load of stores at the top. So we are planning a lift by Bev, Jim-H, Wilkie, Al-B, Abdul and me to Advance Base then Camp 1. Not sure how the future plan will work out—difficult to predict, but if weather keeps up we should get higher. Glance through the window of the dining tent, and over Jim-H's shoulder. Chogolisa ('Bride Peak') looks as magnificent as always down at Concordia corner. He nods at the mountain, 'Nice innit', he says. It wasn't what I had been thinking. Plan to leave 4 am tomorrow for Advance Base and Camp 1 the same day. Cut a dishdasha out of a sheet sleeping bag; a white shroud to keep me cool.

Once again John Porter sums up for the A-Team (19th—24th June):

For the next few days, everything was climbing. The Burgesses went up to establish Camp 2, then Al and I took over the next day. We carried big loads and spent the afternoon transferring the dump on the col to the camp and making home improvements. There was never any need to discuss what to do or how to go about it. By this stage of the trip, we simply did things without wasting effort on plans. We alternated the chores of cooking, clearing and fetching snow, and making the effort in the morning, but never had to discuss whose turn it was.

The next two days (22, 23 June) were superb climbing days. We worked hard, pushing ropes to 7,400m and carrying up as much hardware and spare ropes as we could. The weather was perfect and the mountains began to fall away beneath us like a receding tide. A selfish scheme, born of the pleasure of being high, and pain at the thought of going down, entered our conversation. There was enough food at 2 for a push for the top. We could see the great couloir that led to the north ridge only a few rope lengths to the left of our high point. Two days up and one down would do it. No more spirit-sapping rope fixing. A little voice inside kept saying, "go for it," loud and clear above the sounds of the tent flapping and the rasp of air entering tired lungs. But during the second night, Al developed a cough. In the morning, we again selected ropes and hardware for the sacs, and dismissed the food and bivi tent.

'We'll fix for one more day, then go down for a couple of days' rest at Camp 1 before going for it,' Al told me, his voice a hoarse rasp that just got through above the creaking of boots and crampons. 'That will give us a chance to talk to the others and work out the teams for the first go.'

It was a decision that saved my life and postponed Al's death by a month. No further progress was made for the next three weeks. We all returned to Base and awoke each morning to the sound of snow scudding down the sides of tents. On two occasions, we returned to Camp 1, but only to realise that we had been fooled by brief interludes in the storm. We were soon back down in Base again.

24th June 5pm (Base Camp to Camp 1). A single call on 23rd from Aid had indicated that all was well at Camp 2 where they had arrived that day. Weather fine, still and warm. John and Al-R fixed some more rope—possibly a total of 11 ropes. Good going. Aid said that John and Al-R were returning to Base Camp that night. Since we were off early the next day we did not wait up for them. (They

135

came in late.) Up at 4, off by 5 with Al-B, Wilkie, Bev, Jim and Abdul, who carries a monstrous load. Negotiate the Ice Fall without too much difficulty to the point where we have been leaving our skis. Abdul has forgotten his goggles. Bev donates his and flees with barely concealed glee back to Base Camp. We continue, Wilkie, Al-B and I on skis; Jim and Abdul on foot, joined with tape. Conditions are superb and we in shade. Some crevasses are beginning to open quite wide. All arrive at Advance Base within minutes of one another. Sort some gear. Jim-H brews. We show him what to carry next day and, leaving him at Advance Base continue to Camp 1. Good going until sun hits me. Then I wilt a bit. But a slight breeze and my new whites help. Then hot sun, soft snow, slow ropes to Camp 1. Torpid. I arrive 20 minutes after Al-B, Wilkie 20 minutes later. Almost immediately the sky clouds over (that breeze brought them from the south) and it starts to snow heavily. Mid pm: Aid and Phil arrive down from Camp 2 where they say that conditions were terrible all night. The Denali (a sturdy tent) blew down in strong winds and snow. No work can be done so they have come down. Phil says you could hardly breathe against the wind. They are continuing to Base Camp. (We had seen wisps of wind whipping across the NW Ridge from Advance Base that morning and could hear the winds roar for miles: a mighty roar on the ridge at 23,000 feet; a zephyr at Advance Base at 17,500 feet.) Discuss tactics: it looks pretty hopeless but we decide to sit it out to see what tomorrow brings. Aid's spare sleeping bag which Al-B has just carried up goes back down with Aid.

25th June (Camp 1 to Base Camp). Wake to a wild night. Lots of new snow. What to do? Seems no point in staying. Impossible to work in these winds higher up. Has snowed all night and the wind is still ferocious. Talk to Base Camp at 10 o'clock and to Jim-H at Advance Base. Jim has had a bad night and complains of a headache. Al-B and Wilkie vote to go down. I demur. Down we go. Slow ski in deep snow to Advance Base. Great glowering clouds coming in from south do not look good. Find Jim-H and Abdul in good form, Jim's head notwithstanding. We have brought snow shoes from Camp 1 for them which with all the new soft snow is just as well. Shut up Advance Base tight (as we did for Camp 1) and continue on down. Jim-H who with Abdul, is slower on snowshoes than we on skis, asks me to wait to go with him across the Ice Fall—which I am more than happy to do for my old friend. Slow ski, rotten snow, rocks appearing, slots opening. Dump skis. Wilkie and Al-B shoot off; I wait for Jim-H and Abdul. Jim says he's been down a crevasse, was held by Abdul. The others are not critical of our retreat. They agree that there was nothing else to be done in the circumstances. There is a rumour that 6 climbers reached the top of K2 on the 23rd but that two are missing and that even the whereabouts of the other four is uncertain. Sleep well.

26th June (Base Camp). Cross to The Strip. Now there is an Austrian team too, a friendly lot who have smuggled in beer camouflaged in orange juice cans. Take a dozen varieties of tea with Koreans and watch a K2 film on a solar powered video of theirs. There is something odd about sitting at the bottom of K2 watching a film of it when you could step outside the tent to see the real thing in half a stride. On towards the US team, stopped by an L.O. Captain who insists on giving us more tea. He tells us of his Broad Peak adventure on which he claims to have been to 7,300 metres. Clearly pleased with himself. Not sure I believe him. Strange man, polite but an evil eye. Apparently it does their careers good to go high. Onto Americans. They are in good spirits. They are waiting for porters. Selling off gear. We need rope and perhaps another pair of snow shoes. Jim-C is wondering what to mention about their accident in his ITN report. Chelsea says she will give us a statement. On way home we are collared by Benoît of the Italian 8,000-metre operation who takes us into his dining dome (tables, neon/solar light and cappuccino coffee) for a brew. Here a real-life drama is being enacted. Story so far:

22nd. 6 climbers, 2 Spaniards, Mari Abrego and Joseme Casinero plus Wanda, Michel, Maurice and Liliane Barrard leave Camp 3 on Abruzzi (7,900m) and bivouac at 8,300m—1 tent for 4, no sleeping bags. Wanda takes $2^1/2$ Mogadons. Liliane gives Maurice an injection of what we cannot ascertain. **23rd.** All 6 reach summit and descend to same bivouac at 8,300m. **24th.** All 6 set out for Camp 3. 4 arrive. Maurice and Liliane are lost. **25th.** Wanda and the 2 Spaniards continue down, now joined by Benoît Chamoux of the '8,000m Challenge' team (who met them, on his way up, solo). Michel refuses to leave Camp 3 and waits for his 2 companions, Maurice and Liliane. Wanda and Spaniards stop after $1/2$ hour (bad weather; poor visibility) and erect a tent, ignoring Benoît's pleas to continue. Benoît climbs down to Base Camp. **26th.** Still no sign of Maurice and Liliane. Michel attempts to descend alone. We are in tent as Benoît guides him on the radio. Great drama as Benoît tries to describe whereabouts of fixed rope to Michel who is staggering around at 26,000 feet in a blizzard muttering into his radio 'grande vide, grande vide' (big emptiness). Benoît urges him to look out for Rentes de Glaces with a urine stain.

'Has Michel a tent and a sleeping bag?' we ask.

'I told him to take one,' Benoît replies.

Michel comes up 3 or 4 times on the radio. Only two hours of daylight left, but no panic in his voice despite being lost, alone at nearly 8,000 metres on the second highest mountain in the world. Maybe he has passed Wanda and the Spaniards in the murk without seeing them. Still no news of Wanda and Spaniards. Worried that Michel will descend below fixed ropes and will have to climb again, which after three nights at 8,000 metres may be more than even his spirit can bear. We make a solemn way back to our camp, vainly questioning, vain questions.

Sixth Week: 27th June–3rd July

27th June (Base Camp). Hear that the Spaniards and Wanda and Michel have radioed from Camp 1. A urine stain has saved Michel's life. Helicopters buzzing about all day. Weather improving though still cloudy. A roll call of teams reveals:

West Germans	—	Broad Peak and S. Face of K2
Austrians	—	Abruzzi
Americans	—	SW Ridge
Italians	—	Broad Peak—K2 by SW Ridge and Abruzzi
S. Koreans	—	Abruzzi
French/Polish	—	Abruzzi

Casarotto (solo)	—	SW Ridge
Poles	—	SW Ridge
British	—	NW Ridge

and the two Spaniards who shared Casarotto's permission but who had detached themselves and climbed the Abruzzi. Cacophonous music al fresco on boogie box. Home brew beer, not bad but a bit sugary sweet.

28th June (Base Camp). Middling weather. Buy all sorts of goodies from the Americans, food especially. Hallelujah! At last Al-R produces a climbing plan, part of which entails Al-B and myself going to Camp 2 to fix—tomorrow. Will leave about 4 am with some rope and personal gear. Wanda and Michel are down. Maurice and Liliane are lost. Wanda looks exhausted with good reason. Michel looks surprisingly fresh. The 2 Spaniards also down. Benoît and some others went part way up (6,000+). It is said that Wanda took $2^1/2$ Mogadon and then, to wake up the next day, Dexedrine and then Ephedrine. Anyway they are down. John, Jim-H and Phil all booking flights home.

29th June (Base Camp to Camp 1). Up at 4.15. The whole team sets off: twins, Al-R, John, Wilkie, Phil. I have 600 feet of rope in sac. Al-B has trouble with a ski-skin that refuses to stick, which slows him to about my pace. He warms it on a bonfire of rubbish at Advance Base. His problem solved. Mine begun. He goes on like a rocket. Merciful clouds on ropes. John and I discuss love, of all things. Reach Camp 1 in good order at 11.45. Re-dig tents, sleeping bag organisation getting complicated. We have two each but they are required in four places—Base Camp, Advance Base, Camp 1, Camp 2. It usually means carrying one which is tiresome. On 1200 radio schedule we are told Ghulam has arrived. 'Do you want your letters read on air?' Jim-H asks. I apologise to Phil for some sharp words yesterday. John apologises for some moaning. He is worried about a work deadline he must make if he is to keep his job. Huge evening meal. Trying to move as light as possible tomorrow. Borrowing John's sleeping bag and down-suit which are already at Camp 2. Excited and hopeful. Went down. It snowed all night.

30th June (Camp 1 to Base Camp). Awoke at 3; snowing hard and windy. Back to sleep. Awoke 7; snowing harder. Reluctantly decide to go down: no question of climbing today. Avalanches just behind tent. Even so I am tempted to stay up; it might be worthwhile waiting. Only John, who says Poles would be climbing this weather, agrees with me. Start down. Snow sliding off rocks. Skis are well buried. A blind ski for a few minutes then a clearing and a swoop to Advance Base, and down to Base Camp. Discover Ghulam has been dishonest. A letter Brian has sent back from Skardu says so. He has been caught falsifying receipts (much too western a ploy to fool us). Ghulam is sacked. The L.O. is utterly despondent. He and Jim-H at permanent loggerheads. A situation that is not helped by the L.O.'s discovery that Jim was a mere staff sergeant in the army which causes him to regard and treat Jim as a subordinate. Jim-H much better at being an insubordinate. All this has nothing to do with religious, cultural, socio-economic gulfs between East and West. It's much simpler. The L.O. is a snob. But he's unhappy and we had hoped to resolve the problem by sending him back to Skardu, a mutually satisfactory solution. Sadly, for all, the Major, the senior L.O.

of all the expeditions, and an honourable and straight man, won't countenance such a dereliction of duty. Agha has been told he must stay and do his job. But at least he is moving house, across The Strip to be with his friends. Now he sits while Jim-H (some valet) packs food for him. A sad and dejected figure with a lower lip pout a foot wide. In his truculence he has threatened to censor all our mail; to report John as a CIA spy; to close down the entire expedition for breach of (unspecified) regulations.

When Agha threatened Jim-H with the censorship of his mail, Jim replied, 'fine, but you'll do it from the bottom of a crevasse'. Agha reported this threat to the Major who, a reasonable man, treated it as no more than a robust jest. But we who knew Jim was sometimes not such a reasonable man, were less dismissive—there were men with sore heads all over North Wales who would have thought the Major foolhardy.

Boys sound fine in my first letter from them both: in a Sport Aid run Tank has run 2 miles, Bongs 6. Wonderful boys, I am homesick. Weather is poor. I'm bored, worried, sad. The National Trust have withdrawn their offer of a job because I haven't guaranteed that I can be back on 15th July. What price K2? Jim-C, Jim-H, Al-R yesterday visited The Strip and had a drink with Casarotto's team. John and Jim-H decide to go home. This will leave us thin. Wilkie not going well and Al-R still has his sore throat. Al says 'there is no climbing on our route', meaning that it is a plod, which is just about right.

1st July (Base Camp). Awake to poor weather. Great breakfast with new food purchased from Americans. Steve, the American doc, was up here at 7 am with a rebreather for Al-R's throat—Al all wired in bed to the contraption. Michel comes for tea. He's climbed Kangchenjunga and now K2. Not bad for someone who doesn't call himself a mountaineer. He is a pleasant fellow dividing his time between Paris, Chamonix and Beirut where he is a journalist. John prepares to leave with Jim-H and with Abdul as a bearer. Rest of us prepare to go up to Camp 1 if weather is fine tomorrow. Colossal avalanche off Broad Peak.

2nd July (Base Camp to Camp 1). Wake at 4 am. Weather clear apart from odd cloud, and cold. Wilkie feels ill, Al-R coughing; they remain behind. Phil, Jim-C, twins, and I set off for Advance Base. Light loads and 150 feet of rope each. Easy going, feel good. Jim-C arrives at Advance Base only a few minutes behind us but decides not to go on to Camp 1. John has come as far as Advance Base to get some gaz for his walk out. 'Thanks for your words', he says with obvious sadness, as we say our goodbyes. He'd anguished the day before about whether to go back; a letter from home said he would be in trouble and his job at risk if he didn't. A hard decision. I had told him to go with a clear conscience; jobs were more important than mountains. Conscientious as ever, his parting words to Al-B were, 'get a Lowe rucksack piccie on the top' (Lowe had given us some kit).

John wrote to me later about his decision to go home:

Then another inner debate began. "It's only a job, jack it," said one side. "It's only a mountain, think ahead," said the other. The days moved past slowly. Boredom and doubt overcame my energy. Rather than kick against time and commitments, I let it

*take me away. I looked back from Concordia and wondered why I was leaving. K2
was etched against a stainless blue sky. Not a single cloud, no hint of cirrus, and in
every direction the solid bright colours of high mountains stood against the horizon.
On the glacier, the warm air was working in the last of the drifted snow. Small
streams glided across the ice, and vanished into crevasses. Fifty miles away at the
glacier snout, the water reappeared, multiplied a million times. The rapids roared
and leapt through the high desert. A hundred miles further, the Indus gathered its
tributaries and forced a way out of the Karakoram, then on through the Himalayas
before sprawling across the plain toward the Indian Ocean. The waters of summer
were flowing at last. Like the water, I felt the passive hand of gravity. The wet
tarmac of Heathrow mirrored the blankness of my mind. I knew only that weeks of
work and missed opportunities were in the past. Chance might have been kinder to Al
and me, but surely I could console myself that Al and some of the others would reach
that unlikely summit seen so clearly from Concordia, perched on an arrow of ice and
rock.*

So Jim and John were gone, and with Jim went much of the humour, and with
John much of the drive.

Phil and I decide to try to ski all the way to Camp 1 via a route that he's spotted
from the ropes above Camp 1 thus avoiding the fixed ropes, shortening the ascent,
and accelerating the descent—individual expertise on skis allowing! This was easy
until sun got us. Then it was desperate. *Sabots de neige sous les skis* and
exhaustion. At last, top a slight rise, and there is Camp 1. As we approached Phil
had stopped to let me know that it was not far, a thoughtfulness for which I was
immensely grateful. Twins had just arrived via the fixed ropes. Said it was their
worst trailbreak. Once literally up to the armpits. Fester a hot afternoon with
brews and *I Claudius*. Plan: Day 1—Al-B + self to go to C2 to stay, Phil + Aid to
carry loads to C2. Day 2; Self + Al-B to fix above high point. Phil + Aid up to
C2 to stay. One light sac for whoever is the trailbreaker, 3 normal sacs, and swop
around.

3rd July (Camp 1 to Camp 2). Hellish wind all night. Feared the tent would
blow away. Sleeping pill didn't work. No-one had any sleep. Woke at 3, dozed till
4, away by 5. On skis this time to foot of the big slope. Works well. Fixed rope
completely buried. Steady jug up to the arete. Going well. Viciously cold in
spindrift. Phil and I tighten, adjust, spruce the fixed-rope system as we climb
swopping some thin ropes for thick. (Thin ropes are lighter—to be used higher
up). Sun hits us on snow arete and the purgatory begins. Phil goes down from
arete saying that he won't be able to carry tomorrow if he goes all way to Camp 2
today. We see 3 figures approaching Camp 1 from below by the new ski route;
presumably Al-R, Wilkie and Jim-C. Al-B breaks our trail. Lots of deep settled
snow despite last night's wind. Takes me 1 hour to the arete—the first 1,500 feet;
then 5 hours from there—the second 1,500 feet. Avalanche in couloir, I cower
behind a rock; concentrates the mind. Sun directly overhead. Arrive C2 at one
o'clock to find 3 feet of new snow. Tents are snowed-in to roof height. Radio at 6.
Bev reports from Base Camp that the American and French accidents have been
mentioned on BBC. Also an L.O. Captain is escorting the Spaniards to Islamabad

to answer charges of climbing the wrong route (Abruzzi).

Fantastic views; half (or is it all?) of China, and behind us the Muztagh Tower, the Latoks; and other mountains of dreams as yet undreamt. Disaster! Spill a full can of water from stove! Massive mopping-up session. No sign of the Americans across on the N. Ridge. Possibly too much snow for them at the moment. Above Camp 2 the mountain rears in colossal proportions, something like 5,000 feet to the top. The first obstacle, a minor one, was the snow dome (already fixed by the twins) maybe five hundred feet high. This led onto a second plateau, a corner shelf that nestled between the remaining NW Ridge and the N Face—that is the vast triangular chunk of mountainside that stretched between the NW Ridge and the N Ridge—the two about a mile apart at this level, but, of course, converging to join at the summit. (Al Rouse and John had already fixed the first thousand feet on this face.) The NW Ridge, from here upwards, is less ridge than corner between Northern and Western aspects of the mountain. The simplest route still appears to us to lie up the North Face in a series of snowy couloirs and ledges. This was, as far as we could tell, the route the Poles had taken, before they were stopped at 27,000 feet.

Seventh Week: 4th July–10th July

4th July (Camp 2 and above). Slept like a log and slept in—Al-B and I both tired. Brewing when Aid and Phil arrived at 0900, to stay. Phil going well today, after yesterday's hiccup. Al-R and Wilkie arrive later. Jim-C attempting to carry camera and tripod to the arete half-way up the fixed ropes between Camp 1 and Camp 2. Hope he makes it. Al-B and I carry rope and replace thick for thin on snow dome above Camp 2. Leave at 10 o'clock. Trail breaking, knee deep, is absolute hell; and then wind dies and sun gets up. These days are so hot it is hard to believe. From top of snow dome the view is gobsmacking but still no sign of Americans on N. Ridge. Lots of new snow. Phil and Aid put up their tent and rest. Aid offers to break trail for us but that seems unfair. We decline. Al-R can't resist noting that Wilkie has light sac. Return to Camp 2 at 1,500 feet tired. Maybe I should eat more in the day. Bev tells us on the radio that evening that he's going to a 4th July party across at the Americans' camp.

5th July (Camp 2 to Camp 2a and Camp 2). Al-B and I up early 0500. Have to re-break trail to top of snow dome. It has blown in. Up to top of dome and across plateau to foot of N. Face. Al-B breaking trail all way, often up to his thighs. Spend an hour finding the rope that Al-R and John fixed. When we do I realise that I do not have the energy to fix more at the top end of it. I am stuffed as never before. Al-B says he will break a trail to the top of it which will be handy for the future—if it stays in. This he does in a fine tour de force. I fall alseep on a pedestal at the foot of the ropes. Awake to see 6 Americans on the North ridge forging up snow slope to what we presume is their Camp 2 at about 22,000 feet. The N Ridge is easy angled but long. I return to top of snow dome where Phil and Aid are siting a camp (Camp 2a) so that we don't have such a flog to start of the North Face. Aid is in fine fettle. Phil not too bad either. Looking up we can see Al-B on face—descending. He is soon with us. Phil and I descend to Camp 2. I am tired. Spend afternoon brewing brew after brew but never seem to be able to quite fill the tank. Al-B does all the work. I lie feeling sorry for myself. We discuss chances and alternatives. I have a Mark I English cold. Now where did I get that? Sneezing, running nose—the last thing I need. Also pains in calf and excruciating pins and needles and a pain in my right chest. What a hypo.

Al-R, Wilkie and Jim-C are coming up again tomorrow. We think Al-R and Wilkie should go on to Camp 2, but not sure how they will take that; we'll see. Would be great to see Jim-C at Camp 2. Losing appetite. Force down some food. Sleeping pill. Sleep well. Night is big with stars. Open door to see them. Wouldn't like to be Al-R with this decision to make, the decision on what to do next. We will soon need more food/gas up here.

6th July (Camp 2). Slept well but woke with sore throat. Brew then lie around. Rest day. Al-R arrives at 10.00-ish with Wilkie. Then we spot Phil coming down from Camp 2c. He's had a very bad night; blinding headaches and difficulty in breathing. Decide that Al-B should replace him. (Aid had gone up to the high point and fixed a couple of rope lengths anyway, until ground got too technical for one person. It only took him 1$^{1}/_{2}$ hours from Camp 2a to the top of the ropes thanks to Al-B's trail breaking the day before.) Al-B readily agrees to join his brother at Camp 2a and leaves about 1300 hours. The rest of us doss and bullshit. Phil notes, 'there's a lot of lying around on these big trips'. About 5 pm Phil, feeling worse, decides to go down to Camp 1 where Jim-C—who had set out ahead of Wilkie and Al-R from Camp 1 this morning but couldn't find the fixed ropes and got frightened by stone fall and retreated—is languishing. This leaves a tent all to me which means I can cook inside and in comfort and lounge around. Trying Turkey Pieces tonight to see if I can find my appetite. They are foul. Tomorrow twins will fix. Wilkie and Al-R will carry and I will try. Have felt lousy all day. 4th night at 22,950 feet. Suffering a bit. Miss my boys. There's some high cirrus coming in from Pakistan, previously always a harbinger of bad weather. Al-R hears on 6 pm radio schedule that Benoît Chamoux has climbed Abruzzi in 29 hours; that 5 more Italians have reached the top: that Kurt Diemberger and Julie Tullis are at Camp 3 at 25,910 feet and should make it tomorrow if weather holds—all on the Abruzzi. He says, 'climbing is meaningless'. On that, at least, we are agreed. There must be 40 folk on the Abruzzi.

7th July (Camp 2 to Base Camp). Al-B goes off first at agonisingly slow pace. Not feeling too bad until I've gone 100 yards then feel weak; absolutely weak. Clouds still building from the south. Cirrus as before. Go down convinced this was a good day for a rest because of weather and that others would soon follow: down to Camp 1 where Phil and Jim-C are waiting. They go on to Base Camp. Marvellous snow to Advance Base and Jim-C's first ski lesson. Phil goes ahead.

Imagine your first ever ski lesson at 20,000 feet! And not only that, but with a fifty-pound rucksack as ballast, to boot. That was Curran's reward for weeks of dogged effort and of unstinting devotion to his film-making task. I could not but admire the man as he screwed his courage to the sticking place, his jaw to the resolute setting and set manfully about the business of translating my glib didacticism into practicable manoeuvres via lungs that had long read empty. Phil was a great help. 'Perfect snow conditions', he yelled with what passes for enthusiasm in taciturn northern society. He proved it by crouching like Klammer and hurtling off towards Advance Base. It was to be several hours before we saw him again.

'Weight on the down-hill ski, Jim.' 'Keep forward, Jim.' 'No, from the knees, Jim.' 'Well done mate.' 'Oops never mind mate.' ''Appens to the best of us.' 'Damn! see what I mean?' 'Steady does it, Jim.' 'Nice one, Jim.' 'Well nearly a nice one, Jim.' 'Doin' well, Jim.' 'No the rucksack doesn't help, Jim.' 'Equivalent of a black-run, Jim.' 'Hang on there and I'll untangle you, Jim.' 'Try stopping and then do a kick-turn, Jim.' 'Try stopping before you do a kick-turn, Jim.' 'Try stopping Jim.' 'Och let's just lie here and take a breather, Jim.' And so we made it to Advance Base with far fewer spills than anyone has right to expect in the circumstances.

At one point Jim noticed some stones rolling down a ridge that lay to our left side. They were accelerating alarmingly and Jim thought that they were heading in our direction and voiced his concern.

'Look at them fucking stones'.

'No probs mate, all to do with the fall line, and we're not in the fall line'.

The stones tumbled on leaving deep, straight furrows in their path and, paying no heed to the laws of the fall line, rolled inexorably towards Jim. They collided. Jim was unhurt but subsequent smooth instructional assurances lacked their earlier authority.

The three of us are sitting at Advance Base when two figures hove into sight: the twins. Phil spots, at a distance, they have their crampons on their sacs—and interprets that sign before I can. They had told Al-R that the Abruzzi was the only way to the top and Al-R had agreed—they say.

We are quitting the NW Ridge. I'm disappointed. We have 3 weeks left at least.

Reasons: team too small (Poles had over twenty climbers on same route), route too long.

Abruzzi a clear run.

Al-R skis in to Advance Base after twins have gone on down. Says he was going like a train to C2a. I tell him that he's fooling himself. Says he was reluctant to agree with the twins but appears to have offered no resistance. Continues to express regret on the way down to Base Camp. Consciences have a habit of solidifying at lower altitudes.

8th July (Base Camp). Bev: 'Council-of-War?'

Al: 'S'pose so'. And then seeing the weather is fine says, 'looks like we've blown it'. Jim-C privately questions Al's sanity.

Couldn't find *Other Men's Flowers*, in which I sought solace. Jim-C receives a letter from Janet Scott—Doug's wife. The word was, she wrote, that if we made the top for the Royal Wedding we'd be knighted, if not it would be the Tower. It was a painful reminder of our fatuous hype to be on top for the Royal Wedding. The things you say, the promises you make in order to raise sponsorship—or to justify that sponsorship having raised it.

There's an argument about the division of spoils—and we haven't climbed the thing yet—or even finished trying! Or have we? There are interminable anti-Bonehead stories. The only Bonehead story that's never circulated is the one about him being so good at what he does that every other bugger is riven with envy and driven to denunciation. And, I suspect, the truth never stood long in the way of a good denunciation. Al-R babbles on about the desirability of freedom and equality in our society. I say both are desirable but mutually exclusive and, given the choice, I'd choose freedom with reluctance.

Al says 'But one man's freedom is another's equality.'

I say, 'Precisely. Mutually exclusive.' And we both think we've won.

Agha has been spared by a devious wheeze. Bev has pronounced him medically unfit for work at high altitude. He is to be sent to convalesce in Skardu. Everyone is happy. Even the Major thinks he can sanction this. There are teams departing The Strip and porters all over the place. Two report to carry for Agha. They must sleep in the stones. We won't even loan them the tarpaulin that is stretched over our food dump in case it snows in the night! I give them a space blanket.

There's great secrecy surrounding our switch to the Abruzzi. Al-R doesn't wish to be banned from Pakistan for ten years; which he says is what the punishment would be. Phil says that it would be a reward. I'm beyond caring. Expeditions are only authorised to climb on one route per permission, per peak fee—and that route is specified by letter. It may cost us another £3,000 peak fee if we are caught and we wonder whether it is worth it; which of the original eight climbers should contribute; which of the supporting crew; who exactly has made the decision; which of us were consulted; who is responsible; and why we are going on to a different route. There are no satisfactory answers. It becomes clear that Al-R still hankers after the North-West Ridge, which shows laudable determination. But why has he allowed so much gear to be brought down? Did he originally agree to the Abruzzi but is now having a change of heart as the implications sink in? It is impossible to be sure. Over dinner Al-B produces a nice new definition of monogamous—one girl at a time.

9th July (Base Camp). Wake at 3.30 with the intention of going up to Camp 1 for some of the gear that we've left there. Weather appalling. A Base Camp dossing day. Arguments all day, ranging from unemployment to equality versus freedom (again) to better dead than red, to UFO's. Agha leaves but not before parading us all in the dining tent for a public reading of a report he has written on each of us. Mine is pretty bad, though I had worse in the Marines. We are not sure whether he is serious or if it is a heavy-handed joke—so we are not sure whether to be amused or embarrassed. Snowing heavily. Nothing has been heard of Julie Tullis or Kurt Diemberger for 4 days when they were thought to be at 26,900 feet on the Abruzzi.

10th July (Base Camp). Invited for dinner by Italians. Great food as expected. Benoît a perfect host. Hear that Tullis and Diemberger are down—came down slowly using Korean camps. They had reached 27,200 feet in good order where they waited a day for good weather which didn't come. A fine effort. They may have another go. Wilkie pounces ferociously on any food going. We previously had had usual round of arguments. Twins pushing hard for Abruzzi and planning a move that way. Al-R still dragging his heels a bit. Twins gradually taking over the leadership.

Eighth week: 11th July–17th July

11th July (Base Camp, Camp 1, Base Camp). Up 3.30. Good ski up to Camp 1 almost without stopping at a cracking pace. For once, I keep up with the twins—by dint of not talking while they chat away amiably as if this is a Sunday stroll. Al-R going slowly and well behind. He's not well. Begin packing up Camp 1 into enormous sacs (60-70lb). (Phil has sunburnt his ankles at base and can't wear boots so no move for him.) Jim-C and Bev are helping out by packing up Advance Base and carrying loads down to Base Camp. There's another 4/5 loads to come from Camp 1. We'll have to go up again. Take kit for Abruzzi—personal stuff can come later. Thigh bursting slog to Advance Base. From there not too bad but some tenuous snow bridges. Jim-C has hurt his back attempting to carry 50lb through a crevassed glacier on his second day's skiing! Austrian L.O. visits, a Captain Khan of the Khyber Rifles and his mate from the Border Guides. Asks us not to talk about the Agha 'unpleasantness'. He assures us that he will be of service. 'It is very better.' As I lie in the sun I reckon that I'm on my sixth nose and at least my fourth bottom lip.

'Look how much older we all look', Al says. 'And the same ageing is going on internally too; and in your brain.' He adds cheerfully.

12th July (Base Camp). Discuss the merits of the Abruzzi as a route. Al-R claims that he is only contemplating it because he has no choice, that he has been, in effect, presented with a *fait accompli*. Says that the Abruzzi is too easy a route for satisfaction. Opinions on this vary. I recall a letter that Pete Boardman sent me saying that it was an impressive route, and also hazily recall reading of other opinions on the same subject. Note to look them up on return.

And on return a browse turned up the following opinions:

'K2 is so terrible that it's as much a wonder today as it ever was if it's climbed at all.'

(Galen Rowell 1978)

'There should be no difficulty in walking up the snow slopes on the east-south-east to the snowy shoulder. From this point, which is just over 25,000 feet the summit could be reached without question given one fine day.'

(Alister Crowley of the Abruzzi 1902)

'K2 will surely never be climbed.'

(Luigi Amedeo of Savoy 1909)

'With a degree of luck our successors will reach the summit'.

(Charles Houston of the Abruzzi 1953)

'So we switched to the Abruzzi thinking it would be a piece of piss, which we soon found it isn't—it's by far the finest piece of climbing done in the Himalayas before the war—and arguably in the 50s and 60s as well. Bloody desperate, with tatty fixed rope tempting mephistophelian lovelies.'

(Peter Boardman in a letter from Urdukas 2nd August 1980)

But all that is later knowledge.

It is worth taking stock of what had happened and was happening elsewhere on

K2 so far that summer. This task was competently completed by Bernard Newman, in *Mountain* magazine.

At the beginning of the season, an unprecedented total of eleven separate expeditions were booked to climb on the mountain. Circumstances would dictate that the fate of many of the climbers involved would be tragically bound together. Listing the expeditions in a clockwise order of routes: an Austrian team of seven mountain guides led by Alread Imitzer were to attempt the SE (Abruzzi) Ridge. A large South Korean expedition on the Abruzzi Ridge used over 450 porters during the approach march and started up the mountain, fixing their own ropes and ignoring old ones. Later, on August 4 one of their porters, Muhammed ali, was killed by stonefall near Camp 1.

A French group of four climbers led by Maurice Barrard completed an ascent of the Abruzzi Ridge, having their last bivouac at 8300m, above the 'bottle-neck' (a weakness in the line of cliffs which guards the upper part of the ridge and is overhung by seracs). The following day, June 23, they all reached the summit: Wanda Rutkiewicz (Polish), Michel Parmentier, Maurice and Liliane Barrard. On the way down, they decided to repeat their bivouac at 8300m, but next day, June 24th, the weather deteriorated and made the descent hazardous. The Barrards were gradually falling behind and eventually disappeared out of sight at about 7900m. Later, Parmentier stayed to wait for them at one of the camps, while Wanda completed the descent with two Basques. Having lost all hope of finding the missing couple, Parmentier and a group of Italians, who tried to help, came down as well.

The Barrards were among the finest of French climbers. Maurice made his first appearance on the Himalayan scene with his alpine-style ascent of Hidden Peak, together with Georges Narbaud, in 1980. Since then, he and Liliane climbed together Gasherbrum 11 (1982) and Nanga Parbat (1984) and almost reached the summit of Makalu in 1985. With the present ascent, Liliane Barrard and Wanda Rutkiewicz had become the first women to climb K2. Climbers from Poland have now ascended 12 of the main 8000ers, as well as another five subsidiary summits over 8000m. As for Michel Parmentier, this is his second 8000er, having climbed Kangchenjunga (1981), also in tragic circumstances.

Two Basques, Mari Abrego and Josema Casimiro, officially members (for mutual convenience) of Renato Casarotto's expedition but in practice acting independently, made a swift ascent of the Abruzzi Ridge in a five-day alpine push. On June 23 they left their bivouac tent (8100m) at the foot of the bottle-neck, and reached the summit a couple of hours after the previous group, in excellent weather. They returned to their last bivouac point and the following day, June 24, started a painful descent in deteriorating weather conditions, joined for part of the way by Wanda Rutkiewicz, and arriving three days later at Base Camp, with slight frostbite in hands and feet. This was the tenth 8000er by climbers from Spain, and Abrego's second.

An American expedition from Portland, Oregon, comprising nine members led by John Smolich, were trying the SSW Ridge but soon met with disaster. On June 21, a massive avalanche was triggered by a falling boulder on the snow high above them, at 6000m. John Smolich and Alan Pennington died as a result, Pennington's body being *retrieved by his friends and brought down for burial at Arthur Gilkey's memorial, near Base Camp. The expedition was abandoned.*

The Italian expedition, part of the programme called 'Quota 8000' was led by Agostino da Polenza, with a total of 20 members, among them several non-Italians. They tried first the long SSW Ridge (also referred to as South Pillar), with the intention of following the Magic Line suggested by Messner in 1979. After the avalanche to the Americans, they changed their plans and passed to operate on the Abruzzi Ridge, in order to secure the summit. Then, on July 5, six members reached the top: Gianni Calcagno, Tullio Vidoni, Soro Dorotei and Martino Moretti (Italians), Josepf Rakoncaj (Czechoslovakian) and Benoît Chamoux (French). The following day, Kurt Diemberger (Austrian) and Julie Tullis (British), who formed the film crew of the expedition, reached the bottle-neck (8200m) and withdrew, in view of the worsening weather. For Calcagno and Vidoni this was their fourth 8000er, whereas Josef Rakoncaj is now the only person to have climbed K2 twice, since he had already reached the top from the North side of the mountain in 1983, while attached to another Italian expedition. Benoît Chamoux made a lightning ascent, in under 24 hours from Base Camp, this being his fourth 8000er in less than thirteen months.

The international expedition led by Karl Herrligkoffer (69) had as members 8 Germans, 4 Swiss, 2 Poles, 2 Austrians and 2 Pakistanis. During the first stages, the leader suffered from mountain sickness and had to be evacuated by helicopter. Then the members split into several groups, the majority moving to Broad Peak, the other objective of the expedition. And so only the two Poles, helped by a young German, were left to concentrate on the expedition's original plan for K2, that is, a new route following 'the central rib of the South Face'.

After having climbed Broad Peak with various other people, Swiss members Beda Furster and Rolf Zemp moved to the Abruzzi Ridge of K2 and managed to reach the summit on July 5, only half an hour after the previous Italian team.

In the meantime, the Poles Jerzy Kukuczka (38) and Tadeusz Piotrowski (46), after a first attempt in which they reached 7400m in June, started the ascent of the central rib on July 5, reaching the summit in alpine style on July 8, after four consecutive bivouacs. The most difficult section of the climb was encountered on the third day, in which they only progressed from 8100 to 8200m having to overcome a difficult 25-metre wall with climbing estimated by Kukuczka as 5+ (UIAA Grading). Finally the summit was reached in bad weather, which forced them to bivouac on the way down, first at 8300m (the same spot used by the French group) and then at 7900m. On July 10, with appalling conditions of visibility and a coat of fresh snow over hard frozen surfaces, they tried to find their way down the Abruzzi Ridge. Then Piotrowski, who was behind Kukczka, lost both crampons and fell to his death from about 7800m, down the 55 degrees icefield. In extremely tough conditions, Kukuczka managed to reach the upper camp of the South Korean expedition, from where he radioed for help to the Polish team active on the SSW Ridge. Eventually he completed the descent, but nothing could be done about his companion.'

And back to the diary where the tale is taken up again with an entry dated 13th

July, at which time we were preparing for a clandestine scramble on the Abruzzi Spur.

13th July (Base Camp). Prepare for Abruzzi. Scramble for food, Phil and I last and don't get much of a choice. Twins in first. Phil has decided to stay which is great. Discussion of teamwork and keeping together and waiting for slow team members on the way down. Twins not keen on this strategy; clearly want to work as an independent unit which they see as their best hope. Plan to go on the first fair day (which could be today) and to sneak past The Strip in dead ground to avoid detection. Have sounded out Koreans—don't think they will mind—but all a bit delicate. Italians now finished so they won't care. Casarotto going up for yet another go on SW pillar. Koreans sitting it out at Camp 2. Say it's windy, Al-B very superstitious—keeps knife handy by his sleeping bag in the night to head off I'm not sure what. Worries about noises from the graveyard. Strange. Someone asked on the walk-in, on seeing an open knife that he carried, 'Al, why do you always carry that little knife with you?' and he'd replied 'Cos me big one's in me sac.'

Al-R makes outrageous statements about Messner being past it. Another big argument on dividing up gear. Al-R gets angry at twins' suggestion that we have paid too much for tents etc. Al says he did all the work organising it—not they—and they have had nearly a free trip out of it.

Helicopter lifts Kukuczka from The Strip. Benoît comes over, pm, for a chat. He has plenty of gen on the Abruzzi. Doesn't think anyone other than the L.O. captain will mind. When he's gone big argument about when and whether we should go—usual circular performance. Will we take, 2, 3, or 4 days? Benoît thinks 3. Says 'you are strong and acclimatized'. Windy, clouds. Al-R shaves and looks very young.

14th July (Base Camp). Jim-C and Bev go to Advance Base to collect some gear. Hear Bev say that we should have gone yesterday. Maybe he's right. We seem to have lost drive and now there's no leadership at all. All kinds of subterfuges are being contemplated to get past other teams on The Strip without being spotted.

15th July (Base Camp, Austrians' Camp 2, Base Camp). Al-R has woken in a great agitation; intent on going on hill. Yet conditions the same as yesterday, exactly. But Al convinces himself that things are spot on. Al-R refuses to address problems of the return journey—porters, dates, etc.—blocks our every move. In mid discussion, he just walks away and sets off for the Abruzzi. In the end we ask Bev (who returned at 11 o'clock) to order porters through our new L.O. for 26th July—2 days earlier than Al-R wants.

Circumnavigate Strip avoiding detection. Pairs are: twins, Wilkie and Al-R, self and Phil. Long walk up glacier to Ice Fall and a difficult-to-follow route through it. (Pass descending Austrian on way and tell him we're doing a recce for an intended traverse of the mountain via the NW Ridge.) Long flog up to Camp 1 in a superb position (19,675 feet). Tents all over the place. Koreans already in residence say we can use their spare tents—which we do. Twins away early on 16th. Rest of us follow 8.30-ish. Koreans are using high-altitude porters. There are sleeping bags in every tent and big gaz stoves and all sorts of luxuries. Little need to carry anything other than the barest necessities. We have 30lb in our sacs. Fixed ropes well fixed. Some ladders on steeper sections—which are quite steep. As I jumar up, rope after rope after rope I wonder what this game we are playing today is called. Whatever it is, it certainly isn't a 'games climbers play' game. There is no climbing involved; jumar, jumar, jumar; rest: jumar, jumar, jumar; rest: unclip. Clip the next rope; jumar . . . Phil and I reach the Austrians' Camp 2 below House's Chimney. We stop for a brew. A few minutes later the twins descend past us. The weather is not good. Al-R and Wilkie pass—going down. Phil and I consider staying but some Austrians come down too—and it's more than an hour to next camp. We go down. There's cloud and the barometer is dropping rapidly. We overtake two Koreans wobbling with exhaustion—and go on to the glacier where three of us stack sacs for another go. An act of faith? Flog down to Base. Very tired and thirsty. We have been on the go since 4 am. Up to 22,950 feet and back to Base Camp in 24 hours. Al-R confesses to mounting pressure. I feel sorry for him. To bed, tired and still thirsty, at 10-ish. An hour later we are woken by Wanda. Casarotto is dying. He has fallen into a crevasse, the last crevasse on K2, after 3 months of climbing solo on SW pillar. He was giving up and going home. It would have been his last descent. We go up to help, weary. Cross to Austrian camp which seems to be the rescue HQ. I have no axe and pinch one from a Korean tent. Coffee. On to the Italian camp. Wanda is a bit hysterical. Julie Tullis more rational. She doesn't think there is any point in going up but Bev thinks we should. Wanda leads us to Ice Fall. Bev falls behind. Others wait for him. Casarotto needs a doctor. Al-R and I go on up. Kurt is with Casarotto who is lying inert by the crevasse from which he has been pulled. He is dead. Bev agrees. We pass this on by radio to the Italian camp. Say we can't get the body down. Goretta (Casarotto's wife) wants to come up. We descend leaving two climbers to wait for Goretta. She changes her mind. The body is buried in the crevasse.

For three months Casarotto had soldiered alone on the SW Ridge. Up and down a dozen times; up to 27,230 feet this last time; the last time. 'One last go', he had told Goretta. And on this last go he had climbed very high (above 8000m) before being forced to retreat in bad weather—for the umpteenth time, but also for the last time. His wife had watched him descend that steep ridge, steadily, surely, always safely—all the way to an easy snow slope that led in minutes (for him, no more than twenty) to Base Camp. A couple of crevasses: he would have stepped over them. Suddenly, even as she watched he disappeared; fallen into a crevasse. It was deep, fifty or sixty feet, but he wasn't dead yet. From his pocket he took a radio and spoke to his wife for the last time. 'I'm dying inside', he said. Even so, when the first climber to arrive on the scene hauled him out he was still alive. He stood up, took a step, keeled over, died.

The crevasse was no more than three feet across, no gulf at all for any of us, a trifle for an athlete like Casarotto. The far lip had broken away as he has stepped out that slightly longer step, stepped out for the last time, on the last crevasse on K2. You could see where it had broken. We stood about as a grey day dawned exchanging the sort of trifles that men do when they are confronted by irrefutable evidence that their game is lethal. Two things killed Casarotto; bad luck—and

149

climbing. Or was there a third thing? He'd been with Messner on K2 in 1979. Great things had been expected of him but he hadn't gone well. Messner later wrote a book, *'K2, Mountain of Mountains'*. In it he said 'I invited Renato Casarotto because I believed him at the time to be one of the ablest European climbers . . . Six weeks after the start of the expedition I wrote in my diary "I ought not to have brought along anyone for their climbing merit alone." The insight came too late. I felt let down by Renato as a climber'. Later in the same book Alessandro Gogna, co-author, writes 'Reinhold says point-blank that as four, we stand less chance of making it than as three—meaning without Renato. He waits for Renato to withdraw as he says that not everyone is equally strong at altitude, and it's no tragedy if someone doesn't make it. I have the impression that no-one else realised what Reinhold is getting at. But it's superfluous anyway. Renato has already given up.'

'At 23.00 Renato and I are in our tent. My rucksack is still unpacked. After a short silence, Renato speaks. It's a sour business. I admire Renato's inner strength; he convinces himself that there will be other chances to make up for things in the future. He says, as if he means it, that all things considered, this expedition has been a useful experience, opening his eyes to new perspectives and he has begun to learn how to relate to other people. All the same he hadn't expected the price to be so high. Secretly he had seen himself as a second Reinhold—that was all over now.'

Who dares say what killed Casarotto now?

We stopped at the Italian 8000-m camp on the way back to our tents. Goretta Casarotto was broken and sobbing, beyond grief, beyond reach. I looked the other way. A group of international climbers shuffled about finding tasks, wondering how to close this chapter. Quite suddenly Al-R made a speech. I wouldn't have dared and I admired his courage. I hadn't the faintest idea what made him do it but it was a fine dignified speech and fitted an impossible situation very well. Statesmanlike. I recall Al's equally fitting little speech at the Fullers' dinner months before. He's good at these things.

Back again at Base Camp at 0600 hours. Some 24 hours! There are eggs for breakfast—Abdul has returned while we were up the hill. Dozens of brews to rehydrate. Weather not good. Austrians and Koreans coming down so perhaps we may have made right decision in quitting the Abruzzi this time. Reckon we have the time and the inclination for one more go. The body of Liliane Barrard is discovered on the Godwin-Austen Glacier, swept there from high on K2 by avalanche. It is buried at Puchoz's grave.

Al Rouse now sole resident on the Abruzzi Close. He says it's spooky with all those bodies just over his shoulder. Jim-C says 'I shouldn't think Liliane will be down to see you, she's only just got there!' Bluebottles attracted by bodies are invading our camp. Not many days left and 'monsoonal' weather still with us. Rained this afternoon. Bev signs a death certificate for Casarotto. Jim-C gets a letter to say that his skiing piece has made ITV. Aid plans now to go it alone on the Abruzzi and to take no tent, rather to use those in situ. Phil and Al-R horrify me by declaring that they haven't washed their hair since they began. Last mail chance. Austrians, Koreans and Tullis demand to know what our plans are. Hear that Dai Lampart's team didn't get up Gasherbrum IV. Wished they had—I liked their style and spontaneity; 'in the rash lustihead of their young powers'.

Ninth Week: 18th July–25th July

17th—19th July (Base Camp to Advance Base). Weather bad. Al-R and Phil argue. Phil decides to leave with Al-B who has dates to meet elsewhere. Al-R can remember exactly how many ropes he fixed but forgets how badly he was going. Says decision to change route wasn't his. There is still equipment to be collected at Advance Base and Camp 1. We go to Advance Base on foot. Big crevasses are opening. Pick up all the gear we can carry and burn what we can't. Collect the rebroadcasting solar panels.

20th July (Advance Base). Al-B and Phil leave for home at 5 am with 2 porters. Deaf between headphones, I miss an avalanche, thanks to Eric Clapton. Jim hand holds to film it; but to his irritation Kurt and Julie have a tripod at Puchoz grave and get the whole thing—a huge belch from Angelus—right across the valley. Begin packing up camp.

Poles for dinner. Aftab complains 'my colleague is in bed the bloody Balti bastard.'

22nd July (Advance Base). Cloudy.

23rd July (Advance Base). Rains. Al-R voices disappointment at those who have already gone home. We will go up to Camp 1 on the NW Ridge to get the remainder of our gear and tents tomorrow. Work out that if I'm still here at Base when porters arrive on 28th I'll have to go out with them to keep a contract I have for work with a TV company. There are 2 Koreans at the Abruzzi Advance Base, otherwise K2 is deserted.

24th July (Advance Base, Camp 1, Base Camp). Low mist. Set off at about 10.30 when weather clears up. At the last moment Aid says he's not coming. Al-R voices bitter disappoinment that Aid is not helping us to dismantle C1. And greater disappointment that Aid has announced that he intends to climb the Abruzzi alone because he is faster than we are and doesn't want to be held back. Al-R talks of contracts and job-descriptions for future expeditions. He seems not to understand that it is all part of a greater disappointment, a greater failure. We are all very tired as we approach Camp 1 having had no liquid or food all day. Some 'gnarly' crevasses have opened up. And there are disturbing thuds as we approach Camp 1, caused by the snow sagging suddenly. We are exhausted. Brew and strike camp. Ski down to the glacier unroped. Rope up for glacier; some comical performances while we remain on skis. We are late at the Ice Fall and it's getting dark. Wilkie decides to bivouac. Al-R and I continue in gloom. Bev is waiting with torch. We have visitors at Base—a girl from the Polish team, Dobroslawa, and the British Chogolisa team led by Andy Fanshawe. Great young lads—more of youth's 'prime vigour'; no hopes of fame or fortune, no posturing; nothing more than a love of climbing brings them here. Sit outside round a lamp chatting for hours.

25th July (Base Camp). The Chogolisa team (who have slept at our Base Camp) volunteer to go up to collect sacs (which Al and I dumped at the Ice Fall), skis and Wilkie as an acclimatization exercise. Al-R had gone to see Dobroslawa. She was to have gone up hill with the rest of the Polish SW Ridge team but decided not to when Al promised to do the Abruzzi with her. We worry about film and sponsors. Raining hard. Barometer low but we are still hopeful of anothe r go. Jim-C and Wilkie can't decide what to do after the 28th until Al-R makes up his mind what he is going to do. He's staying, he's not staying. He's climbing w th the Polish girl; he's not. A visiting Australian says the mulberries will be fir ished when we go out but that apricots will be in season.

26th July (Base Camp). Poor weather. We are discussing Al's behaviour after breakfast when he turns up. 'Just talking about you', we say.

'Nothing derogatory I hope.'

'All derogatory.'

'At least I know where I stand.' Al declares that he is now committed to climbing with Dobroslawa. He says he's made a promise; he can't break it. 'But what about your committment to this team, at least to Wilkie? He has always declared to stay.'

Big row. I tell Al-R that I think he's a fool. Al goes off to tent in tears. Jim-C follows to comfort him. But still there is no apology or commitment to Wilkie. Wilkie pulls out. Jim-C stays. Jim-C and Al-R plan to move to Polish Base Camp. We spend the day packing up but keep options open in case tomorrow is fine. It's sad packing without finishing with a good fight. There are midges at Base Camp now. Kurt and Julie come round. Kurt is making a film for German TV and is doggedly persevering. Julie says that she has to get back soon to prepare lecture tour. She is doing a book which, she says with disarming honesty, is about herself. A huge avalanche sweeps the Abruzzi. We give the Koreans a bottle of Champagne that we had bought long before, when hopes were bigger.

27th July (Base Camp). A dismal day. Woken by Wilkie stomping the quarter deck and muttering such inconsequences as whether the Gortex on Jim-C's tent is delaminating—at 6.30 am! 'Jackie will want to know if UV light delaminates Goretex', he claims. 'That's probably the last thing Jackie will want to know', counters Curran with commendable early morning wit. Al-R is an increasingly lonely, sad and pathetic figure—stalking about in white grandfather longjohns, white shorts over them, and duvet. Koreans visit with a video Kung Fu film. Stay for lunch. Three Australians visit. They have discovered a body on Broad Peak. No sign of porters by 7 pm. Poles are back down from the SW pillar. They say they will have one more go. Jim-C recounts a story of a friend of his who had visited a mortuary with the purpose of identifying the body of a dead climbing friend.

'He doesn't look too bad, does he?' he said to the undertaker.

'I've certainly seen him looking worse', the undertaker replied.

28th July (Base Camp). More dismal weather and a clamping fog. Porters arrive about 7 am. But only 13 instead of 28. Rambling discussion on what to do. Visit Strip to say goodbye to all and sundry. Al wanders about talking to himself. I have a dark thought that this was what Captain Quigg of the Cain might have been like. Seven more porters arrive 3 pm. Absolute chaos. Their leader is a crook. Says he's a Sirdar and won't carry a load but that he is to be paid for supervising. His men won't carry without him. Confrontation. In the end he says he'll co-operate for the price of a gift. We give him a Karrimat. He takes three. As the afternoon wears on more porters collect a load and leave. Aid, Wilkie and Bev depart, singly. I hang on until the last of the porters has collected his load; 28 in all. It's getting late. We are spiritually bankrupt. Bathos.

Labyrinthine Ways

'I fled Him, down the nights and down the days;
I fled Him, down the arches of the years;
I fled Him, down the labyrinthine ways
Of my own mind; and in the midst of tears
I hid from Him, and under running laughter.'

(*Hound of Heaven*, Francis Thompson)

'Yes, to dance beneath the diamond sky with one hand waving free . . .'

(Bob Dylan 1965)

I hate goodbyes and had been thinking of leaving with Aid, Wilkie and Bev before Al came back from The Strip. But I couldn't; too much had gone wrong to quit without a cheerio. I hung around. At last, about four in the afternoon, Al appeared looking younger and less careworn than at any time in the last three months. The team, the porters, the loads, Base Camp—they'd all gone and with them much of his own burden. He was almost his old chirpy self, ringmaster once more, albeit of a much smaller circus. Perhaps his new audience would be more appreciative. Jim was standing with him.

'See you Jim.'

'See you mate, and don't forget those letters and phone calls'. I had been entrusted with a handful of letters to post, and a list of phone calls to make on his behalf.

'Don't worry. See you Al. Good luck. I hope you get up the damn thing.' I managed to mean it all.

'See you JB.'

I shouldered my rucksack and set off back down the glacier that we had walked up those months before, eyes wide and big with hope. Now hope had to be postponed. It would seep again, well-up maybe, but some other time, some other place. Not here, not this year, perhaps never *here* again. I hadn't asked myself if I wanted to come back, or if I had, I hadn't answered, but there was nothing now for hope and so it was postponed.

The parting was an unsatisfactory sorrow. I was pleased to be going, sad to be leaving. I hated leaving a three-month job unfinished but I had work with a TV company to get back to and the first cash in three months. That was justification wasn't it? Well wasn't it? But I envied Al his staying and his being able to stay, even though, had I been really honest with myself, the same choice was mine. I admired Al's determination to finish the job. I admired Curran too. He had no hope of getting much above twenty thousand feet—and probably no desire to go that high—but he had come to make a film and while there was chance of some summit footage he thought his place of duty to be K2. And I think there was more. He was a close and loyal friend of Al's and he saw that Al needed a mate, now more than ever. So Jim quietly and determinedly stayed on. In some ways, he was in an enviable position. He had taken unpaid leave of absence from Bristol Polytechnic in order to join the expedition but now his summer vacation had begun so, ironically, he was being paid again.

'Oh good', he had said one morning about three days previously. 'My holiday starts today, I'm getting paid again!'

'Bloody teachers. What difference does it make? You were on strike before!'

I set off towards Chogolisa without looking back until I could be sure that Jim and Al had been lost to view: a final glance, a final wave would have made a terrible dent in the thin shell I had grown around my conscience. The views about were less spectacular than the same scenes on the walk-in. Three months accustoms the mind and eye to most things and now Broad Peak, the Gasherbrums, Chogolisa, were merely mountains on which mortals had trod this summer long. Not so much that they had shrunk; rather that imagination's scale had grown, and the mind had recalibrated—as a mind must. I walked fast, jogged and trotted to catch the others, but the glacier was so black with stones now, that an army could have been hidden there and I wouldn't have known. I overtook Aftab, crucified under his cross of spoils, Abdul loyally walking at half-speed with him. 'See you at Concordia', they said as I left them behind. Thoughts crowded in but I blasted them away with rock music from a Walkman that Jim had loaned me. I didn't want to think. I had to go home; there was no turning. I needed to earn that cash. Didn't I?

I trotted across the foot of Broad Peak and past the German, Yugoslav and Australian camps. 'G'diy, G'diy', but no Aid or Dave or Bev.

Two full sides of Fleetwood Mac's 'Rumours' later I came to Concordia, which, I had forgotten, is miles wide. There was no snow, no tracks. I stood on a rock in a vast Force 12 rubble sea and shouted at all Concordia for Aid and Wilkie and Bev. There was no reply, no echo. The shout was too small and the place too big to be bothered. In the end, as darkness grew, I took out my sleeping bag and lay down, wonderfully alone in this biggest of bivouacs. But the content was shortlived and before long thoughts crowded in again and introspection and sleep skirmished in equal struggle. The next morning I woke from a half-sleep with no conclusions to carry into a bleary day.

I was away by four, at first light. After an hour I came upon a gaggle of porters brewing tea and then Aid and Bev. We all claimed to have spent the night at Concordia. Aid was surprised to find that Wilkie was not with me. No one had seen him since we'd left Base Camp the day before. We debated what we should do while Aftab failed to coax a flame from any of the stoves that we had brought for the walk out. It was well over twelve hours since I had drunk anything and I was gasping for liquid. Just then a Balti who had been brewing tea on a few twigs—bits of Paiyu I imagined—recognised my thirst and with a great rascally grin offered me a pour from his pot. I took as much as my conscience would allow—which wasn't anyting like the quantity my thirst was asking—and thanked him. We both grinned, forging a small bond between us—and thereafter grinned whenever our eyes met, all the way home to Dassu. Not for the first time I was puzzled how the men from this area had earned such a reputation for recalcitrance, strikes and bloody mindedness.

Aid and I retraced our steps to my Concordia of the previous night to look for Wilkie. We looked fearfully into the great black-sided water-filled holes, often hundreds of feet across and at least as deep, searching for some sign of Dave. It was not inconceivable that he'd fallen into one in the darkness. At length we gave up and while Aid made his way back I stopped to gaze, racked with inner torment, at a K2 that rose cleaner and sharper than ever it had these past two months, into a cloudless blue sky. Should I go back? It was a ridiculous notion but I thought it all the same—and more than once. I took some photographs and turned away for the last time.

Later there was a stunning view of the Muztagh Tower looking like a Walt Disney mountain, but between setting down my rucksack and extracting my camera, tumultuous clouds rolled quickly over it and it had gone. We were slightly cheered by those clouds and the bad weather that appeared to be following them for they all meant that this wasn't a climbing day. The clouds were a particular relief for me. Today was the last possible day that I could have embarked on the Abruzzi, climbed to the top and back, sprinted to Skardu, taken the first plane to Islamabad, caught an immediate connection back to Britain and made it all in time for the TV job. Now that that possibility had gone I felt justified, vindicated. My conscience cleared, even as the view clouded over. Al would probably be hard on our heels. Certainly, we reasoned, he would not be setting out for the hill today.

We stopped at Gore, now black like all the rest and sweltering in a bake of hot stones and blown over with a summer population of flies. Abdul, lovely Abdul, was there before us and we were welcomed with a big brown brew of tea. Never was tea more welcome.

Other teams from other mountains drifted by in general retreat. One, an Austrian, stopped for a chat. He looked fresher than a man who'd been toiling on big mountains should and I remarked on it. Yes, he said, he'd been at Broad Peak Base Camp for only a week when, during a preliminary recce, he'd come up against a glacial stream. For reasons which he didn't explain and which didn't seem worth pursuing, he'd apparently elected to throw his boots to the far bank rather than carry them. They never made it and he'd had to watch as they sank out of sight. Now he was going home. It seemed strange to me that he somehow couldn't have cobbled a spare pair from somewhere, or that he wasn't more angry. But he was philosophical about it.

'Maybe he'd read that Zen book of yours.' I said, pulling Aid's leg.

Along the broken trail to Urdukas Aid related how Al had one day announced to the A-Team, while the B-Team were on the hill that they, the A-Team, would be awarded the first summit bid because they had done the most work. It seemed to me to be a curiously divisive way to climb a mountain and it made me sad to hear it because it reminded me of all that squandered hope, and made vanity of all those dreams: dreams which now embarrass the inward mind. And considering that Al's promise must have been made somewhere below 7,300 metres it was somewhat premature too.

We reached Urdukas around four in the afternoon. It looked like an oasis, a patchwork of impossibly green grass made greener to eyes that had grown stale on black and white. There were bushes and flowers and improbable roses and the scents and the smells of all those things. It was wonderful.

The Duke's ledges were all taken, fully occupied with a retreating German team, so that we were given no choice but to descend a hundred feet to the glacier and there to carve a flat spot for the night.

Aid and I lay around admiring views, only half-glimpsed those months before, of the famous Baltoro backcloth—the Cathedrals, Trango, Paiyu Peak and all the rest—and I wondered aloud what on earth had happened to Wilkie.

'Musta fallen down a hole after all!' laughed Aid.

Then there he was, up there in the platforms amongst the emerald green, sniffing about for a spot big enough to lie on. We called to him and waved and he started down. He was an altogether unprepossessing sight in voluminous grey nylon running shorts into which were tucked, not very successfully, a shirt that looked as if it had once been raw silk but that was now considerably overdone, the kind of shirt that looked lost without its coat and tie; a gentleman's shirt. A white sun hat, well pulled down, sat on his head and above the lot an umbrella hovered. It gave Wilkie shade but not shade enough to hide the red blotchy wounds that he'd inflicted on himself with a blunt razor a few days before when removing the best, but by no means entire part, of two months' growth of beard. Not at all a prepossessing sight. But he was chirpy as could be.

'Hey we thought we'd lost you Wilkie.'

'Yes. Must have missed you. Fabulous here though.'

Wilkie loved mountains, practically lived for them, and I knew it had grieved him to be effectively denied a second go at the Abruzzi by Al's 'labyrinthine ways'. Later, when we were home, I asked him what his thoughts had been as we walked away from K2. He wrote;

'I had been committed to stay on for the Abruzzi till the end. But sadly, Al had made that impossible, so I was obliged to leave with the others. The continuing unsettled weather made the departure from Base Camp a bit easier to take. Needless to say, soon after we left, the weather changed to perfect. This stirred my mind to a chaos of conflicting thoughts and emotions, the dominant ones being black feelings of envy and resentment towards Al — which then led to a counter-current of guilt that I should be so uncharitable. As the walk-out ended, so did the good weather, after 4 days. Another morning of endless blue gave way to a mackerel-skyed afternoon, and an evening jeep drive to Skardu in glowering clouds and a gathering dust storm. Next day, it was raining in Skardu. The ensuing drive to Islamabad lasted 4 days as road

and bridges were engulfed by rain-washed mud slides. Once again, this changed weather had its effect on my mental state. I had a premonition of disaster. The good weather appeared to have lasted long enough to get high on the mountain, or reach the top, but to get down? From 100 miles distant, the change had been rapid, total and enduring: a well scripted setting for tragedy. Such speculations also had their rebound: were they rational or brought on by malevolent wishes?'

A little later, Aftab tottered in, Abdul scampering at his side. Aftab looked exhausted. He'd quit Base Camp weighed down by booty and the best part of the contents of the kitchen tent, including tables, folding chairs and a horrid plastic bowl that passed for the kitchen sink (and he would have had a go at taking the tent itself, had we not promised it to another climbing team). Faithful Abdul, no mean pillager himself, but blessed with build the equal of his acquisitions, had taken on board all that Aftab had jettisoned along the way, so that by Urdukas he carried an Ideal Home exhibition on his back, a boogie-box in one hand and most of Aftab in the other. Abdul, grinning as he saw us, dropped his burdens to the ground and rustled up a cup of tea in about the same time that it took Aftab to fall asleep. Next day Aftab hired his own porter to carry his plunder.

The sunset was terrific. It was still good to be among these mountains. Lying in the tent the next morning savouring a vast mug of tea that Abdul had cheerfully pushed through the door twenty minutes before, I overheard Aid, who had risen earlier, talking with one of the porters.

'You carry this too. On top.' Aid said.

'No, too heavy.'

'But you Balti, you strong.'

'You stronger, you K2.'

There was no answer.

The path to Lilligo was broken, bouldered, dusty and very hot. Yet here was a rose bush seven feet tall and in full bloom, surviving—flourishing. Before Lilligo we encountered a German team walking in to Gasherbrum II—one of the 8,000-metre dwarfs down the road from K2—followed by a French team lying disconsolate on a patch of sand by a lovely stream on the Baltoro's flank. They had an injured girl among them and were waiting for a helicopter to fly her out. They had been waiting there five days.

The stream, lovely as it was, presented an obstacle. It was gathering power and width by the minute as the sun's melt fed it. Aid pronounced it unfordable and set off upstream to find a crossing point. As I prevaricated, Ali, one of the Ovetts among our Baltis, dashed into the torrent with his double load—60 kg (for which he earned double)—and waded the thing with ease, though it was waist deep. Then, dumping his burden at the far bank, he returned to take me by the arm and half-escort, half-carry me over and set me down in safety. I was as grateful as I was impressed. Later, as we were waiting for Aid to reappear Ali turned to me, and pointing at my Karrimat asked:

'Baksheesh, Dassu?'

I replied, 'Baksheesh now.' He looked grateful. Maybe he was also impressed, but that night, my bones hard on the Karakoram's floor, I was to regret my generosity.

At last, a good half hour after he'd departed, Aid reappeared.

'Hey man, you're not goin' to believe this but crossing upstream I just passed a group of trekkers.'

'And I suppose they were streaked-blonde Swedish girls.'

'No, Californians.'

Wilkie wanted to know what they looked like. Aid gave the question a moment's thought then said:

'Dunno, they all had shorts on.'

Wilkie spent the rest of the day thinking about that.

We went on to Lilligo, the place of that orographical opera two months before, and arrived there about mid-day. We took a fly-blown siesta, simmering gently under parasols until, unable to bear this sweating idleness longer, we set sore foot for Paiyu. We were going downhill and losing thousands of feet a day, but you wouldn't have thought it because for every down there seemed to be an equal up. Al had said as much on the way in. 'It's all uphill on the way down', he'd said. And of course we hadn't believed him. But it had proved to be one of his more accurate exaggerations.

I was overheating and my rucksack was beginning to feel overheavy. It must have been all of thirty pounds. Then there it was—the wisp of Paiyu wood, not yet entirely plucked, green against the ochre hillside and still clinging, clinging on to the damp crutch of that frail stream.

I sat on a boulder to rest, to gaze, and railed ridiculously against the sun's scorch. Just then an old porter, about 50 years old, no more than four foot six and all of that rags and bone, scuttled by in that curious quick-stepping shuffle that over-loaded men adopt to stop their knees from buckling. His head was bent to his chest and his load continued upwards from where the head should have been for some distance. On the top were tied his own things, a pot and woollen rag that might, just might, have once been a blanket. He shuffled and grunted with the effort. As he passed I could see that he was a simpleton: the village idiot. He smiled and coughed a chirpy 'Salam'. 'Salam a lekud', I replied with a grin that I also hoped he would see, chin half way to his knees as it was. But he'd seen it all right, pointed to my parasol and asked 'Baksheesh, Dassu?' Some idiot. He got it sooner than that.

We had always thought of Dassu as the beginning of the living world, but, now that everything we owned was the subject of a 'Baksheesh Dassu?' request, we were beginning to feel that that fetid little place might actually be the end of it.

A descent began at last, down the snout of the mighty Baltoro, toward the desert of the Braldu: Baltoro dust for Braldu dust. The Cathedrals, the Trango Towers and Paiyu Peak were falling abaft.

They had looked sharp, lucent and pure from Urdukas in the morning but now they were hazy, dull and disappearing into clouds that boiled up the valley towards—towards K2. It had been the same every day, tidy forenoons, very untidy afternoons. We wondered how far up they boiled, those clouds, and worried lest they simmered around the corner to K2. And what if Al had gone on the hill? No, he'd soon be catching us. Surely he would.

159

For the last few miles to Paiyu we plodded along the dry earthen bank of the nascent Braldu river spewing from the snout of the Baltoro. The bank was a hundred feet high in places, a hundred feet of vertical crumbling earth. At one place, where the path ran about a yard from the edge on my left, I noticed, just another yard to my right, a great crack several feet wide and too dark to see its depth. This slice of the Karakoram was destined for Karachi beach. I stepped to the right, over the crack and onto terra-more-firma, and walked on a hundred yards, from where, looking back, I saw that the slice was vastly undercut as if cantilevered on a hinge of dust. It was hard to see what kept it there. But I was too dulled by heat and thirst to give the phenomenon or its certain—and imminent—fate a second thought.

Paiyu at last. Abdul offered me a swill of his water in a very dirty bottle. I declined, pretending that I wasn't thirsty. I doubt that I was convincing. Next he unfolded a rag and proffered a chunk of what was certainly the least appetizing paratta I had ever seen. I was touched by his generosity though and, already embarrassed by my earlier refusal, took it from the rag and forced it, as Abdul watched for reaction, straight to my mouth. I took as small a bite as I felt would pass for politeness and feigning interesting in a porter's load that had been set down a few yards away, moved over to smuggle the rest of the paratta to a pocket, to be disposed of later.

Later a clutch of porters who had left K2 Base Camp the day after us came in bearing gear surplus to Julie's and Kurt's plans. Again we wondered if Julie and Kurt were following, and if they were, how far behind.

Bev counted the money. We had five thousand rupees with which to pay off our porters, hire a jeep and tractors for the Dassu-to-Skardu leg and a lorry or bus for the journey from Skardu to Islamabad, pay Abdul and Aftab their three months' wages, and feed ourselves. It didn't seem a lot. Bev said it wasn't enough. He was right in theory, but in practice money is an elastic thing.

Paiyu stank. I was glad to be gone at 3 the next morning. We were aiming to get the best part of the day's walk done before the sun really got going and the river swelled. But it wasn't soon enough. About eight o'clock Aid and I who, lightly loaded, had been strolling along somewhere near the front of our little caravan, stopped on a sandy spit for a wash. I laundered my tee-shirt, pants and shorts and had to seek out protective shade while they dried on a rock. In ten minutes they were as dry as dust. Afterwards we came across a group of young doctors from Guy's Hospital, their hopes on Lobsang Spire, a pinnacle as commonplace on the Baltoro as it would have been remarkable anywhere else. Was it far to Paiyu, they wanted to know. 'Depends what you mean by far', Aid replied with that coded caution of Northern folk. It was uncharacteristic of him for he was half-American now and more usually as open-hearted as Americans tend to be. An atavistic lapse perhaps, but anyhow one which he soon corrected with a deluge of advice, information and good-natured chit-chat. A pretty girl who had joined their number might have been responsible for the cordial conversion.

By eleven we were being steadily shrivelled by a wind that must have blown straight from Hell's front gate. We stepped behind an enormous boulder to find its shade already occupied by a dozen porters. They made room for us and we sat

160

together for half an hour before anyone made a move. I was relieved to see that the natives were suffering from the heat as badly as we foreigners. It made me feel better.

We had thought when we set out that morning that we might get to Askole that night. But the sun had different ideas. Jola was a good place to stop Abdul said, and it had water, good clean spring water. Jola, a name given to a patch of dust no more distinguishable than any other, was gained by means of the Jola Bridge, though to call it a bridge was as great an optimism as Icarus' bid for the sun. The bridge consisted of a single cable strung across the Panmar River, which is technically a tributary of the Braldu, but actually a mighty tumult of its own. From this single cable an orange-box-like contraption was suspended by means of a pulley and a hank of plainly ancient wire. One at a time a porter and his load squeezed into the box which would be released to run down into the bottom of the vee of the cable at the middle of the river and some twenty feet above it. (Al had warned that the bridge was five hundred feet above the river, which claim Wilkie, our second mathematician, now said was 'an exaggeration by a Rouse-factor of twenty five'. We were accustomed to applying only a factor of ten to Al's estimations.) From here the orange box was pulled, uphill now, to the far bank where the porter, whose thoughts would have been exclusively of Allah, disembarked. It was an exhilarating little adventure and one for which the keeper of the bridge exacted a toll of 8 rupees per passenger—if passenger is the word. Aviator might be better.

Abdul was as good as his word. Half a mile from the Jola Bridge on the track to Askole there was a limpid brook bubbling out of the rocks. More, it was a flat, fresh-smelling site with an arresting view of Bakor Das towering into the sky—arresting that is even by Baltoro's high standards—and, so far as I can find, not yet climbed, though it deserves to be. But above all, the site was in the shade and by evening, comparatively cool. This was luxury indeed. The world seemed, quite suddenly, a softer, kinder place. We decided that we might as well complete the comfort and, I think without asking Aftab's permission, untied what were now *his* table and *his* chairs from their bundles and set them up for a supper fit for kings. Aftab, catching the mood, produced his finest curry and we ate as hungry men should. It was the best evening for months and balm on my bitterness. We talked long after the meal and talked easily, lightly. Everyone had a story. The chat turned from mountaineering to medicine to mountaineering medicine and so to pulmonary oedema (an altitude-related illness) of which Bev had made something of a study. All mountaineers have a practical interest in the illness (and its close relative cerebral oedema) and each of us held forth for longer than our knowledge of the subject could possibly warrant. Aid's last word was the very essence of northern practicality. He recalled:

'Met this Japanese lass once, 'bout 18,000 feet over Khumbu way. She was sufferin' from pulmonary oedema. Real bad she was. Could see she was going to die. So I told her mates to get her down lower. And they argued. So I lost me rag a bit and said "Either get her down tonight or get paraffin up in the morning" ', adding by way of explanation, 'see, they burn bodies in Nepal.'

Later I sat looking at the stars and wondered what was beyond them and beyond that and beyond again, and chased my thoughts as far into that darkness as I dared. Introspection had begun in earnest; no particularly healthy thing. Mountaineers should stay roped to whatever sanity they can hitch their minds to. I remembered that there was a passage in the *Seven Pillars of Wisdom* about such star-wondering and determined to find it when I got home. Lawrence writes:

> 'When we see them all, there will be no night in heaven'.
> 'Why are the Westerners always wanting all?' said Auda, provokingly
> 'Behind our stars we can see God, who is not behind your millions'
> 'We want the world's end, Auda'. 'But that is God's,' complained Zaal, half angry. Mohammed would not have his subject turned. 'Are there men on these greater worlds?' he asked. 'God knows'. 'And has each the Prophet and heaven and hell?' Auda broke in on him. 'Lads, we know our districts, our camels, our women. The excess and the glory are to God. If the end of wisdom is to add star to star our foolishness is pleasing.'

I'm still not sure that I can understand Lawrence here but then, I couldn't understand the heaven, or the stars, or the beyond, that night at Jola either, the night I tried to throw my mind beyond the stars.

A very early start the next day got us to Askole before the sun scorched us again. The village was brighter than before and the poplars even more elegant. In fact it looked beautiful. Curious that, for I'm sure that apart from ripened crops and the always pleasing pastorale of harvest time, the place hadn't changed at all. Curious what sixty days in a wilderness do to eye and mind. The campsite, however, was worse than before, worse for the wear of dozens of expeditions and trekking parties. Where there had been some grass, now all was dust.

That afternoon was the hottest yet. We lazed, drank tea, drew up plans for the journey from Skardu to Islamabad, discarded them and drew others, reminisced and argued. Most of the porters had disappeared into the village. For some this was home. Others knew someone who lived here and had gone visiting. I spent an hour cleaning and cannabalising a bag of stoves in order to improve our cooking range. '£40,000 and one stove working', one of us had said with just a hint of bitterness. I succeeded in repairing a second, an MSR; positive turbo in the right hands, damp squib in the wrong hands; utterly lifeless in Balti hands.

'OK Abdul I've got another stove working, see how long it takes you to louse it up.'

He took me at my word and had it loused up in two brews. Sarcasm's just deserts perhaps. What was much worse was that half-way through my repair I had had an asinine argument with Aftab. I had need of some tools and remembered that about a week earlier I had loaned Aftab my Swiss Army knife. Since then I'd asked for it on a number of occasions but Aftab had always denied being able to find it. No matter. Now I asked more plainly and Aftab answered that he had thought it a gift. I grew angry and raised my voice. Then I grew angrier with myself for losing my temper with him. We had always got along well and now I had broken a bond more delicate to repair than any stove. Repairs of this sort take time. Later, when it was cooler, I said sorry with as much dignity as a ridiculous situation could allow. When Aftab replied, 'Sahib, I keep the knife?' I felt better. Well he always was a smart-arse.

With better reason I was angry again but this time kept it to myself. Two of our party had talked freely within earshot of Aftab, whose English was good, of wogs and coons and kafirs. I doubt that he was acquainted with the first two but the origin of the last was not so far away and I thought it certain that association and context would make the insulting nature of the others pretty plain—if not the insults themselves. But since Aftab showed no discomfort it seemed better not to risk causing any by dissenting.

During the afternoon two groups of British trekkers arrived and set up camp with greater efficiency than had characterised our laagers. I lay in the meagre shade of an old tree and eyed them with curiosity. Both groups were on their way to Concordia. I hoped that they would be as impressed with the place as I had been. They appeared to be of all ages and were clearly from many backgrounds. Indeed, one old lady was dressed in a sort of habit which set me wondering if she was a nun and what order was it that required such costume to be worn at Concordia. Then, scolding myself that the British must be the only race under the sun who would not walk ten yards to say hello to a compatriot in a foreign land, I got to my feet and went over. No, she wasn't a nun but wore this 'I Claudius' garb, as we had christened it, for comfort and coolness and because this was fundamental Islam where more usual hot-weather gear like shorts and tee shirt caused offence when worn by women. Bev came over to deliver a learned medical discourse on the perils of their way and Aid joined us to be friendly because that was his nature. The ten yards' haul through the sun turned out to be a profitable one. Both groups were equipped with huge vacuum-lined containers full of a cool fruit drink. When they offered me a drink I grabbed it, and a second, third and fourth—just about enough liquid to get back to my patch of shade.

A number of local entrepreneurs came to try to sell us prayer mats. None succeeded. Aid and Wilkie tried to sell the Hadji Mhadi a tarpaulin. They didn't succeed either.

That evening over dinner our conversation roamed over the usual topics: Al and what would be happening now on the mountain; our own plans from hereon; the chances of flying from Skardu to Islamabad; food, beer and sex—or was it sex, beer and food?

Wilkie was more bitter now that the weather appeared to be stable. He felt that should Al succeed then he would be obliged to 'tell all'. He also said that he thought Jim Curran could have played a more positive role in persuading Al to stick with his team—but that applied to us all. Only now did it strike me that no-one had tried to reason with Al or to persuade him from his advertised plan. At the time I had openly condemned both the plan and Al, but that was hardly the same thing as reasoning; hardly a useful thing. Bev was cross with Al rather than bitter. He would have stayed too so that, though Al's defection had not cost him a chance of the top, he was leaving with a feeling that his job was not fully done. At one point, very cross, he said that he'd make sure that Al never led another major expedition. We weren't to know how small our querulousness was later to seem, how shaming our petty whinges.

The best immediate plan came from Ali, the lad with the Olympic legs and the double cargo. He suggested that he and his brother, who was travelling light with only slightly heavier than regulation freight, should sprint the two-day stage, Askole to Dassu, in a day, so that they could have a jeep and tractor ready for our arrival. All this for a few tens of rupees and some kit in the way of baksheesh. Was he sure he could carry his double cargo that far that fast? 'Of course.' Had he not carried a double load all the way to Broad Peak Base Camp in half the normal time? It must have been an ancestor of this lad that had Kipling rabbiting on about:

> 'With that he whistled his only song, that dropped from a mountain crest—
> He trod the ling like a buck in spring, and he looked like a lance at rest.'

We readily sanctioned the plan. I wondered what the brothers Ali would do to an Olympic 1500-metre field. 'Not much', Bev said and broke a little Wilson-of-the-Wizard-romance with brutal fact—the last thing I needed. Then, warm to the discourse, Bev announced that he was thinking of writing a psychiatric profile as an appendix to the expedition report. The threat was too awful to contemplate. Our horror must have showed for Bev took his leave of our after-dinner parlez and went off to the village to hold surgery. Hours later he returned with shocking tales of grief and pain, and complaints that in the West would be quickly and easily remedied with hot water, aspirin and antibiotic but which, in Askhole, village of medieval hygiene, were but pre-ambles to short stories of certain death. As with most experienced physicians, years of practice had immunised Bev's emotions against another's suffering. I envied him his hardness—even if it was only superficial.

For breakfast on the 2nd August we ate fresh eggs: two apiece. They were wonderful and we went to work on them, strolling off through poplar, juniper and willow, and by fields dense with wheat, maize, potatoes and other vegetable crops. The fields were irrigated by a complexity of moats and channels that not only took water to the parched earth but fed energy to watermills on the way. I counted the grains on an ear of wheat—between six and eight—good farming. Indeed the whole agricultural system was a deal more sophisticated than you would expect of a shut community: they were surviving comfortably—and a little more—masters of their harsh environment, an autarchy.

For two hours we rambled pleasurably through this comparative bliss of shady lanes, terraced fields, babbling water and confident homesteads; civilising ourselves by degrees. On the way we splashed in the hot sulphur springs, leaner, sleeker, splashes than the tidal waves we had caused at the same place on the walk-in. Now we were eminently filmable, fit for any celluloid, but Curran had stayed, a self-declared 'refusnik' and there was no-one to record our metamorphosis.

A few miles further the valley pinched in, shaping itself for the infamous Braldu Gorge which lay not far ahead now. We wondered whether we would take the high or the low road. The first, a necessity when the river is high, climbs thousands of feet to skip the dangers of the gorge. The second stays so low that the Braldu is snatching at your heels. The low route can only be taken when the river is comparatively meek. In the event we followed our noses and any number of locals who claimed they knew the best way, and got the worst of both worlds, high and low.

By the time we arrived at the entrance to the Gorge it was ten o'clock and promising to be a very hot day. To begin with we took the high road and climbed nearly two thousand feet. By midday some of the porters had had enough. They found shade, squatted in it and said, in Balti to Abdul who passed it on to Aftab in Urdu who gave it to us in English, that they would not move again till the sun had gone. You could hardly blame them. The Gorge was stiflingly hot, the sun relentless, the land tinderbox dry. You had the feeling that if you lit a match the whole thing would burst into flame.

Sometimes when close to the banks of the Braldu, the river was so mighty that it threw up a following wind that swept and cooled us for yards. Walking in this windy corridor was tolerable. But any rise in the path took us above it and into a terrible heat.

The entire way was corrugated with nullahs—ravines cut by the tributary streams of the Braldu—that were nearly always at right angles so that we had to traverse every one, down to the bed, up to the crest. One nullah was particularly unappealing. It must have been close to 300 metres deep and the sides little more than steep banked mud slides: a very temporary bit of geography indeed. Down we went—fortunately perhaps with brains aboil and three parts insensible to the hazard—until at the bottom we reached a viscous sludge that served as stream. Then it was up again, a full thousand feet on the other side. By now most of the porters had found shade and taken refuge. Only a handful mad-dogged on with the Europeans. Now the path led across a loose 40° sand bank that sifted directly into a turbid Braldu, open mouthed and hungry, 60 metres below. Had it been a snow slope it would have been crampons and axes and maybe even second thoughts about ropes for porters but we were wearied beyond worry and pressed on anyhow. Did I have any water left, Wilkie wanted to know. I did and offered him the bottle. He took it and drained it. I was too thirsty to complain. Silence is a form of economy.

We arrived at the campsite at 4.30—the one of the first night on the walk-in with a two-plank bridge and no name. Abdul had assured us that there would be water but we could only find a puddle under a rock, half a brown-inch deep. We scooped it dry. Abdul hadn't arrived yet so we scouted for more but there was none. I returned to the scene of the puddle a little later. It was filling again. There must be a spring; frail and brown, but wet and what the hell. We bled it until it would bleed no more and then took our thirst to the Braldu. The water here was too turbid for even our thirst to consider so we manned the Katadyn filter pumps and half-cup by half-cup kept the thirst at bay: a sort of baling-out in reverse: you could never be sure whether you were getting ahead; the pumping demanded energy we were not sure we had. I eyed the sun's descent and wished it speed. It sank at six. Life was cool and wonderful in an instant. My limbs found energy that only a moment before had seemed lost forever. Eyes found renewed beauty in the softened light and pastelled colours. Mountains and nature were lovely now, only minutes after being hateful: fickle nature, affections more fickle. The shade was long and I thought of hope and life and love.

Abdul strolled in late and cheerful and in no time had a brew bubbling over dung and sticks—having forsaken a hundred pounds' worth of stove for this alternative, faster, technology. In no time we were all joshing and persiflage once more. Bev tuned into a report of the Commonwealth Games. We listened to an hysterical commentary on the finish of the men's 400 metres final. It all seemed an irrelevance, a small thing to be shouting so loudly about. But then, what of us, what of our own irrelevance, our own

> 'Tomorrow, and tomorrow, and tomorrow,
> Creeps in this petty pace from day to day,
> To the last syllable of recorded time;
> And all our yesterdays have lighted fools
> The way to dusty death. Out, out brief candle!
> Life's but a walking shadow, a poor player
> That struts and frets his hour upon the stage,
> And then is heard no more; it is a tale
> Told by an idiot, full of sound and fury,
> Signifying nothing.
>
> (*Macbeth:* Act V Sc.v, W. Shakespeare)

The porters came in at all hours, some not 'till midnight. Ours had been a ten-hour day, theirs much longer. We lay about, drinking tea and fretting that the weather now seemed perfect. Should we have stayed? Could we have stayed? Where was Al now? On his way up, no doubt. No doubt.

One of the porters offered me a chunk of his chapatti—Balti bread as Aftab called it. It looked appetisingly crispy and I took it. To our mutual and manifest delight I found it so delicious that misgivings about hygiene were drowned in succulence.

Some Italians came down very late with their porters. Aid chatted to them, speaking, to my amusement, in the same broken English that he used to address the porters. Then I overheard the Italians themselves speaking to their porters in the exact same broken and shortened language. Was this a new form of pidgin, a sort of anglo-esperanto brewed in Baltistan? No doubt as long as language remains a vehicle for the conveyance of ideas and thoughts, expediency and simplicity will triumph over syntax. So that, for Baltis, Balti-Brits, Balti-Italians and all Euro-Baltis 'down-going' will always be preferred to 'going down', 'down-side' to below, 'top-side' to above, and 'what time Dassu arriving?' to 'at what time do you expect to arrive in Dassu?'

The next morning, at four, we stormed up the five-hundred feet of steep path to the jeep track that led, at last, to Dassu. It was great to be swift and fit in the cool. The track itself was easy walking and only downhill now. We stopped at the first village for breakfast which we bought from a house that doubled as the local cafe. We feasted on hard-boiled eggs and parattas from the cafe, tea courtesy of Abdul, and from the tree that we sat against, apricots enough for a glutton, almost enough for Wilkie and a few too many for his digestion. He spent most of the next two days with his trousers round his ankles. Once, his trousers and ankles didn't meet soon enough. Human nature being what it is the rest of us found humour in his discomfort. Wilkie found none.

About four eggs later the Italians' Liaison Officer joined us. His brother was the station-master at Pinner in Greater London and he wanted to know, very reasonably, what Pinner was like and where in the hierarchy of British life stood a station-master. None of us had the least idea, or the imagination to furnish an invention and he went on to Dassu disappointed.

The walking was very pleasant. The villages, fields of corn and orchards now had a slightly Van Gogh look about them; a child-like brushful look. Perhaps it was because we had been starved of colour for so long, perhaps we were now less pre-occupied than on the way in, perhaps we had changed, but whatever the reason the colours splashed riotously on the eye and mind, filling hungry senses.

Not long after breakfast we were greeted by an army patrol that we learned comprised mainly trainee military doctors. They were uniformly polite and greeted us in perfect, unaccented English with cries of, 'How are you?' and, 'Are you well?', shaking our hands as they did so. They were going to camp on the Baltoro as part of their military training. Their cheerfulness and zest reminded me of my own days as a young officer as did the uniform, the accents, the manners and the unbounded hope in which they travelled. The world may be 'wondrous large from marge to marge' but mankind is bound by likenesses—and a good thing too.

Just before Dassu as we were stepping over a stile, Aid and I were stopped by two of our porters. These two were obviously, delightedly and abandonly gay (as we must say these days). Not just because they held hands the day long—that affectation is not uncommon in Pakistan or indeed in many of the Muslim countries—not just because they blew air into their words as they spoke in a high, lisping pitch, but because they were so openly happy—and gay.

I was about to go over the stile when one of them pointed first at my mouth and then, and with more enthusiasm than I considered decent, at his crutch. He repeated the gesture several times until in some embarassment, I turned to Aid for help. 'Hey Aid, what's this bugger trying to tell me?' I pleaded with no thought for the literal. 'He's telling you that he's pissing blood', he said as if it was the most obvious thing in the world. I must have looked confused. 'He's pointing at your scarf. It's red. That's blood. And at his parts. He's bleeding. 'sobvious init.' Might have been to him but as far as I was concerned it had been a close run thing.

About a mile before Dassu we were swung over the Braldu on another wire-guided soap box, a two seater this time. We crossed without incident. The weather was perfect again and it grew hot, then very hot, until at last, Dassu brought relief of sorts. A minor official opened the Rest House for us, showing the Italian L.O. to a separate and senior room and addressing him as Sahib, us as nothing. The quaintly colonially phrased regulations looked down on us from the wall, gently mocking, I felt. Aid persuaded us to go for lunch at a local cafe. It was a dismal place, filthy, fetid and flyblown noticeably so after two comparatively sterile months. A little later we walked up to the centre of the village where a collection of tractors and jeeps awaited us. The brothers Ali had done their work well. They stood there grinning all over in their administrative triumph, their feat of endurance making no mark on their easy smiles, smiles that said they were genuinely pleased to see us and not only because it was pay day.

But pay day, at least for some, looked less than a certainty. At Base Camp, Al had calculated the cost of the walk-out and had given Bev that amount plus 'a little extra' to get us from Skardu to Islamabad. It soon became apparent that he'd calculated too precisely—and that he had judged the walk-out a day short into the bargain. And the 'little extra' wasn't going to be enough to get us to Islamabad either.

To begin with things went fairly well. From each porter in turn, Aid, using his best Anglo-Balti, elicited a name which he called to Bev. In a succession of minor miracles of mental arithmetic Bev calculated what the fellow had carried and for how long and, thereby, how much we owed him. From a stuff bag that held the expedition's entire budget I issued the sum that Bev had authorised. The porters all asked for baksheesh but none took offence when it was refused—as if it was a ritual that had to be played out.

But very soon it began to look as if the stuff bag was diminishing more rapidly than the queue. What would we do if we ran out of rupees? There'd be riot. Or we'd be jailed. Or both.

And both looked a certainty when the Italians' L.O. chose that moment to ask how much we were paying. We told him. But that was not enough he said, it was a whole day's pay too little. The rules stated (and he had them handy) that two rest days were mandatory during the walk-out. We had allowed only for one. Now we *were* in trouble. Porters who had already happily departed were recalled and the process begun again, the routine request for baksheesh included. Again they accepted our refusal and again scuttled away, no happier than before, but now with at least 1,300 rupees apiece, money enough for many years of living as high as you can in Baltistan. Somehow we'd made it—with 73 rupees to spare; rupees which had to finance us as far as Islamabad.

The tractor and a trailer were loaded to the gunwhales and well beyond; 27 separate porter loads improbably stacked, impossibly piled; high even by local standards. It lurched off at an unsteady chug. We climbed aboard the jeep, we being Bev, Aid, Aftab, myself, 3 Italians, the driver and his mate and a pile of gear we hadn't been able to squeeze onto the tractor or trailer. The L.O. was about to board too when he became involved in a heated argument with his Sirdar, a Hunza and a tall, dignified and handsome man. The argument flamed into altercation and then exploded into abuse. Aftab gave us a running commentary. The argument was over money. The L.O. was accusing the Hunza of taking a cut of the fee for the hire of the jeep. The Hunza denied it. The L.O. shouted that it was disgraceful that he, the Hunza, should cheat the Englishmen. I wondered how much of it was show, a sort of compensation for finding fault—fairly found though it most certainly was—with our porter payments. It was all slightly embarrassing. We just wanted to get on, get going, get home. We were beyond caring about a few rupees.

The L.O. was overacting, overplaying his hand, shouting loudly now. And as shouters always do he was losing ground and face; making a fool of himself—and, by association, of us. Then it grew very ugly. The L.O. seized a ski-stick and to my open-mouthed horror set it about the Hunza with cruel sweeping blows. The sweeps were long in coming, such was their arc, and they kept coming, and the Hunza must have seen that first one swinging in, or if not, certainly the second and third—and all the rest. But he made no move to duck, not the first nor those that followed; neither ducked nor flinched, but stood ramrod straight—in any other circumstances almost elegant—and stared with the coldest eyes I have ever seen into the rage-ugly face of his assailant. Only when the stick was bent nearly to right angles did the beating cease. Only then did the Sirdar move. Surely he would hit the L.O. I hoped he would pole-axe him with a mighty punch. But he turned and walked away, all the anger, injury and insult in his eyes. We had, all of us, watched in frozen immobility, unable or unwilling to intervene. There were too many cultural and religious barriers to be vaulted between the jeep and the crime to be all sorted out in the seconds that that foul act had lasted. At last I jumped from the jeep, ran to the Sirdar and held out my hand and apologised. It was a pathetic, a ridiculous gesture, but I could find no other in my reservoir of experience, in my catalogue of responses. But pathetic, ridiculous, or not he accepted. He was cool, but the eyes burned. I was shocked and saddened. The L.O. stepped into the front of the jeep and we drove away across the dusty desert plateau toward Shigar.

The road to Shigar lay between luxuriant harvest crops and orchards, and was overhung, with trees, many heavy with ripe apricots. We played games, trying to grab bunches from the branches as we sped beneath. Sometimes these efforts were rewarded by a clutch of juicy fruit, sometimes by the stinging slap of a branch. Because of our number we were standing in the back of the jeep, squeezed up between the bars of the awning frame, and now, in these apricot avenues, we had to duck and weave as the lowest boughs threatened to remove our heads. After a while we became economical in the ducking, sparing in the weave; like a good boxer who evades only by the tiniest fraction, a miss being as good as a mile and many calories cheaper.

At the same cafe that had welcomed us on the way in we took tea and then onions and then, as our appetites made truce with the filth and the flies, dal and curried lamb and all sorts. Bev, Aid and I nibbled. Wilkie tucked in as if there might be none tomorrow. A few miles on he was retching and vomiting; apricots from way back to breakfast, dal from Dassu, all sorts from Shigar. Since he was now riding in the cab he was vomiting out of the window. Much of it splashed on those at the back. It was an unwholesome experience—if a new one.

We climbed out of the Vale of Shigar and onto a desert plateau again. As the night came down a strange warm wind got up, blowing sand and dust in spectral willy-willy across the loom of the lamps and on into darkness. Dots of light from tractors and jeeps twinkled briefly, and then were lost in the sweeping sand and sea of the night. The wind blew with an eerie sound, unreal, like the wind in a film; not quite right, but you knew what was meant. The storm grew wilder and the night more spectral as the headlights cut great arcs across Baltistan in their sweeping search for the desert track—often no more than a set of tyre marks in the sand. It was a weird night and I left with an impression rather than a picture.

Poor Wilkie got out for a monstrous vomit and then dropped to an urgent squat to vent a new complaint.

'What d'you reckon's wrong with Wilkie, Bev?'

Bev scratched, puckered and pursed: this was a diagnosis for which he would have to look to the very horizons of his vast experience. At length he had it: 'He's not well', he said, managing to look as if the decision had cost his intellect dear. It's a great comfort having an expedition doctor.

As the night grew wilder and weirder we asked aloud what the weather would be doing on K2 and wondered whether this storm would reach the mountain—it was blowing in that direction— and wondered and worried about Al. What was he doing? Where was he? How was he?

We dropped from the desert and drove into Skardu. There was no sign of life and no lights. The town was deserted. The only sounds were the roar of that hot wind, the occasional crash as something blew over, the barking of a dog. A cardboard box blew along the road and across the headlights but I didn't catch the sound of it, the wind was the louder noise. It wasn't late, eight o'clock or so. It was odd that no-one was abroad—Skardu is usually a bustling place—odd that nothing stirred save that wind. Did I imagine then that there was badness about, evil in the air? Or are these later, fancier thoughts?

At the K2 Motel we found out why the place was deserted. There had been a riot that day because a man from out of town had knifed and killed a Skardu man. It was the only murder that anyone could remember, and the first riot. The rioters had torn away or burnt the best part of the bazaar. Folk were uneasy, no-one knew what was going to happen next. A general strike had been declared and the town placed under curfew. Nothing like it had ever happened in Baltistan before, the motel manager told us, shaking his head sorrowfully. He was sorry, there was no food for us. The bazaar was burned and no supplies were getting through because of the strike. There were no planes or buses either. All were on strike.

We were back in the world. How about a cold Coke? There was no Coke and anyway no electricity because of the strike. One of us complained that any civilised place would have cold Coke, which later seemed a strange measure of civilisation. The manager gave Bev a pile of mail that had gathered—presumably since Al Burgess and Phil had left— and as Bev began to sift through it, Aid and I, noticing that Wilkie wasn't with us, went to find him. We found him on the banks of the Indus. He had been very sick and was still very ill. He was not a pretty sight.

We were shown a room. Wilkie cleaned himself up in cold water and lay down to sleep while the rest of us went to the dining room where the manager, industrous as ever, had conjured up a fairly respectable meal out of nowhere. As we were finishing he somehow brought to life his video and a showing of 'Alien' began. I stumbled from the room, exhausted by the long day and no longer certain what world I was in. 'Alien'! A birthday card from my boys reminded me of the world I wanted most and I sat on the lawn in the hot wind reading over and over the simple kind words that my headtorch illuminated. 'Happy Birthday Dad from Joseph and (in a greater scrawl) John Mark'. I took out my sleeping bag, unzipped it, spread it on the lawn, and lay down to sleep—my inward eye focusing in two directions: Al and K2; and home.

It had been an odd day. I drifted from it into an unhappy, restless sleep.

I awoke the next morning, startled by a distant musserein and stirred by an early sun, to find myself next to an enormously fat girl, German as she turned out, who appeared to have grown there in the night. She was immensely ugly and snored. The wind had stopped and had she not been there and not been snoring it would have been a wonderful awakening. But as she was, it seemed for sleepy seconds that the world was growing curiouser and curiouser and that this might be Alice's Wonderland. I stood up, still in my shorts, and stretched and yawned to shake off the sleep. The view was wonderful, so was the morning. Over there, to the north somewhere, was K2 and Al and Jim. As the world began to right itself, I found something near to an even keel.

Aftab had slept on the lawn too, though whereas I had chosen to do so, preferring the space and sky to a crowded room, he had been banished there by Pakistan's own self-inflicted apartheid that separates western tourists' sensibilities from the facts of Eastern life. (I remembered a similar system self-inflicted in Malindi in Kenya years before and considered for a moment that Marx might be right after all; that the greatest god was economics.)

'Sleep well, Aftab?' I asked him as he stirred.

'No Mister John. I worry about our argument. Are you still angry with me?'

I apologised again, profusely and sincerely. And we were both happier for it.

Somehow the manager rustled up a breakfast and we ate loudly and long. Soon after, Agha, our erstwhile L.O. turned up. He had been languishing in Skardu for the past few weeks having been declared unfit for work at altitude by Bev. It was a declaration that afforded him a face-saving 'out', and saved us from more uneccessary hassle. At first I hardly recognised him in his traditional mufti of shalmar and qameez, though his whimpering, querulous voice betrayed him soon enough. Where were Al and Jim, he wanted to know. We answered that to the best of our knowledge they were on their way; would be here in a day or so. Agha readily accepted this explanation. He was anxious to wind-up the expedition and get home to Islamabad. It was about the most co-operative he'd been these three months. He too was happy to accept that since my name was still on the papers as the leader, I could attend the obligatory de-briefing at the ministry. He bade us cheerio and hotfooted it to the airport where he'd secured a flight on a military C130 aircraft—the only transport exempt from the strike. Just as he was leaving we remembered that we had loaned him 2,000 rupees to finance his wait in Skardu. He had 1,600 rupees left and we were solvent again. But we were stuck in Skardu until the dust of the civil disturbance had settled. It was a frustrating prospect.

The motel housed an interesting population. There was a young English lad of about seventeen making his way by thumb from England to Australia, a group of girls from Hong Kong who somehow contrived to look more incongruous here in the Far East than we occidentals, a German innkeeper on a trekking holiday and a team of Australian allsorts trekking and jesting and living a bit larger than life; Les Patersons to a man, but fancying themselves Crocodile Dundees.

As the morning wore on we prepared ourselves psychologically for a long seige. There was, after all, ample precedent. The climbing world abounds with tales of folk stranded for weeks in Skardu awaiting an aircraft, and though that was in the days before the road to Pakistan was built the strike had effectively closed that escape; we could find no one who was prepared to run the blockade. Early in the afternoon the manager appeared, beaming and helpful as ever. 'I have good news, the strike has been called off, but the road has been blocked by landslides.' It was difficult to see what precisely was good about this news but we thanked him for his solicitousness anyway.

At least Wilkie was looking better—and had recovered sufficiently to see the funny side of his earlier misfortune.

Abdul arrived on top of the tractor bringing our gear from Dassu. He had slept the night along the way. We busied ourselves unloading the trailer and tidying the loads. Abdul was immensely cheerful and somehow, somewhere, had changed from his Base Camp rags into his Sunday best shalmar and kurta. We had an embarrassing time explaining to him that since we had no money he would have to accompany us to Islamabad where we hoped we could somehow raise enough to pay him. Despite the fact that he lived just down the road in the opposite direction Abdul bore the news of this three or four-day, several-thousand-kilometre diversion, with all his usual equanimity. He was, as we might have been allowed to say a century ago, a splendid chap. We had no money for Aftab either but since he lived in 'Pindi he at least was spared the geographical inconvenience.

It was impossible to find out if the road was still closed, or whether the buses were running; or anything much else. Rumour supplanted rumour; counter-rumour overtook counter-rumour: eastern promise and all part of the East's infuriating mystique; all very frustrating to westerners in too much of a hurry to countenance a philosophical approach. Except Aid, that is, who had delved into his book, *The Way of Zen* and emerged with the gem that, 'paradoxically, nothing is more artificial than the notion of artificiality'. Something in the notion seemed to fortify him but it did nothing for my Irish impatience—and anyway I couldn't see the paradox for the life of me.

Aftab, who had been uncharacteristically energetic, stimulated perhaps by all this new oxygen—or more likely by the threat of a delay in regaining home comforts—brought good news. He had found a driver and a lorry—a cement lorry—but a lorry that was willing to take us all and our gear to Islamabad. It was leaving within the hour (which, applying the Eastern rule, meant sometime this week) and the driver had accepted that we couldn't pay him until after he delivered us.

Aftab was as good as his word. There was indeed a lorry and the great white cloud under which it was parked testified that it was indeed a cement lorry. (It left on time too, for which I owe Pakistan an apology.) The driver was a fat, devious-looking cove dressed in the greasiest robes imaginable. His chubby black cheeks (from dirt and ethnicity both) billowed beneath a once-white circular cap. He looked the prototype from which the stereotype music hall villain-of-foreign-extraction had been derived. But he was going to Islamabad and he wasn't fussy about his cargo. We loaded our stuff into the canopied rear of the truck, stacked it all for comfort, unfolded some of Aftab's chairs and made a veritable Pullman of this dusty truck. Aftab pulled rank and *droit de translator* and climbed into the cab, alongside our unsavoury-looking driver. We told the motel manager that Al would settle our bill when he passed through; only a matter of a day or two, as we assured him. He didn't look very happy with the arrangement but, because of the British reputation for fair dealing (a reputation that has somehow survived the post-colonial shenanigans of expeditions such as ours, as well as hippies, Beatle/guru daftness, and drug runners), he accepted it and wished us luck as he shook our hands.

Through the back of the truck we were able to see that Skardu bore the smouldering scars of riot and arson. The townsfolk, those of the bazaar in particular, wore the sullen and shocked expressions of a people who have, to their own greatest surprise, behaved badly and who were now astonished that they could have done all this; aghast at their own collective wantonness, their shame borne on hunched shoulders, their contrition mutely eloquent.

The truck stopped for petrol. An apricot vendor appeared at the tailgate. We bought a bagful and Wilkie, his appetite now fully recovered, tucked in. Not much later he could be seen leaping from the back of the truck, which was fortunately moving only slowly at the time and running off in search of a superloo, or any boulder that would serve instead. As any less urgent man could have told him there was nothing for miles. To cries of sympathy and encouragement, he hung from a milestone and thrust his backside out over the Indus which surged a thousand feet beneath. It was not an altogether successful operation.

'Serves the silly bugger right for being such a pig with the apricots' Bev said, all bed-side manner and concern.

We stopped at six at a filthy roadside shack of a cafe that served, amongst the flies, a meal of spinach, dal, chapattis and tea. Wilkie, conscious of his delicate intestinal state and doubtless anxious to be spared any more of Bev's bed-side manner, exercised great self-restraint and ate only twice as much as the rest of us. The result was as predictable as Bev's diagnosis.

Replete, we continued down and around the bends of this mighty road, sleeping, reading or boogie-box listening; snug in our silicotic sedan, rumbling along somewhere between the Indus and the sky. We had lurched round just another bend when we squealed to a violent halt. From within our canopy we were distantly aware of voices and lights and the hum of other engines. A mud-slide, triggered by yesterday's storm, had swept across this tenuous tarmac ribbon. The road was blocked, our escape cut. The driver reversed, turned and drove back to his Routiers. We slept soundly. There was nothing to be done.

After a Routiers breakfast the next morning we argued out a plan. The mud slide could take days, even weeks to clear and I argued that there would be as many vehicles the other side of the slide as there were on ours. I ventured that some enterprising lad probably had a bus ready and waiting for the captive passengers he knew must emerge from the Skardu side. But what about the gear? We'd never be able to carry it across—it was after all 27-porters' loads heavy—and we simply couldn't abandon it. It was Wilkie who was noble enough to volunteer to remain with the cement lorry and our gear. He didn't need to be back for work until early September and this was August 5th. Aftab opted to remain too, his concern for his newly acquired merchandise now outweighing his desire to be home. The rest of us, Abdul, Aid, Bev, and I, persuaded another truck-driver to take us back down the road to the beginning of the mud-slide. We rode on his balconied roof which, on the sharpest corners of the road, projected well out over the precipice, affording us an uninterrupted glance of the Indus far, far below. At other places we had to duck for the road had roofs as well as cantilevers.

The mud was knee deep, stiff and coarse with gravel. It was hard on the legs and scraped my bare legs barer. A train of like-plighted refugees followed us, including the troupe of girls from Hong Kong who giggled their way across this adventure and an old man, so frail that he could hardly draw his legs from the mud. When he stumbled I offered him a lift which he accepted with a weak smile and together we piggy-backed it the mile to the far side. At one place a stream cut through the mud slide on its way to join the Indus. The old man and I arrived there to find that Aid had established himself as a latter day St. Christopher and was ferrying the giggling troupe, one at a time (though he could have hefted them all at once) across the torrent. They were enjoying themselves enormously. So was St. Christopher.

When we regained the road we were welcomed by a bus—just as we'd hoped. Bev was already there, seated on his sac and sipping tea and looking exceedingly pleased with himself.

'Where the heck did you get that cup of tea, Bev?'

'Well, y'know, I find that when you're in these odd places, if you behave like an Englishman people tend to treat you like one—and it *is* four o'clock.' That was the only explanation on offer and I can't improve on it for I'm still not sure how he did it, but there he was drinking tea, and from a cup.

I boarded the bus, sat down, and, addressing the back of the two Pakistani heads immediately in front asked: 'Excuse me, do you know where this bus is going?'

Both heads turned and were equally helpful: one said, 'Islamabad', the other, 'Gilgit'.

'But they're in opposite directions!'

Both heads agreed. No more. Precisely, equally helpful. And with precisely equal obstinacy neither was prepared to enlarge on his opinion.

The bus pulled away and a conductor began his rounds, collecting fares with no more fuss than had we all been aboard the Clapham omnibus. The most remarkable thing was how it all went unremarked. Only the troupe from Hong Kong made anything of it and sang as kids do on school outings—which, I suppose, was all it was to them.

In the event, when we reached the KKH proper the bus turned north to Gilgit—just as Allah had presumably willed it. This was unhelpful. Islamabad lay some hundreds of miles to the south. My two guides showed no signs of either triumph or alarm, despite the fact that one was diametrically wrong, the other absolutely right. There's some sort of inner peace to be found in this Allah-wills-it business. Certainly it renders all navigation superfluous (any other kind of plan or scheme too), and there's advantage in all of that.

In Gilgit we ate a superb dinner, slept well in a wonderfully comfortable, ridiculously cheap hotel, and the next morning ate a breakfast at least as good as the dinner. Abdul, who was hesitant at first in the face of all this unaccustomed luxury, soon relaxed sufficiently to enjoy himself enormously, though he remained wide-eyed to the end.

We had booked on a bus to Islamabad which was due to depart the next morning. The booking had been made by telephone from the hotel and was by far the easiest transaction of the entire expedition. We had even been given the choice of a ride in a standard bus or, for a few rupees extra, in a 'Super Deluxe', and impecunious though we were, we splashed out on the latter. Hell, we might as well finish in style. Next morning, full of fried eggs and toast and tea I decided to afford myself a further treat—a shave by a local barber. The shave turned out to be what is euphemistically known as an 'experience'; more education than treat. The barber, who had brothers and offspring and cousins the length and breadth of Britain, was an economical man and saved water by spitting on the brush to wet it.

He yanked my face this way and that, tugging at ear, nose or whatever came handiest, and renewed the lather with that same expectoral economy, two or three times over. My upper lip, not greatly different from that of any other human, seemed to be giving him particular trouble which he solved by hooking two fingers inside my mouth and pulling the whole assembly well beyond the tip of my nose, to a point where he could wield his razor with greater efficiency and precision. A neat ploy, though not one likely to bring customers beating a path to his door, but at 3 rupees it might be thought that the experience was good value.

The 'Super Deluxe' was waiting at the bus station. We were grateful for those very words painted in bright proclamation down the sides, for there was nothing else to suggest that it might be going anywhere other than the nearest scrap heap—provided that that was not too far. What earned it the Super Deluxe label defied imagination, since one simply could not conceive of a lower order of vehicle than the wreck that stood before us. I sympathised with anyone having to travel on the standard service. When we got inside, though, there was a pleasant surprise—each passenger was given a seat to himself—a fairly novel arrangement on the Indian sub-continent. Aid offered the theory that the guarantee of a seat was in fact the difference between the two classes of bus. He may have been right. An officious conductor showed us to our seats and gave us our tickets which he had first to fashion from scraps of paper that he kept folded in his pocket for that purpose. When all the passengers had been seen to he took his place in a seat alongside the driver, stretched sideways and rang a very loud bell. Since the driver was closer to him than the bell it was difficult to see how it served better than a 'let's go mate' or some Urdu equivalent. But it was always the bell, loud and clear after every stop—and there were many stops.

Sitting across the aisle were two European women dressed in Pakistani clothes. It was a long time since I had spoken to a woman and the prospect was a mildly pleasant one. We chatted amiably for a bit and then I asked one what it was that brought her to Pakistan.

'God sent me', she replied with a devastating lack of embarrassment.

'What did you do to upset Him?' I asked. The conversation ended soon after. In a different conversation Aid later learned that they were missionaries, here to rescue Pakistani women from Islam. 'From the fire into the frying pan. Could be worse', I thought and no longer felt so bad about my earlier bad-tasting joke.

We reached Islamabad at 3 am on the 6th August after twenty bone-shaking hours, a thousand uneccessary bell rings and about half a ton of delicious dal and nan spread—literally—over three or four fly-blown pit-stops.

We four (Abdul was by now a constant companion) took a taxi to Karen Rushworth's house—she had generously agreed that we could stay there even though she was away on holiday. The chowkidar let us in and we made straightway to the fridge where we found what we really needed—beer.

The next day it was breakfast at the Brit Club, a breakfast of beans and bacon and eggs and tomatoes and sausages and fried bread and beans: above all beans. Afterwards we had a swim, sorted our gear, booked our air tickets, cashed a cheque with the Club for £600 that I wasn't sure I had in order to pay Abdul; tried to find the Ministry of Tourism open and failed on every one of the three days we tried; and wondered how Al was faring and where he was, and about Wilkie too. By chance I bumped into an old friend who was tooling around in a primrose-yellow, chauffeur-driven Mercedes on business that he was careful not to be too specific about. We were about to order a taxi to take Abdul, now fully paid, to the bus station when my friend offered to let his chauffeur run him there. The phrase 'culture-shock' hardly does justice to Abdul's utter bewilderment as we bundled him and his £600 into the limmo, shook his hand, and dispatched him to the bus station. The boy from Kaphlu started for home in an air-conditioned Mercedes. He was grinning as wide as the moon as he was swept away from the tree-shaded avenue. I won't forget his smile or his leaving.

We loafed and festered in Islamabad for two more days, on the first of which Wilkie arrived with the lorry. He was cemented to the Brit Club bar when we found him. It was good to see him again, good to know he'd made it unscathed, more or less; the gear too.

Now we had a new problem. We had seats to fly on the 10th but had not been able to make arrangements to air-freight our equipment. Again Wilkie was noble and volunteered to stay behind until this job too was done.

Aid, Bev and I flew back to Britain on the 10th. Almost immediately I began work for the television company responsible for bringing me home.

A few days later Brian rang with the bad news.

* * *

'Are we to take it that Al is dead then?' I asked at length.

'Yes. He's dead.' Brian straight and steady as always. For a week I was beseiged by calls from the press, radio and television, but I had almost no idea what had happened and no story to give them. I wondered sometimes if they believed me. Gradually, from information via calls from Wilkie, still in Islamabad, and scraps from a dozen other sources we were able to piece the story together but though it was clear from the outset that a terrible tragedy had overtaken Al and others, a lucid account was never given until *Mountain* magazine reported the facts, with a great deal of help from Jim Curran, some months later. This sad story is perhaps best told as plainly as *Mountain* gives it:

Towards the end of July, the weather had improved considerably and a complex group of people started out for the summit via the Abruzzi Ridge. They included members of five different expeditions: Alan Rouse, leader of the mentioned British group, Kurt Diemberger (Austrian), Julie Tullis (British) and Dobroslawa Wolf (Polish), Alfred Imitzer, Willi Bauer and Hannes Wiesser, all members of the Austrian expedition active on this route; and also several members of the South Korean expedition who had so thoroughly prepared the route up to and beyond the SE Shoulder (7800m).

By August 2, the group had reached the site of a large Camp 4 (c.8000m) from their Camp 5 (8300m), in fine weather. On August 3, whilst the remaining climbers presumably recuperated at Camp 4, the summit was reached by three Koreans, Bong-Wan Chang (34), Chang-Son Kim (26) and Byong-Ho Chang (25) who had used oxygen (the only expedition to have it). Shortly after leaving the summit, the Koreans were caught up by the Polish team, who had just reached the summit via the SSW Ridge, and both parties continued the descent. Darkness fell before the climbers reached Camp 4. One Korean was forced to bivouac, and Wojciech Wróż failed to reach Camp 4, presumably having abseiled off the end of a fixed rope.

Eventually his companions managed to complete the descent without further mishap. Wojciech Wróż (44) was a very well known mountaineer in Poland and had previously climbed Kangchenjunga South (1978) and Yalung Kang (1984), as well as having been above 8000m on K2 in 1976 and 1982.

On August 4, while the previous group was descending, futher ascents to the summit were made, in rapidly deteriorating weather conditions. The first, by Austrians Imitzer and Bauer, was at about 4pm, shortly followed by Alan Rouse. Rouse then descended quickly to help Wolf, who had reached c.8450m and was very tired, back to Camp 4. Later in the day, at about 7pm, Diemberger and Tullis also reached the top, but during the descent Tullis suffered a fall that dragged them both down for about 100 metres, fortunately without injury. Being too late to reach Camp 4, they were forced to bivouac in the open.

On August 5 the weather deteriorated further and a long, fierce storm began. Diemberger and Mrs Tullis, who was suffering from eye problems, managed to reach Camp 4, joining the rest of the climbers who had been involved in the attempts of the previous day.

No more news was received after that at Base Camp and a week later (August 11) no trace of the missing climbers had been found. Messages were then sent to Europe, stating that all seven climbers were missing, presumed dead. However, by late on August 11, Willi Bauer had arrived at Base Camp and the entire chain of events was finally revealed:

The storm that had started on August 4 developed full force during the following days, with heavy snowfall, winds in the region of 150 kph and temperatures of minus 30°C. Their tents having been wrecked, Tullis moved in with the Austrians Bauer, Wiesser and Imitzer, while Diemberger joined Rouse.

On August 7 Julie Tullis (47) died in her sleep.

The storm continued unabated, and by August 8 the trapped climbers had run out

177

of food and fuel. On August 10 the sky began to clear and the snowfall stopped, but the fierce wind continued. Bauer, Diemberger, Imitzer, Wolf and Wiesser started to descend. Alan Rouse (34), was unable to move, had drifted into delirium and was left in his tent, as there was absolutely no hope of evacuating him from the mountain.

Almost immediately, Imitzer and Wiesser collapsed. The remaining three, Wolf, Diemberger and Bauer, continued the descent but failed to find shelter in the remains of Camp 3 (7350m), which had been avalanched prior to the ascent. Now descending fixed ropes from the Shoulder, Bauer and Diemberger managed to reach Camp 2 (6900m), which was stocked with sufficient food and fuel, late in the evening, and spent the night there. They had last seen Dobroslawa Wolf a couple of hours before their arrival, when she was lagging behind on the fixed ropes. She failed to arrive at the camp, presumably having been killed above 7000m.

The following day, August 11, the two survivors continued the descent. Bauer (44), who was the stronger, went ahead by evening to reach Base Camp, which was still occupied by the Polish and South Korean expeditions, as well as two or three climbers of other nationalities. Immediately, a search party, including Jim Curran the film cameraman for the British expedition, was formed, and eventually found Diemberger at the foot of the mountain shortly before midnight, painfully moving towards Advance Base Camp. Both Austrians had suffered severe frostbite to finger and toes.

After several days of waiting, on August 16 a helicopter arrived at Base Camp and evacuated the two Austrians to Skardu.

The information which chronicles these events has come from several sources, but has been carefully studied and confirmed by Jim Curran, who was present throughout the whole episode. He is anxious to point out that the above is correct, to the best of his knowledge, and should hopefully put an end to the speculation that has been rife in the 'popular' press and amongst the climbing fraternity.

This is by far the greatest climbing tragedy that has occurred in the Karakoram range. Although sudden avalanches elsewhere in various 8000ers have taken a greater toll of victims on several occasions, a long gradual ordeal of this magnitude has only been surpassed by the catastrophe to the German 1934 expedition on Nanga Parbat.

Julie Tullis, whose third attempt on the mountain this was, had previously tried mountains such as Nanga Parbat and Everest, always accompanied by her filming colleague, Kurt Diemberger, who had formerly climbed five 8000ers. Together they climbed Broad Peak in 1984, a second ascent for Diemberger. Julie still remains the only British woman ever to have climbed an 8000er.'

What did we make of it now? What were our true thoughts, our honest feelings? I hardly knew my own then and can't bring them out of whatever recess of my mind they are skulking now. Certainly some of us felt guilty. If I had stayed, would Wilkie have stayed? And then would a stronger team have got down safely? Or would we have died too? Questions we all tormented ourselves with, but vain questioning all the same. There is no answer; will never be an answer.

We had broken the only rule. We had left Al. Al had died. There was no connection in fact: the two are unrelated. But our guilt made a connection and our consciences made close cousins of the unrelated facts. There was no escape. There never will be.

Wilkie, straightforward as ever told me later what his feelings were:

No sooner had John, Bev and Aid flown home, than a telegram came from Jim giving the news that Al and company were missing.

The black reality restored my normal high regard for Al. I could not bring myself to fly off and leave Jim to carry the burden alone. I settled in for a long wait. I waited 3 weeks, with an endless succession of journalists pressing me for more information which I didn't have. This pressure was amply offset by the hospitality and sympathy of my hosts at the British Embassy club.

A too brief conversation with a frost-bitten Diemberger en route to hospital in Europe, revealed curiously few extra facts, but gave an all too realistic impression of the flavour of the struggle and tragedy. Then one day my limbo state suddenly ended without warning, as Jim made his appearance at the club, as if transported by some science fiction beaming device. I could switch my life state over to the 'busy' mode, with practical arrangements for the return to England. A few months have now passed and I can reflect with more perspective. There are still some details missing from the crucial events on the mountain. Diemberger's account of the timings leave a few questions unanswered. Why was a day apparently spent resting (if that is possible at 8000 metres) at Camp 4 prior to the summit? When Kurt and Julie successfully reached Camp 4 the morning after the summit, why had Al and co. not set off for Camp 3, or if they were waiting for these two, why did they not then leave straight away? Perhaps we will never know. In any case, although I feel justified in resenting Al's behaviour which denied me a chance of climbing K2, I must also feel a bizzare gratitude—he may well have saved my life!'

Mine were, typically, less straightforward, a deal more confused. One of the film crew asked me whether Al's death was the result of a misjudgement. I answered that of course it was and thought just after that life itself was probably just a tottering series of misjudgements—unless your deserts are small and you put nothing to the touch.

What are the lessons, the same fellow wanted to know. None, I said, there are no lessons. Mountaineering is dangerous. People die, but the circumstances are always unique. There's nothing to be learned. He evidently thought that an unsatisfactory reply and wandered away.

Another approached and said chirpily, 'Bet you're glad you came back to do this programme'. (Ironically it was called 'Survival of the Fittest'—but the irony escaped me at the time.)

I answered that I wasn't, particularly. He asked if I meant it. I said I did. 'But it saved your life, you'd be dead, you don't mean that.' I said yes again and have wondered since if I meant it then: if I mean it now.

Al brought light to many darknesses and glittering gifts to dull days. Faults he had in plenty. But these were small things; seeming smaller now. How I wish this had all been a novel. How I wish that he were here now to say that it was.

I had said that I would never go back to K2. It had cost too much in life and human dignity and in honour. I didn't hate the mountain even though it had taken 13 lives that summer. It would have been daft to squander the energy of hatred on so much inanimate rubble. Nor was it because I had returned home body-weary and mind-weary. Those are the normal scars of duels with very big mountains; they would heal; both would grow young again. No it was something deeper than all that; my mortal soul had aged quicker and more permanently than the mind and body that it inhabited; had aged beyond growing young again and had grown sad and tired with that age. I would not return to K2. I vowed it. Whatever was left of life, it was too precious to squander three months of it on some gigantic bump on the earth's surface.

*　*　*

A few months after our return Andrzej Zawada asked me if I'd join him on the first winter attempt on K2 in December 1987.

'But I vowed that I'd never go back', I told him.

'But what is your answer?'

'Yes, I'll come.'

I had no choice.

Appendix 1 – K2 Film

The following is taken from a circular sent to all team members, by Jim Curran, the expedition cameraman.

Now that we have a film deal (of sorts) I thought it worthwhile to circulate everyone with a few notes about how I see the film going, and, more important, some bits of advice to help make it a good one.

FILM

We will attempt to get high quality 16 mm film as far as possible on the mountain, using one of two Cannon Scoopics. The Scoopic is easy to use and gives results comparable with Arriflex or Aarton cameras which are far more sophisticated and very heavy. High on the mountain we will be using Super 8 cameras which are hopefully 'idiot proof'! Nevertheless a few basic principles are given here which can make all the difference between 'home movies' and professional documentary footage.

1. *Always remember that 'movie' as in 'movie-camera' refers to the* **film** *moving, not the camera.*
   Always keep the camera still whether hand holding or on a tripod (monopod).
2. *Avoid zooms and pans unless there is a very good reason for them, and even then avoid them. Use the zoom to frame a shot (as with a zoom lens on a still camera) not as a trombone.*
   If in doubt shoot on wide angle.
   Focus on full zoom then pull back to frame.
3. *Make shots too long rather than too short. A thirty second shot can be cut, a two second shot goes in the bin.*
4. *Use* **close ups** *whenever possible. Figures filling the frame, heads feet etc, are far more dynamic than two minute black blobs only visible on a cinema screen.*
5. *Film* **sequences** *rather than single shots, e.g, digging a snow cave might be a sequence of ten shots including big close ups of shovel in snow, gritted teeth of digger, snow rolling down the slope etc, as well as the straightforward shot of a person on a slope digging a hole. By shooting sequences an editor has far more flexibility in cutting.*
6. *Keep all cameras warm in inside pockets, sleeping bags etc.*
   Check that exposure apertures are not iced up, or covered in snow.

7. *If using 16 mm Scoopic* **always** *use a changing bag* **particularly for removing exposed film.** *(I will go over the Scoopic with anyone who is interested in using it.)*
8. *If possible, try to rehearse shots without incurring the wrath of the 'actors'.*
9. *Remember, as with still photography, the best images tend to be early morning and later afternoon/evening. Side lighting gives detail and three dimensions also, (more important) exposures will be more manageable. (You can only change the aperture on a movie camera—not the shutter speed.)*
10. *However good the rest of the footage may be the success of the film does largely depend on how much is shot above say 25,000 feet. We have around 80 cassettes of super 8 (4 hours) so don't be afraid to use it and make mistakes.*
11. *Finally when being filmed* **never look at the camera.**

SOUND

Sound is often seen as the poor relation to film, yet can, and often does, make mediocre footage seem brilliant and more alarmingly, good footage desperately boring. Again I am trying to make all tape recorders 'user friendly' and am relying on various models of the Sony Walkman for the bulk of sound recording. I would urge every member to keep a tape diary and hope that you will not feel inhibited in using it to reveal your most profound and earth shattering revelations about yourself and your companions. Naturally in the finished film you would have the final say as to what does or doesn't get in but it is important that people do record personal impressions of the trip. I am trying to ensure we have enough external mikes to use on all the Walkmen. This is important as the built-in mike tends to record the motor noise of the Walkman itself. By and large JH and I will attempt to cover most if not all, sound up to and hopefully beyond Camp 1. Above that I hope that the team will make an effort to record conversations and effects. Even with Super 8 it is occasionally worth attempting sync. sound by clapping in front of the camera and clearly identifying the shot.

N.B. Keep the mike as far away from the camera as possible.

On the walk-in I would like to ensure that a 'portrait' of everyone is acquired, both on film and with some sort of 'soliloquy' as to what brings you to K2. For this I would want to spend a part or all of a day with each member. I hope you will endure some time being told what to do and will believe me when I lie and say it won't happen again!

Appendix II – Equipment

The dramatic rise in the standards of Himalayan climbing has been helped significantly by improvements in equipment, both technically and psychologically. Gear is lighter, more efficient and reliable, which has enabled mountaineers to climb faster, for longer periods on difficult routes without massive high-altitude porter support and numerous camps. However climbers are only human and even when well acclimatized and very fit can easily succumb to the overwhelming power of nature, particularly at altitude.

Choosing what equipment to take was based on experience, the main problem generally occurred due to personal preferences or obligations. The gear requirements can be divided into three: walk-in, Base Camp and on the mountain.

Walk-in

The dramatic and beautiful walk to K2 Base Camp passes through some of the most varied terrain imaginable; from dry hot desert to snow and moraine-covered glaciers. Sun stroke is a real possibility on a clear day low down; frostbite a lurking danger for the unwary in a storm at Concordia. You need equipment to combat the vagaries of the climate, yet if you are lucky the walk could be completed in tracksuit, trainers, three-season sleeping bag and lightweight tent. However to cover all eventualities warm clothing such as fleece or down jackets should be near at hand along with walking boots, gaiters, thermal underwear, balaclava, waterproofs and umbrella (for sun and rain). It can get pretty cold at night so a good four-season sleeping bag is ideal as it can be used at Base Camp as well; a zip gives extra flexibility low down. Tent can also be the Base Camp tent so a 2/3 man dome tent is excellent. If you can handle the luxury of a foamy then it is well worth it, leaving thin closed cell mats for the hill.

Every morning the porters like to get away as quickly as possible so it is best if their loads are not disturbed too much. Carry as much of your own gear as practical (though after 20lb weight it saps the energy for the mountain). In the evening this also has the advantage that you don't have to wait for the porters to arrive before you can get at your gear. A 60 to 70-litre rucsac should accommodate what you require for the walk-in.

Most of the kitchen can be bought in Pakistan though good quality large paraffin stoves are best brought from Europe. A large communal tent is a good idea but often impractical to put up and down every night, better for the walk-in is a large polythene sheet which can be spread over all the loads which are arranged in a circle to produce a cooking and eating area inside (load security is also improved). Hygiene is paramount and a water purifying pump is ideal; in the morning everybody should fill their water bottles for the coming day.

All the porter loads have to be packed very carefully and in polythene in case of rain. Strong semi waterproof cardboard boxes are good though even better are plastic drums. All loads need to be marked and their contents logged and made secure.

The rules and regulations of the Pakistan government state the porter and staff requirements. For your liaison officer, cooks, Base Camp helpers and mail runner these should be good quality and brought from Europe. All the porter requirements can be obtained in Pakistan, though it is best if possible to bring polythene sheets or lightweight tarpaulins for their night's shelter with you. A small though important item is sunglasses; a fresh fall of snow followed by a sunny day is a recipe for painful snowblindness. Cheap and adequate glasses can be purchased in Pakistan, though the porters break them easily so spares should be at hand.

Although there are tracks most of the way to Base Camp, in bad weather the glaciers can be dangerous and ice axe, crampons and rope should be readily available. Low down there are several river crossings some with 'exciting' bridges, a rope can help porter morale.

Base Camp

For a long stay at Base a tent each is ideal, and the modern geodesic domes are perfect; they are big enough for all your personal gear and can withstand very bad weather. They also are sufficiently strong yet light to be used on the hill if the mountain tents are destroyed. A communal eating area is vital; we used an excellent North Face 'conference' dome which we furnished in luxury with lightweight camping chairs and tables. A cooking shelter is equally important and here a large family tent just survived the many heavy snow falls.

Clothing varies as to personal choice, but the same as the walk-in is normally used, though a pair of insulated 'moon' boots are standard bad-weather footwear.

Evenings are short, and adequate lighting is always a problem. We used Hurricane lamps which always caused problems, though the alternatives are equally problematic (i.e. batteries do not last long and are very heavy to transport in quantity). Communal music and multiband radio (especially short wave) are also important.

Cooking at altitude is a problem. Paraffin stoves do not work as well and even with the 'highest' quality fuel available they clog continually and many spares and prickers are required. By mistake we were supplied with silent burners which compounded the problems. Pressure cookers are vital for many bulk foods such as rice and dahl and they save fuel. Good quality plastic mugs, plates etc are ideal but there never seem to be enough mugs.

On the hill

We had a wide variety of clothing and who wore what and when, varied enormously. Plastic boots with foam inners were standard, covered with Yeti gaiters low down and full neoprene overboots higher on the mountain. Clothing was based on the layering principle. Loop stitched socks and thin thermal underwear provided the base layer, then a layer of fleece of polar plus; high on the hill a Gore-Tex covered down suit was used but lower down (the majority of the time) a Gore-Tex shell layer was adequate (this was either a light one-piece suit or sallopettes and jacket). Thin thermal gloves were worn under pile/Gore-Tex mits. Expedition-weight, Gore-Tex-covered, down sleeping bags are quite bulky and heavy but are necessary on a mountain like K2. A full length Karrimat is equally important.

At Advance Base and Camp 1 we used a variety of Dome tents from Wild Country (Mountain Super Nova), Phoenix (Phorum Extreme) and North Face (VE 24 and North Star). Higher we used small, lightweight tents such as the Phoenix Phearless and Photon and Wild Country Gemini. None were perfect but all survived and considering the conditions they performed remarkably well.

Because of the position of the route we had a long, relatively easy snow-covered glacier to traverse much of the way between Base and Camp 1. Skis fitted with ski mountaineering bindings and skins saved many hours in ascent and descent whilst small plastic kids' sledges towed behind helped load carrying. The Emery bindings fitted just about adequately on the Scarpa plastic boots.

Everybody had their own choice of technical gear but we all used clip-on crampons such as footfangs or Salewa Scissor type and the Wild Country 'Littlejohn' harnesses were excellent. Petzl ascenders are lighter and just as safe as the other makes, and were used on the thousands of feet of fixed rope supplied by Beal. The size depended on the position and varied from 7mm to 11mm.

Cooking was on modified gas stoves, low down from Epigas, higher from Hursch, with special high-altitude gas mix. MSR stoves were also useful up to 22,000 feet, particularly for melting snow, but after this height they started to falter.

Communication was a difficult problem to solve due to the complex nature of the route, resulting in Base Camp being out of line of sight of the route. A series of radios in each camp and a rebroadcasting unit between Base Camp and Advance Base Camp solved the problem, all supplied by Plessey, and with the batteries recharged by Sola-Pak solar panels.

There were few complaints about the gear and it all worked well in difficult conditions. All the manufacturers should be praised for their generous help.

BRIAN HALL

Appendix III – Sponsors

The following companies, to a greater or lesser extent, generously helped the expedition by supplying equipment or food vital to the smooth running and success of the trip. All members of the team thank these companies for their generosity and help:

Bachelors
Beal
Berghaus
British Mountaineering Council
British Vita—Middleton
British Wool
Carrington Performance Fabrics
CAN UK
Danial Quiggans
DMM
DRG Plastics
Drinkmaster
Duracell
Europa Sport
EPI Gaz
Fuji
Fullers Brewery
Henry Sutcliffe
Hampton Works
How & Bainbridge Ltd
Javlin
John Bunch
J.W. Collier
John West
Jones and Bebb—Llanwrst
Jordans
Jaradine Cargo Int
Karrimor

KP
Linston Industrial Sales
Lowe Alpine Systems
Mount Everest Foundation
Mountain Equipment
National Westminster Bank
New Balance
North Face
Optimus
Peter Onslow Ltd
PIA
Pentax
Petzl
Plessey Military Communications
Phoenix
Quaker Oats
Rab
Racal
Ringtons Tea
Rowntree MacIntosh
RTZ
Solapak
Sport Extreme Chamonix
Sunpak
St Ivel
Tate & Lyle
Texaco
The Wild Water Centre
Thorntons
Vango
Walter Hughes
W.L. Gore
Wild Country
Wilson Engineering
Wool Council